P9-BZR-856

100 Greatest Literary Detectives

100 Greatest Literary Detectives

Edited by

Eric Sandberg

ROWMAN & LITTLEFIELD
Lanham • Boulder • New York • London

Published by Rowman & Littlefield
An imprint of The Rowman & Littlefield Publishing Group, Inc.
4501 Forbes Boulevard, Suite 200, Lanham, Maryland 20706
www.rowman.com

Unit A, Whitacre Mews, 26-34 Stannary Street, London SE11 4AB

British Library Cataloguing in Publication Information Available

Library of Congress Cataloging-in-Publication Data

Names: Sandberg, Eric, editor.
Title: 100 greatest literary detectives / edited by Eric Sandberg.
Other titles: One hundred greatest literary detectives
Description: Lanham, Maryland : Rowman & Littlefield, 2018. | Includes bibliographical references and index. |
Identifiers: LCCN 2017050362 (print) | LCCN 2017055749 (ebook) | ISBN 9781442278233 (electronic) | ISBN 9781442278226 (cloth : alk. paper)
Subjects: LCSH: Detectives in literature—Dictionaries. | Fictitious characters—Dictionaries.
Classification: LCC PN3448.D4 (ebook) | LCC PN3448.D4 A16 2018 (print) | DDC 809.3/872—dc23
LC record available at https://lccn.loc.gov/2017050362

∞™ The paper used in this publication meets the minimum requirements of American National Standard for Information Sciences—Permanence of Paper for Printed Library Materials, ANSI/NISO Z39.48-1992.

Printed in the United States of America

Contents

Acknowledgments ix

Introduction: The Character of Crime xi

Jean-Baptiste Adamsberg 1

Kogorō Akechi 3

Lew Archer 4

Bob Arctor 6

Byomkesh Bakshi 9

Inspector Hans Bärlach 11

Brother William of Baskerville 12

Martin Beck 14

Héctor Belascoarán Shayne 16

Detective Inspector Napoleon Bonaparte 18

Inspector Tyador Borlú 20

Lieutenant Boruvka 22

Dame Beatrice Adela Lestrange Bradley 24

Simon Brenner 26

Valeria Brinton (Woodville/Macallan) 28

Father Brown 29

Inspector Bucket 31

Brother Cadfael 34

Inspector Cadin 36

Albert Campion 38

Steve Carella 39

Thomas Carnacki, The Ghost-Finder 41

Pepe Carvalho 43
Mario Conde 45
Sergeant Cuff 47
Commander Adam Dalgliesh 49
Detective Superintendent Andrew Dalziel and DCI Peter Pascoe 51
Stephanie Delacour 53
C. Auguste Dupin 54
Inspector "Benedito" Espinosa 57
Erast Petrovich Fandorin 59
Professor Kate Fansler 61
Dr. Gideon Fell 63
Gervase Fen 65
Mrs. Gladden 67
Inspector Alan Grant 69
Cordelia Gray 71
Detective Benny Griessel 72
Ebenezer Gryce 74
Bernie Günther 76
Mike Hammer 79
Cliff Hardy 81
Inspector Costas Haritos 83
Timo Harjunpää 84
Tony Hill 86
Harry Hole 88
Sherlock Holmes 90
Hong Jun 92
Huo Sang 94
Inspector Eitaro Imanishi 97
Venus Johnson 100
Kemal Kayankaya 103
Kōsuke Kindaichi 105

Lieutenant David Klein 106
Aunt Lalli 109
Duca Lamberti 111
Judith Lee 112
Lituma 114
DI Thomas Lynley and DS Barbara Havers 116
Chief Inspector Jules Maigret 119
Philip Marlowe 121
Miss Jane Marple 123
Sharon McCone 125
Travis McGee 127
Kinsey Millhone 129
Kiyoshi Mitarai 130
Eberhard Mock 132
Inspector Salvo Montalbano 134
Inspector Morse 136
Inspector Grazia Negro 139
Thursday Next 141
Don Isidro Parodi 143
Joseph Peters 144
Hercule Poirot 146
Ellery Queen 149
Daniel Quinn 151
Quirke 152
Mma Precious Ramotswe 155
Ezekiel "Easy" Rawlins 157
DI John Rebus 159
Bernard Grimes Rhodenbarr 161
Commissario Luigi Alfredo Ricciardi 162
Kay Scarpetta 165
Sam Spade 167

Spenser 168
Doc Sportello 170
Nigel Strangeways 172
Fahnderwachtmeister Jakob Studer 174
Inspector Erlendur Sveinsson 176
Teodor Szacki 178
Philip Trent 181
Camille Verhœven 184
Inspector Kurt Wallander 187
Mei Wang 189
V. I. Warshawski 191
Chief Inspector Reginald Wexford 193
Lord Peter Wimsey 195
Nero Wolfe 197
Lily Wu 199
Detective Sergeant X 202

Notes 205
Index 219
About the Editor and Contributors 227

Acknowledgments

This book is a collective endeavor. It would not have been possible to present such a wide range of detectives without drawing on the experience, expertise, and enthusiasm of the many talented contributors to this volume; my first thanks are due to them. I would also like to acknowledge the important role played by the Crime Studies Network, the International Crime Fiction Research Group, and particularly the International Crime Fiction Association, run by Fiona Peters, Agnieszka Sienkiewicz-Charlish, and Joanne Ella Parsons, in developing this project and in promoting the study of crime fiction in general. Professor Elise Kärkkäinen from the University of Oulu has been tremendously supportive of my work, for which my sincere thanks. Finally, I want to thank Johanna and the World's Greatest Detectives, who have shared with me for many happy years the delights of crime.

Introduction

The Character of Crime

It's never easy trying to figure out a detective.[1]

If you love crime fiction, you will hate this book. Why? You will hate it because a list of the hundred greatest fictional detectives will almost certainly be missing one, if not several, of your favorite hard-boiled private eyes, dedicated police officers, or amateur sleuths. The world of crime fiction is vast, the tastes of crime readers varied, and no selection of investigators could possibly satisfy everyone. Your outrage at the omission of your personal favorite is as inevitable as it is justifiable. But more important than this anger is what it tells us about both the idea of greatness and the nature of crime fiction.

First, greatness, despite the title of this book, is a concept that needs to be handled with considerable caution. This is not to say there is no such thing as literary greatness. If Sir Arthur Conan Doyle is not a great mystery writer, and if Sherlock Holmes is not a great fictional detective, what are they? But difficulties arise nonetheless in attaching the label to particular writers and their creations, even in a case as seemingly clear-cut and as indisputably canonical as this, and agreement on the assignment of the term is elusive. Marshall McLuhan, for example, in his admittedly generally negative comments on crime fiction, reserves his most withering invective for Conan Doyle: "Obsessed with the psychic stench that rose from his own splintered ego," and his creation, "the arrogant, sterile Holmes."[2] And if Holmes cannot be safely considered great, what then of the many less well-known, less thoroughly established detectives to be found in these pages, and outside of them?

Many critics would simply reject the idea of greatness, in literature or elsewhere, full stop. Barbara Smith has argued that "all value is radically contingent." It is not a "fixed attribute, an inherent quality, or an objective property" of, for example, a work of fiction; value does not belong properly to the work itself. It exists instead, Smith explains, as the "effect of multiple, continuously changing, and continuously interacting variables," such as economic, social, and personal factors. If we accept Smith's argument, it would be axiomatically impossible to identify greatness with any reliability.[3] Yet as Smith acknowledges, there are "extensive demotic languages of popular criticism," the hits and flops, the masterpieces and epic fails of daily conversation, the very existence of which shows us that value judgments are "among the most fundamental forms of social communication."[4] While we may thus sensibly mistrust the practice of valuation, it is not something we can simply stop doing.

We might say, then, that the idea of literary greatness, in this case great crime writing, is not—or is not only—a fixed quality of authors and their works but a social construct, a necessary agreement, as it were, among readers, writers, and critics to embrace and reward certain traits, be they ways of writing sentences, ways of structuring plots, or ways of developing and presenting characters. And since an agreement is subject to development, evolution, and even radical change, the investigative figures discussed here represent not a definitive statement of greatness but a contribution to an ongoing discussion of crime fiction.

This still leaves us, however, with a problem, and one that is particularly relevant to a work of this sort: the fact that the assertion of value—of greatness—can, and frequently does, become self-perpetuating. "The recommendation of value represented by the repeated inclusion of a particular work in anthologies," Smith writes, "not only promotes but goes some distance towards *creating* the value of that work."[5] Canon formation, in other words, is far from being an innocent activity, a bland and objective *recognition* of literary value. Instead, it is an active *assertion* of—even an attempt to create—the value it ostensibly identifies. There is nothing wrong with this, but it does mean that we must be aware of what we are doing when we contribute to the construction of a canon by creating lists like the one in this book. It is on these grounds, in part, that this volume attempts to cast its net as widely as possible over the vast body of international crime fiction; if your favorite detectives are not featured on these pages, as they no doubt deserve to be, it may well be that their absence is a strategic recognition of the need to constantly challenge any tendency toward stability in the canon, and to actively look for new voices (be they contemporary or historical) who bring new elements to our vision of greatness in crime fiction and of the great detective.

The second thing we can learn from our outrage at discovering that Sergeant X or Detective Chief Inspector Y has not made the cut is that crime fiction matters. While the form has long occupied a culturally central position as one of the most broadly, reliably, and persistently popular forms of literature, it has also been seen as faintly disreputable and undeserving of serious consideration. At its mildest this type of criticism has coolly discussed crime writing as "mere detective-story"; at its strongest it sees the genre as "a menace to civilization."[6] Part of the function of a book like this is to refute these aspersions by contributing to the now substantial body of work that recognizes crime fiction as a distinctive and valuable element of literature that cannot, or should not, be segregated into the ghetto of genre fiction. It is, in short, a form that it is worth getting angry over.

CRIME FICTION AND LITERARY CRITICISM

Most readers and critics would locate the emergence of the genre in the nineteenth and twentieth centuries, with Edgar Allan Poe's 1845 story "The Purloined Letter" frequently cited as an inaugural text. This alone demonstrates the formidable endurance of the genre, but it is not difficult to trace a much longer tradition of crime as a prominent feature of fictional narrative. Consider the story of Cain and Abel, which revolves around a murder motivated by jealousy, an act of divine detection based on what we would now call either a clue or forensic evidence ("the voice of thy brother's blood crieth unto me from the ground"), and a punishment for the discovered perpetrator.[7] This interest in crime occurs in diverse literary forms and traditions, from classical Greek drama to *One Thousand and One Nights*, from Ming Dynasty *gong'an*, or court-case fiction, to the lurid tales of the *Newgate Calendar or Malefactors' Bloody Register*. But it was not until the development in the early nineteenth century of a proto-criminology and the introduction of official state police forces with London's New Metropolitan Police in 1829 that crime fiction began to develop as a separate, distinct, and recognizable genre.[8]

From this point on, the story of crime fiction has been one of extraordinary success, as it has developed and transformed its own conventions, adapted to changing sociohistorical circumstances, and spread around the globe. It has been claimed that no other genre can today compete with crime fiction in terms of a diverse, wide-ranging popularity.[9] While this is not the place to test this claim with any rigor, one example might be in order: the latest library-borrowing data compiled by the British Society of Authors reveals that with one exception *all* of the ten most-borrowed authors, excluding children's writers, write crime fiction.[10]

Yet despite this cultural centrality, crime fiction has long languished at the periphery of literary study, alongside other forms of genre fiction derided as, in Michael Chabon's words, "fundamentally, perhaps inherently debased, infantile, commercialized, unworthy of the serious person's attention."[11] This situation is, however, beginning to change, as once seemingly impermeable divisions between "literary" and "genre" fiction erode, both in theoretical and practical terms. There is an increasing recognition that, as Ursula K. Le Guin has argued, "genrification is a political tactic and that the type of fiction . . . distinguish[ed] as serious, mainstream, literary, etc., is itself a genre without any inherent superiority to any other."[12] It is also increasingly common to find authors operating on both sides of the ostensible divide—"literary" writers producing "crime fiction," and "crime writers" producing "literature." The selection of detectives appearing in this book is intended to recognize this phenomenon, and indeed the long and honorable history of the detective in literature.

Many critics and scholars are now placing crime fiction at the center of their interpretative endeavors, recognizing it both as a form capable of shedding valuable light on diverse cultural configurations and as an inherently valuable literary tradition. This attention is unquestionably positive, both for readers of crime fiction who wish to develop a broader and richer understanding of the genre and for literary scholarship in general, which cannot help but gain from sustained engagement with a type of writing that has played such a central role in literary history and remains so enduringly popular. Yet there is a gap in the study of crime fiction, and here, too, our initial dismay at discovering the absence of a beloved character from the pages of this book is relevant.

CRIME FICTION AND CHARACTER

Much of the attention that has been, and is now being, directed at crime fiction has focused on either its social implications—the way it is able to articulate, examine, and potentially critique particular social anxieties over, for instance, the boundaries of justice—or its unique narrative structures built around the clear, and clearly analyzable, stages of crime, detection, and punishment. These are of course perfectly viable—in fact extremely powerful—interpretative approaches. What is missing, however, is a sense of crime fiction as a genre if not dedicated to, at least very capable of, the creation and exploration of character, a sense that at the very heart of the genre, its power, and its appeal, lie its characters: murderers, informants, witnesses, and victims, but most notably its detective figures. French crime writer Pierre Lemaitre has argued that "the unparalleled success of crime fiction clearly demonstrates the visceral need people have for death. And for mystery."[13] Yet I would argue that it also indicates the powerful need people have for character, although this is not a perspective that has been widely adopted in academic criticism.

There are a number of possible explanations for this. For many years now, academic criticism has shied away from character as an interpretative or evaluative category.[14] It has been seen as a blind alley best avoided by "sophisticated critics" interested in, for example, "the truly important matters of language."[15] Similarly, character has frequently been seen as an outmoded construct, a fictional analogue of a particular way of thinking about human identity no longer relevant to modern experience. "The novel of characters," as writer Alain Robbe-Grillet argued in 1957, "belongs entirely to the past, it describes a period: that which marked the apogee of the individual."[16]

Like all literature, the study of crime fiction has suffered from this rejection of character, but it also labors under other, more specific, critical difficulties. First, there is the close association of crime fiction with plot. This involves both the fact that crime stories involve more or less elaborate plots (often to get away with murder) and the fact that they often rely on elaborate narrative plotting intended to control the reader's access to information about these plots. Historically, this has aligned crime fiction with the "novel of plot" rather than the "novel of character." For example, in his introduction to Charles Dickens's *The Mystery of Edwin Drood,* G. K. Chesterton (creator of Father Brown, discussed later in this book) argues that as the novel is "a detective story first and last" any discussion of it, "alone among the Dickens novels," need "speak of the plot and of the plot alone."[17] Similarly, Wilkie Collins (whose detectives Valeria Brinton and Sergeant Cuff have entries in this volume) felt forced to defend himself in his 1861 preface to *The Woman in White* against the imputation that "his labyrinthine, suspenseful (and often implausible) plots came at the expense of his characters."[18] Collins himself rejected the bifurcation between plot and character, arguing that it is "not possible to tell a story successfully without presenting characters: their existence, as recognizable realities, being the sole condition on which the story can be effectively told."[19] Yet if one were tempted to accept, in however nuanced a form, the proposition that some types of fiction rely more than others on plot for their overall effect, it would be understandable to classify crime fiction in this way.

And certainly many critics have done exactly this. Dorothy L. Sayers, one of the leading Golden Age detective writers (her detective Lord Peter Wimsey features in these pages), and one of the form's earliest and most acute theorists, paraphrases Aristotle to argue that "the first essential, the life and soul, so to speak of the detective story is the Plot, and the Characters come second."[20] Or consider

Canadian critic Northrop Frye's definition of what he saw as a fundamental problem with "murder stories," all of which "conceal an essential clue: the murderous character of the murderer. Hence there's a clash between the detective interest in the plot and the novelist's interest in character."[21] If the author of a crime story is compelled to conceal or withhold key information about one, and often more, of the characters in their story in order to serve the plot, she inevitably damages the work's capacity for characterization. Frye has even gone so far as to describe crime fiction as "pure caricature of the novel form" since "the novel is designed to reveal character, the detective story to conceal it."[22]

Yet as any reader of crime fiction will tell you, and as the contents of this volume attest, crime stories offer some of the most memorably vivid and fascinating characters in all of literature. And when we read crime writing, our engagement with the text is (almost always) mediated through the strong central figure of the investigator. This tendency is so powerful that when authors attempt to decenter the investigative figure, he (or increasingly she) has a way of creeping back from the periphery. Maj Sjöwall and Per Wahlöö's ten-volume series, *The Story of a Crime* (1965–1975), works very hard indeed to shift the focus of attention from the individual investigator to the group, and from the individual mystery to the broader, systematic social context within which crime occurs. Yet the series is now almost universally referred to as the "Martin Beck novels" after their investigative protagonist. Similarly, Lisbeth Salander dominates in spectacular fashion Stieg Larsson's *Millennium* trilogy, despite the fact that these are ostensibly police procedurals and as such should not focus on a single character.[23] If we cannot account for these characters with our normal theoretical tools, it does not mean that something is wrong with the characters but that something is wrong with the theory.

How, then, does character function in crime fiction? What is it about the form that produces such memorable and resonant characters? The individual entries in this book will go far toward answering these questions, demonstrating in a hundred different ways that the genre is capable of creating magnificent characters. But it may be worth making a few more general observations before allowing the detectives to speak for themselves.

THE FIGURE OF THE DETECTIVE

One thing that may need to be clarified is why the detective figure, as opposed to the victim or the perpetrator, is the object of particular interest here. In part, the question answers itself, and generally in the first few pages of a crime novel, or even before it has formally begun, for crime stories, in their classical form, open with a death.[24] The victim thus cannot take center stage as a character. It is true that the process of investigation often reveals a great deal about the victim's character, often to their detriment, in order to provide a motive. Think, for example, of Lanfranco Cassetti, alias Mr. Ratchett, in Agatha Christie's *Murder on the Orient Express* (1934), whose real character, his identity and past, *is* the solution to his murder. But this is perhaps an exception to the rule of the emptiness of the figure of the victim in crime fiction, the way in which a character like Rusty Regan in Raymond Chandler's *Big Sleep* (1939) operates as an organizing absence, a black hole around which the crime novel orbits. Indeed, this may be one of the wrongs the genre exists to right: the unforgivable erasure of identity inherent to the act of taking a life.

On the other hand, crime fiction has certainly produced many notable villains. Holmes would be incomplete without his nemesis Moriarty, and although Thomas Harris's Clarice Starling is certainly an interesting character, she has been thoroughly upstaged by Dr. Hannibal Lecter. These are notable exceptions, however, within the mainstream of detective fiction in which criminals tend to occupy a peripheral position. While a reader's attention is often directed toward them—their identity or whereabouts are after all the object of the investigation—they tend to remain obscure or marginal characters. As Frye points out, the closer we come to knowing them as they really are, the closer they come to apprehension and punishment. Of course this does not apply to crime writing—often described as *noir*—that rejects the investigative model. A novel like Ted Lewis's *GBH* (1980), which focuses on George Fowler, porn king, gangster, torturer, and murderer, clearly places the character of the criminal in the spotlight. But this form, for all its strength and popularity, does not provide the main model for crime fiction, in which the villains are only gradually revealed, dragged from concealment by the persistence and perspicuity of the investigator, and then quickly disposed of.

The opposite, however, is true of the figure of the detective, who tends to occupy ever more of the reader's attention. Part of this may have to do with the way the serial nature of some detective fiction encourages a form of characterization in which repeated appearances over multiple texts allow for the gradual accretion of characterizing detail. In many series, this process is carried out over time, offering fictional lives lived in parallel to our own, albeit generally at a slower pace. This allows crime writers to offer developed, rich, and detailed representations of their investigators, and to register the impact of social transformations on them as they move through history. Readers of Sara Paretsky's V. I. Warshawski series, for example, have been able to follow the hard-boiled heroine through more than three decades of her, and their, lives, growing as she grows, changing as she changes. And given that crime writing often has a political impetus, this means that the form also excels at examining the impact of the political on the individual.

The peculiar emotional stresses that characters—and readers—encounter in the crime novel, through the inevitable encounters with danger, violence, and death, are also important. Just as we can learn more about the personalities, or character, of real people by observing them at times of stress, the investigative figures of crime fiction must frequently confront, and react to, the most trying of circumstances. Finally, the plot-driven nature of the crime novel somewhat ironically demands the elaboration of character to generate and sustain the reader's interest. Investigative routines—be they the close examination of the scene of the crime for the proverbial cigarette butt, the questioning of a closed group of suspects, or the creation and examination of elaborate timelines and schedules—are in a sense, just that: routine. And routines, however comforting and efficient they may be, both in life and in narrative, seldom hold our interest. Thus space is created for the development of character: the routines may not be riveting, but if the fictional person who carries them out is, all is well.

These are, however, simply some of the ways that the character of the investigator works in crime fiction. In Vera Caspary's novel *Laura* (1943), the eponymous heroine—in this case a suspect, not the investigator—claims that "there are two kinds" of fictional detective: "the hard-boiled ones who are always drunk and talk out of the corners of their mouths and do it all by instinct; and the cold, dry, scientific kind who split hairs under a microscope."[25] There is certainly some truth here, and much wry, self-aware humor, but Laura is, as Caspary knows, guilty of a radical oversimplification. Indeed, the novel's own investigator, Detective Mark McPherson (who does not appear in this book, although he is a fascinating figure), matches neither of these two stereotypes. Instead, as is demonstrated in the pages of this book, there are many different types of investigator, who function in many different ways to achieve many different ends. Here you will find one hundred examples, some very familiar, some much less so, of the startling diversity—of method and motive, of technique and tone, and of significance and style—of the figure of the detective. You will find characters from both sides of the Atlantic but also from across Europe, from Asia, and from Africa. You will find men and women of different ages, cultural backgrounds, and political persuasions. Yet while they are all different, the sleuths, private eyes, and police featured in these pages have two things in common: through their investigations they can help us to understand the complexities, perils, and potentials of our world and, while doing so, provide us with one of the purest and deepest sources of the inimitable pleasures of reading.

JEAN-BAPTISTE ADAMSBERG

Fred Vargas (Frédérique Audoin-Rouzeau)
(1957–)

Commissaire Jean-Baptiste Adamsberg is perhaps the most fascinating detective in contemporary French crime fiction. He works at the famous *brigade criminelle* in Paris, but his origins in the Pyrenees in southern France give this unruly character an affinity to nature that enables him to relate to local people in the rural areas his investigations lead him to. These include the Alpes-Mercantour region in *Seeking Whom He May Devour* (1999 [2004]) and small cities and villages in Normandy in *This Night's Foul Work* (2006 [2008]) and *The Ghost Riders of Ordebec* (2015 [2016]). Adamsberg travels to a distant Serbian village in *An Uncertain Place* (2008 [2011]) and to Iceland's northernmost community in *A Climate of Fear* (2015 [2016]), while *Wash This Blood Clean from My Hand* (2004 [2007]) introduces him to the vast wilderness of Canada.

In all of these places, Adamsberg encounters people whose habits, beliefs, and speech patterns contribute much to the humor and witty linguistic play that characterize the novels. Many secondary characters are deeply eccentric, such as former seaman Joss Le Guern, who discusses life with the ghost of his late great-great-grandfather in *Have Mercy on Us All* (2001 [2003]). Sympathetic and informed descriptions of regional peculiarities and ancient legends enhance our enjoyment as we discover, or rediscover, different corners of the world.

No matter what part of the world he is in, Adamsberg displays a striking disinterest in systematic investigative methods. He is in fact incapable of active thinking. Instead he lets his thoughts drift, "peacefully waiting for ideas to rise to the surface of his mind."[1] This is a clear break with the tradition of ratiocination in the detective genre. Adamsberg relies on intuition and hunches, which usually prove to be correct at the end of tortuous investigations that may at first seem entirely erratic. Adamsberg's far-fetched ideas and lack of focus often exasperate his loyal partner Adrien Danglard, walking encyclopedia and single father of five, who believes in proof, method, and reason but cannot help being seduced by his superior's gentle, evasive, and charming personality. In the later novels, Adamsberg's brigade is divided into two camps as tensions rise between those who continue to support the *commissaire* despite his strange ideas and behavior, and those who reject his unorthodox way of conducting investigations.

Adamsberg's approach is not limited to instinct. He also relies on his senses but not primarily, as is typical in crime fiction, on sight; it is claimed he can feel or smell guilt. He is further endowed with seemingly extrasensory, even supernatural, powers. He is able, for instance, to put children and animals to sleep by simply placing his hand on their heads. This skill comes in handy in *An Uncertain Place* when a neighbor's cat risks dying from distress and pain while giving birth. Adamsberg's touch calms the animal, so that the kittens can be delivered safely. Given these abilities, it is unsurprising that Adamsberg is open to all possibilities, even those that lie beyond everyday experience, and gets entangled in investigations revolving around werewolves, ghosts, vampires, and other apparently otherworldly forces. He is indifferent to social norms and expectations, and he never dismisses even the most surprising explanations, treating people, no matter how marginal and odd, with respect—unless they are evil.

Adamsberg's irregular personality spills over into his private life. Despite some brief affairs, he truly cares for only one woman, the transient musician-plumber Camille Forestier, who exits and enters his life at irregular intervals as the two take turns leaving each other. In the early novels, Forestier and Adamsberg's love is undisputed: "At the source of the water there's only her, and me. Downstream there can be quite a crowd."[2] Later on, Forestier gradually becomes a kind but distant friend (despite Adamsberg's efforts), before disappearing from his life altogether. Adamsberg also becomes a father unawares, not once but twice. In *Wash This Blood Clean from My Hand* he goes to Canada, where Forestier has taken refuge after their last breakup, and stumbles across her and their child, about whom he knew nothing. In *An Uncertain Place,* he discovers yet another son, the twenty-nine-year-old Zerk, who was the result of a short fling in the detective's youth.

All of Vargas's "rompols," as she abbreviates the more common *romans policier,* elude categorization. They are a unique blend of fairy tale, legend, and myth combined with police work and spiced up with elements of the thriller.[3] Still, some liken Adamsberg to Georges Simenon's famous Chief Inspector Maigret because of alleged similarities between their investigative methods and because both authors convey an atmosphere of "Parisian poetic realism."[4] While a rational explanation to the events is always given at the end of Vargas's novels, the fantastic seems to become ever more prominent in Adamsberg's latest adventures, where the impact of ghosts and other supernatural beings on people's lives is acknowledged even after the killer's more prosaic motivations and actions are uncovered. Adamsberg is thus a fascinating—and rare—example of a detective who works beyond the limits of the rational, helping us explore the less well-understood, and less comfortable, aspects of life.

Selected Bibliography

The Chalk Circle Man (1991 [2009])
Seeking Whom He May Devour (1999 [2004])
Have Mercy on Us All (2001 [2003])
Wash This Blood Clean from My Hand (2004 [2007])
This Night's Foul Work (2006 [2008])

An Uncertain Place (2008 [2011])
The Ghost Riders of Ordebec (2011 [2013])
A Climate of Fear (2015 [2016])

—Andrea Hynynen

KOGORŌ AKECHI

Rampo Edogawa
(1894–1965)

Rampo Edogawa's debut work "The Two-Sen Copper Coin" (1923 [1956]) cannot be ignored in any discussion of the development of Japanese detective fiction. Many agree it was the first "original" detective story with a distinctive Japanese flavor, in contrast to work "adapted," or even worse "copied," from Western crime fiction. Rampo's creativity was not restricted to mysteries, and he became the central figure in prewar popular fiction by writing a variety of stories from horror to science fiction, much like Edgar Allan Poe, from whom he took his pen name (a phonetic rendering of "Edgar Allan Poe" in Japanese). However, his most memorable creation was the private detective Kogorō Akechi and his group of young assistants, the Boy Detectives Club.

In Akechi's first appearance in "The Case of the Murder on D. Hill" (1925 [2014]), the narrator describes his new friend as an educated idler with an unusual interest in crime and detection. Akechi is no older than twenty-five and is a thin, charming man with long, tangled hair. His plain looks and shabby clothes are counterpointed by his encyclopedic knowledge of criminal psychology. Upon visiting him in a boardinghouse, the narrator is astonished at the state of the room, which has so many books in it that there is nowhere to sleep. Akechi is an avid reader of Western detective fiction and claims to seek the same sort of mystery in real life. His interest, however, lies in human psychology and the criminal mind rather than in the mere clever details of how a crime was committed. When the narrator names Akechi himself as the perpetrator (referring to stories such as Poe's "The Murders in the Rue Morgue" and Gaston LeRoux's *The Mystery of the Yellow Room*), Akechi laughs at this superficial and material approach to detection and claims that his method is instead "to see through the depths of people's hearts."[5] Edogawa used Akechi in other pioneering short stories such as "The Psychological Test" (1925 [1956]) and "The Stalker in the Attic" (1925 [1956]), making him the representative detective of prewar Japan.

As the public demand for detective fiction increased, Akechi moved from a niche youth magazine to the mainstream media, and evolved from a Poe-inspired amateur detective into a Arthur Conan Doyle–inspired professional who takes part in more action-centered investigations. In "The Dwarf" (1926 [2014])—serially published in the major newspaper *Asahi Shimbun*—Akechi is described as a renowned detective who has returned from the frontier of Japan's ongoing colonial expansion in China. In subsequent cases, he displays a foreign air, wearing Fu Manchu–inspired Chinese clothing or sophisticated Western suits. While in his earlier cases eroticism and grotesque crimes were employed to showcase Akechi's psychological method, in the later popular serials these elements gradually become a goal in themselves, embellishing Akechi's at times rather mundane detective work. "The Dwarf" begins with a sensational scene in which the narrator spots a strange person carrying a human arm in his pocket. His interest in this bizarre figure leads him to uncover, with the help of his friend Akechi, a series of nightmarish crimes. Rampo apologetically described the novella as an example of his immoderate inclination toward Gothic horror rather than detective reasoning. The irony is that "The Dwarf" was successful enough, and more importantly graphic enough, to be adapted into a movie the following year (two more films came after the war) and cemented the public image of Akechi, leading to subsequent adventures with sensational titles such as "The Spider-Man," "The Vampire," and "The Clown of Hell."

When public censorship of crime fiction tightened during the war years, Edogawa transformed Akechi once again, catering to a younger audience by eliminating many of his trademark elements. In the first novel in this series, *The Fiend with Twenty Faces* (1936 [2012]), Akechi appears as a father figure, married and living with his thirteen-year-old assistant Yoshio Kobayashi. Kobayashi is at first peripheral, but after he organizes the Boy Detectives Club, his investigations with his school friends are foregrounded. The "Seven Tools" Kobayashi carries, such as a pen flashlight and a pocket utility knife, helped attract young audiences familiar with spy thrillers and their gadgets. The success of the series also owes something to Akechi's foe, the "Fiend of Twenty Faces," who is modeled after Maurice Leblanc's gentleman thief, Arsène Lupin. The Fiend challenges Akechi and Kobayashi not with grotesque murders but with his masterful skills of disguise. Akechi's psychological detective method gives way here to a contest of wits.

The Boy Detectives series was a huge success for Rampo and constituted his major source of income after the war. Indeed, the series was so popular that it was soon adapted as a movie (1954), a radio series (1956), and a television program (1958). These adaptations had a lasting impact on Japanese popular culture, and the broader legacy of the iconic Akechi and the Boy Detectives can be seen in the internationally popular cartoon *Case Closed* (1994–).

Selected Bibliography

The Fiend with Twenty Faces (1936 [2012])
The Edogawa Rampo Reader (2008)
Japanese Tales of Mystery and Imagination (2012)
The Early Cases of Akechi Kogorō (2014)

—Satomi Saito

LEW ARCHER

Ross Macdonald
(1915–1983)

Although Lew Archer is arguably the last great detective of the first wave of American hard-boiled detectives, his prominence in the history and development of the genre is often overlooked. This is in part due to the enduring popularity of many other iconic figures from the period, with characters such as Raymond Chandler's Philip Marlowe or Dashiell Hammett's Sam Spade often positioned as the great, archetypal exemplars of this kind of cynical yet chivalric urban sleuth. Although it is true that in many ways Archer is a straight continuation of the hard-boiled paradigm, he also represents a more nuanced and complex incarnation of this particular type of detective. Solitary, tough talking, and prone to existential musings, Archer is also far more compassionate, pitying, and ruminative than his predecessors, often acting less as the central subject of Macdonald's novels than as a kind of mobile lens, providing intimate access to both the minutia of American family life and the complexities of the human condition. Often poetic and packed full of sociological and psychological insight, these are among the very few instances in which the private-eye novel has been elevated to the status of literary art.

First introduced to us in *The Moving Target* (1949), Archer is hired by the frail and debilitated Elaine Sampson to locate her husband Ralph, a millionaire entrepreneur who has disappeared following another heavy drinking binge in downtown Los Angeles. The novel immediately foregrounds Macdonald's presentation of Archer as a fresh variation on the world-weary hard-boiled detective. When offered a drink by Mrs. Sampson, Archer sarcastically replies, "Not before lunch. I'm the new-type detective."[6] Although of course saturated with irony, this statement makes palpable both Macdonald's indebtedness to his antecedents and his attempt to reinvigorate and modify the genre.

The family-driven plot of *The Moving Target* prefigures Macdonald's enduring preoccupation with the evil that exists at the heart of family life. Archer describes himself as a "private eye at the keyhole of illicit bedrooms," and buried domestic secrets, childhood traumas, and ancestral dysfunction invariably constitute the rotting foundation of the warped American Dream that he inhabits.[7] Placing greater emphasis on observation than scientific detection, Archer is arguably more of a psychoanalyst than a collector of clues. It is through this almost Freudian method of detection that a vision of American suburbia built upon intergenerational violence and Oedipal drama materializes, as Macdonald ultimately undermines and deconstructs the myth of the white, heterosexual nuclear family so central to American national identity. This psychoanalytic emphasis on ancestral memory and ancestral desire is most palpably dramatized in the *The Galton Case* (1959), which essentially functions as a modern rewriting of the Oedipus myth.

Although revealed as divorced and in his midthirties in *The Moving Target*, Archer remains something of an enigmatic and indistinct figure over the course of the eighteen novels in which he appears. He is around six feet tall, strongly built with dark hair and blue eyes, but Macdonald offers very little additional physical description of the detective. Information about his past appears only sporadically and incrementally over the course of the texts. While often vague about his own personal history, we do still learn—obliquely—about Archer's troubled childhood, his military service on Okinawa during the Second World War, and his dismissal from the Long Beach police force.

A perennial loner who is often destitute, Archer traverses the hypnotic plasticity of the California landscape in a dilapidated Ford convertible, charging fifty dollars a day plus expenses for his services. An occasional drinker and heavy smoker—that is until he quits in *The Instant Enemy* (1968)—unlike many hard-boiled detectives Archer eschews violence whenever possible. Not only is this an integral part of his chivalric code, but also it is a way of avoiding infection by the violence and depravity of California's dark, criminal underbelly. When jumped by a stranger in *The Drowning Pool* (1950), for instance, Archer is consumed by a desire for violence. Catching himself, he ruminates, "There had to be a difference between me and the opposition, or I'd have to take the mirror out of my bathroom. It was the only mirror in my house, and I needed it for shaving."[8] Yet at times the greatest threat to Archer's safety appears to be the state of California itself. Throughout the Archer novels, Macdonald presents the Golden State as a modern-day Sodom and Gomorrah. A space of iniquity, vice, and violence, the biblical scale of the sin entrenched in these urban spaces is made clear when Archer reflects that there is "nothing wrong with Southern California that a rise in the ocean wouldn't cure."[9] This apocalyptic representation of California reaches its apotheosis in *The Underground Man* (1971), when an out-of-control forest fire engulfs the city of Los Angeles. Archer may not be able to purify California, but nature can.

A selection of the Archer novels still remains in print today, demonstrating that interest in the great hard-boiled sleuth has not waned. Archer has also been portrayed on both television and the big screen on a number of occasions, most famously by Paul Newman (as "Lew Harper") in both *The Moving Target* (1966) and *The Drowning Pool* (1975). Although often unjustly overlooked, Lew Archer remains one of the greatest of all of the tough-talking private eyes that have traversed the mean streets of postwar California.

Selected Bibliography

The Moving Target (1949)
The Drowning Pool (1950)
The Barbarous Coast (1956)
The Doomsters (1958)
The Galton Case (1959)
The Chill (1964)
The Goodbye Look (1969)
The Underground Man (1971)

—Nathan Ashman

BOB ARCTOR

Philip K. Dick
(1928–1982)

There have been many different versions of the fictional detective, but one of the most unusual comes from the pen of Philip K. Dick, an author described by Fredric Jameson as "the Shakespeare of science fiction."[10] Dick was an extremely prolific writer whose output crosses genre boundaries, but he is not generally considered a crime novelist. Yet his 1977 novel *A Scanner Darkly* offers in the character of undercover narcotics agent Bob Arctor one of the genre's most fascinating, and moving, studies of the figure of the investigator and his relationship to society.

One of the main sources of this fascination is the fact that as an undercover cop, Arctor automatically straddles the ostensibly absolute dividing line between crime and punishment: he is simultaneously part of the underworld of a rampant and lethal drug culture and of the institutions that fight against it. The novel is set in California in a future 1994 in which Substance D, or Death, is alongside more traditional narcotics shredding the last remnants of an already tattered social fabric. Arctor is perfectly aware of the damage that these drugs are doing to society and to individuals. His great fear as an undercover agent is not that he will be discovered and murdered but that he will be slipped a "great hit of some psychedelic that will roll an endless horror feature film in his head for the remainder of his life."[11] The fact that this is the drug dealers' preferred method of punishment indicates, as Arctor reflects, that they know exactly how horrifying the effects of the drugs they sell are, and his commitment to tracking down the high-level distributors of Substance D is real, if at times inflected by a visceral desperation. In an echo of Kurtz's horrifying advice in *Heart of Darkness*, the only solution he can offer to the drug problem is to "kill the pushers."[12]

Yet as a participant in the drop-out drug culture he is investigating, he is equally aware of the lethal hypocrisy and of the cruelty of straight-world culture. Before becoming an undercover agent, he was a family man, until one day realizing that he hated not just his job or his house but also his life, "the whole fucking place and everyone in it," including his wife and daughters.[13] And as a doper, he is repelled by the casual brutality of straights like the wealthy and well-educated Thelma Kornford: when she discovers that a bug she is frightened of is harmless, she comes up with what becomes for Arctor and his doper friends a mantra to remind them of what is wrong with the "real" world: "IF I HAD KNOWN IT WAS HARMLESS I WOULD HAVE KILLED IT MYSELF."[14]

Arctor's dual identity is thus a source of inevitable and potentially irreconcilable conflict. As the undercover agent known as Fred, he loathes and despises the doper Bob and his circle of friends. But as the doper Bob, he loathes and despises the straight world embodied by the police. This all becomes much more complex when Bob becomes Fred's main investigative target, and he begins (or they both begin) to have serious difficulty in holding fast to any sort of unitary, integral identity. Perhaps the clearest symbol of this crisis is the so-called scramble suit he wears when meeting his police supervisors. By projecting fragmentary images of millions of human features onto a shroud-like membrane, it transforms the wearer into an anonymous "Everyman."[15] Arctor is not just two people; he is instead all of us, and the divide in his character between detective and suspect, hero and villain, is thus projected onto all of us. We can never, Dick implies, clearly place ourselves on one side of that line or the other—if the lines even exists.

By proposing the detective figure as a model for a divided human consciousness, Dick's novel looks well past the usual confines of the genre. But he also looks back to the form's roots. In "The Final Problem" (1893), Sir Arthur Conan Doyle had Sherlock Holmes plunge to his death with archvillain James Moriarty. While

Conan Doyle famously backtracked due to fierce public pressure, the model of the detective as a person willing to sacrifice his life for the good of the community was established. It is as if the form has a hidden need to acknowledge that whatever physical, mental, or social skills investigators bring to the quest for justice, however tough and resilient and persistent they are, at some point none of this is good enough. The ultimate good demands the ultimate price.

Bob Arctor pays this price, albeit in a form particularly suited to a novel exploring the boundaries of subjectivity and individuality. In order to infiltrate the production centers of Substance D, it is not enough for "Fred" to become "Bob." Instead, he must undergo the complete mental collapse and loss of self he fears so deeply; it is only by sacrificing not just himself but also his identity as himself that he is able to fulfill his investigative function.

Selected Bibliography

"Minority Report" (1956)
The Man in the High Castle (1962)
"We Can Remember It for You Wholesale" (1966)
Do Androids Dream of Electric Sheep? (1968)
A Maze of Death (1970)

—Eric Sandberg

B

BYOMKESH BAKSHI

Sharadindu Bandyopadhyay
(1899–1970)

Bengali crime writer Sharadindu Bandyopadhyay created a series of detective stories set over a lengthy span of time, all featuring the detective Byomkesh Bakshi. He appeared for the first time in "Satyanweshi" (The Inquisitor) in 1931. Neither a private investigator nor a police officer, Byomkesh's innate tendency toward selfless truth-seeking, and his desire for accurate knowledge, mean that detection is simply his passionate hobby. He detests the nomenclature of official investigation, even rejecting words like "detective" or "spy," and prefers being described as "just an Inquisitor, a Seeker of Truth."[1] Though indifferent to power and material wealth (he never charges a fee), he is elated by feelings of self-satisfaction after solving a case, pleased with his rising fame, and happy to accept an occasional gratuity from clients.

Unlike the superhuman image of many popular Western detectives, Byomkesh's powers of detection suggest neither infallibility nor extraordinary mental faculties—his "reasoning power is moderately developed but not yet mature."[2] He accepts his defeats modestly and never takes his detective skills for granted. Byomkesh thus offers a strong contrast to Sherlock Holmes, the quintessential detective. He is neither an expert in scientific studies nor a skilled violinist. When he is idle he does not resort to cocaine for stimulation. Instead, he enhances his torpor by relaxing with a hot cup of tea. He is, in fact, an educated, wise, and sober middle-class Bengali with no eccentric traits: "From his looks or even his conversation, one wouldn't judge him to be extraordinary in any way."[3]

Byomkesh is also humble enough to give due credit to his friend Ajit Bandyopadhyay, the narrator of many of his adventures, acknowledging that his popularity depends solely on his magnificent writing. Byomkesh and Ajit first meet in "The Inquisitor." In the Chinabazaar neighborhood of Calcutta, several unsolved murders have left the Bengal Police Department in a fix, as the government and the press have been very critical of the department's failure.

Byomkesh arranges to stay in a lodging in the area under an alias to investigate, sharing a room with one Ajit. Thus begins a profound bond of friendship. While the Byomkesh-Ajit duo may be inspired by the Holmes-Watson partnership, the two relationships are quite different. Byomkesh is around twenty-four years old, and Ajit is a year or so younger. Byomkesh originally lived in a rented apartment in Harrison Road with his manservant Pootiram, but due to their increasing attachment, Ajit (who has no family ties, has vowed lifelong celibacy, and has dedicated himself to literature), accepts his friend's invitation to move in. He thus begins his grand role of documenting and narrating Byomkesh's adventures. They live together like brothers and continue to do so even after Byomkesh's marriage to Satyabati, whom he meets for the first time in "Where There's a Will" (1933).[4]

These comparisons to Sherlock Holmes are not coincidental. Byomkesh is a product of the pre-independence era of Indian history. During this time, detective fiction, and particularly the Holmes adventures, contributed to the hegemonic dominance of European culture, reinforcing a sense of racial and cultural inferiority among colonized Indians. When read against a background of globally acclaimed Western detectives, Byomkesh is particularly significant from a postcolonial perspective. He replaces the imperial cultural paradigm with indigenous cultural traits, thus subverting imperial cultural and textual authority. Byomkesh foregrounds an essential Indianness (or more specifically Bengaliness) by carving out a niche as a dhoti-clad Bengali detective.

Many of the Byomkesh adventures are nationalist in sentiment. In "The Inquisitor," Bandyopadhyay begins by portraying the common man's Calcutta. He also refers to the dreams of the new Bengali generation experiencing an identity crisis. In the 1955 "Adim Ripu" (Primeval adversary), Bengal's historical and political metamorphosis in the aftermath of the Second World War and the partition of Bengal and India in 1947 leads to a "steep downfall in the worth of human life."[5] Byomkesh's clientele ranges from ordinary people to Bengali feudal lords and aristocrats. Each time the detective visits a feudal estate, he glories in the rich cultural heritage of Bengal, a rejection of imperial subordination, and throughout his investigations, he praises the local sociocultural identity.

Byomkesh has been a significant figure in Indian popular culture for eighty-five years now. His fame is constantly on the rise, with English-language editions, several regional and national television series, and even a recent Mumbai action thriller, *Detective Byomkesh Bakshy!* (2015). Superhuman feats do not define Byomkesh Bakshi; instead, he is a down-to-earth detective-next-door, with a magnetic personality and a profound sense of humility, compassion, and romance.

Selected Bibliography

Picture Imperfect and Other Byomkesh Bakshi Mysteries (1999)
The Menagerie and Other Byomkesh Bakshi Mysteries (2007)
The Rhythm of Riddles: Three Byomkesh Bakshi Mysteries (2012)

—Anindita Dey

INSPECTOR HANS BÄRLACH

Friedrich Dürrenmatt
(1921–1990)

Inspector Hans Bärlach of the Criminal Investigation Department of the Bern Police is not the detective his mentors, friends, and underlings would like him to be. He is an existentialist who factors the existence of the absurd into his inductions, and who recognizes the "skews" at the very margins of human motive that the scientific community would just as happily overlook. Both *The Judge and His Hangman* (*Der Richter und sein Henker*, 1950) and *Suspicion* (*Der Verdacht*, 1952) position Bärlach as the counterpoint to characters—most tellingly, his superior Dr. Lucius Lutz and war criminal Fritz Emmenberger/Dr. Nehle—who represent modern epistemological reductions of the mysteries at the heart of human behavior, and who favor methods of mastery and control that conceal the interpretive violence at their core. Bärlach, then, is a Sisyphean actor who struggles not just to solve individual cases but also to uncover the metacrime of abstraction and alienation.

As a twentieth-century professional whose career has witnessed numerous advances in scientific criminology—to which Dr. Lutz, back in sleepy Bern after observing the wholly modern investigative apparatuses of New York and Chicago, is wholly committed— Bärlach struggles to continue practicing his craft in the face of both disease and the expectation of forced retirement (whichever destroys him first). The "duty of a criminologist," he believes, is to question reality itself, to suspend one's assumptions about the world in an act of radical Cartesian doubt before embarking upon the construction of a speculative web.[6] Bärlach's method involves looking for and *beginning with* deviations in the fabric of a supposedly well-ordered reality, rather than progressing through the immediate elimination of the unusual. His long-standing rivalry with the brilliant career criminal Gastmann is, in many ways, a contest over the significance of the incalculable, and their devilish two-step occurs on a metaphysical chessboard far removed from the bureaucratic concerns of state and police. Whereas his rival stakes his life's work on the notion that the "incalculable, chaotic element in human relations . . . makes it possible to commit crimes that *cannot* be detected," Bärlach's operative thesis is that "human imperfection . . . guarantees that most crimes will perforce be detected."[7]

For Bärlach, there can be no such thing as a "case-by-case" basis: the mystery of the here and now always reflects backward and forward, covering the span of a lifetime, or even the whole of human history. His motivations as an agent of justice, albeit one who has few illusions about moral perfection, involve psychological manipulation and the keeping of cosmic tallies that would not fit inside a case file (his treatment of Gastmann, whose crimes are real but extend beyond the limits of his assignment, and fellow inspector Tschanz, who is not clearly on one side of the law or another, are cases in point). Every encounter with crime is an encounter with the abyss—of human nature, of the will, and of evil—and he finds himself "steeped in darkness again," feeling the weight of eternity and the "coldness of the universe" descend upon his rickety body as he follows his lonely hunches.[8]

In a sense, Bärlach's experiential and professional horizon is the pathos of post-war Europe in the aftermath of the Holocaust, with new forms of expert management never as far away from the camps as they might appear to those caught up in their hyper-efficient allure. Bärlach's quarry in *Suspicion*, for example, Fritz Emmenberger, is a crossing of Friedrich Nietzsche and Heinrich Himmler, a sadist whose concentration-camp medical experiments are supposedly beyond good and evil. So the void Bärlach traverses continually and holds at bay for "one more year," even as his physiology betrays him, is also the deep time of European cruelty and what Theodor Adorno and Max Horkheimer would describe as the continual "progress" of the Enlightenment resolving into the dark horrors of administrative murder.[9]

The principle that guides the inspector in his encounters with deviations of the human will—but which is also the seat of his anxiety—is the tautology "the law is the law," ultimately grounded in the logical and ontological formula X = X.[10] Although Bärlach knows that this principle of identity has lately given rise to monstrous deeds ("a Jew is a Jew" is but one axiomatic spin-off), he must nevertheless hold on to his tautology as the last gasp of motivation in and for a dying world. Behind each of his cases lies a struggle against the alienations of mechanistic thinking that takes us increasingly further away from understanding the motivations of other people, and that make good and evil mere outputs of an impersonal social apparatus. But Bärlach's final ground is also an abstraction: "the law is the law" is itself an irrational and mechanistic formula that he cannot easily defend.

Though Bärlach does not resolve this paradox, he constantly fights to make friends with it. For as piercing as his investigative intuitions are, as crafty as his manipulations of his fellow human actors can be, he is an existentialist first, always thrown back upon the troubling lack of transcendental meaning in a cold and indifferent universe. He may be a uniquely European figure made for European audiences—his character has primarily been reproduced on European television—but his speculative reach is universal, for the administered society and the personal and psychological crises contained therein (and the need for a principled response to stave off nihilistic surrender to these crises) is now a global condition.

Selected Bibliography

The Judge and His Hangman (*Der Richter und sein Henker*, 1950)
Suspicion (*Der Verdacht*, 1952)

—Zachary Tavlin

BROTHER WILLIAM OF BASKERVILLE

Umberto Eco
(1932–2016)

Although certainly not a prototypical detective, Brother William of Baskerville utilizes traditional crime-solving methods to guide readers through a series of mysterious deaths, with no clear suspect or motive emerging until late in the story. Winding through a labyrinth of evidence, both figuratively and literally, Umberto Eco's *Name of the Rose* (1980) is set in 1327 in a Benedictine abbey in northern Italy. A suspicious death has occurred, and the visiting English monk William is tasked with unraveling the mystery. Superimposed over this detective story is a more complex interrogation of aspects of the late medieval period, including the role of the Inquisition, the tension between religion and politics, the philosophical convergence (and divergence) of science and faith, and the increased focus on the book as a body of knowledge and tangible historical record. With its many layers and plot twists, including illicit sexual desire, constant deception, and the struggle for political power, the novel unfolds like a fourteenth-century soap opera, and at the center of it all is William of Baskerville. Traveling with Brother William is Adso of Melk, his scribe and disciple, who like Sherlock Holmes's companion Watson serves as the narrator of his adventures.

Often described as a doppelganger to Holmes, William is characterized by his sharp and penetrating eyes, beaky nose, and tall, thin frame. His habit of eating herbs gathered during his dangerous journeys leads Adso to "suspect he was in the power of some vegetal substance capable of producing visions."[11] Beyond sharing physical attributes and a penchant for occasional bouts of drug-induced mental clarity and intellectual transcendence, the most obvious correlation between William and Holmes is their attention to detection and reasoning.[12] Importantly, however, William departs from his model with regard to humility, occasionally appearing puzzled, admitting his mistakes, and conceding that he often guesses.[13] He even goes so far as to equate himself and Adso with a pair of clowns. But this humility and self-doubt never interfere with William's quest to solve the series of macabre deaths at the abbey through the application of reason.

Occasionally referring to his friend from Occam (William of Ockham) and guided by the words of (Roger) Bacon, Brother William describes how he arrives at his inferences by using observation to derive the most likely explanation to reconstruct events and thus identify a murderer. William continually teaches Adso to "recognize the evidence through which the world speaks" in order to develop propositions, no matter how uncertain they may at first seem.[14] He reminds Adso on many occasions throughout their criminal investigation of the need to imagine *all* possibilities when attempting to reconstruct the crime in order to discover the murderer.

A learned Franciscan motivated by a love of learning and a powerful desire for truth, William embodies a certain sensibility in relation to the power of reasoning. He is vain when his interpretation of the evidence leads to success, and frustrated when he is led astray by a false line of reasoning. As a (genuine) inquisitor, William focuses on acquiring and evaluating the evidence he needs to help him to arrive at the most reasonable premises, which he can then in turn use to derive conclusions. His investigatory prowess relies in large measure on this logical process. Like his creator Eco, who is famed for his seminal role as a scholar of signs, their uses, and their interpretations, William is a semiotician who reads signs to arrive at inferences, and uses cryptography, or the reading of illegible signs, to uncover perplexing clues that often require further elucidation (sometimes with the help of "medicinal" herbs and reflection).

Although William of Baskerville has sometimes been hastily located in the shadow of Holmes, he has earned his own place as an influential fictional detective. He embodies the dichotomy between religion and criminal detection, teaching the reader that acquired knowledge, coupled with perception, the interpretation of observed signs, and reasoning ultimately leads to the truth. But he is quick to remind us that such guesses always have an element of fallibility: "You perceive a line of reasoning that seems more convincing than the others. . . . But until you reach the end you will never know which predicates to introduce into your reasoning and which to omit. . . . I won, but I might have lost."[15] Unlike most traditional detective stories in which the successful capture of the criminal is accomplished through a linear series of clues waiting to be discovered by the astute, logical detective (regardless of any whimsical character flaws that may present themselves throughout the story), Brother William uncovers the murderer *despite* the fact that his reasoning proves flawed. He is deeply humiliated and has to openly admit his own failings as a detective. Here the reader (as well as the murderer and the trusted sidekick) perceives a weakness that has the potential to jeopardize the case, and it is in this imperfection that Brother William of Baskerville becomes human.

Selected Bibliography

The Name of the Rose (1980, 1983)
Foucault's Pendulum (1988, 1989)
The Prague Cemetery (2010, 2011)

—Michelle D. Miranda

MARTIN BECK

Maj Sjöwall (1935–)
Per Wahlöö (1926–1975)

Martin Beck, first detective, then inspector, and finally chief of Sweden's National Homicide Squad in Stockholm, is a rather lugubrious figure. Hampered by digestive problems, a weak immune system, a runny nose, and a fear of flying, he seems far away from the hard-boiled detectives of an earlier generation. In addition to endless cups of coffee, he occasionally drinks beer (and in *The Abominable Man* [1971 (1972)] even a *Beck* beer!), smokes *Florida* cigarettes (until they are discontinued by the State Tobacco Company), and listens to Bach's sixth Brandenburg Concerto, humanizing habits that foreshadow the hugely popular detectives of Scandinavian noir.

In his spare time Beck reads pulp fiction or historical books and constructs model ships. In the first Sjöwall and Wahlöö novel, *Roseanna* (1965 [1967]), he is portrayed as a quiet, discontented family man living in the quiet Stockholm suburb of Bagarmossen with his two children, Rolf and Ingrid, and his wife Inga. The lack of marital bliss is symbolized by his regular nights on the bed settee, and his only domestic happiness comes from eating breakfast with his daughter Ingrid, or his rare periods as a grass widower. His loathing for his wife peaks in *The Fire Engine That Disappeared* (1969 [1970]) when Beck resorts to the second lie he has ever told. In order to avoid celebrating Midsummer with his wife and brother-in-law, he claims to be on duty over the weekend. Despite feeling "criminal," he enjoys a weekend with his colleague Kollberg in a summer cottage with "considerable quantities of food and life-restoring drink."[16] The pleasures of solitude and gastronomy appear more enticing than any potential erotic ventures. On an official trip to Budapest to investigate the disappearance of Swedish journalist Alf Matsson in *The Man Who Went Up in Smoke* (1966 [1969]), he is seduced by the failed but talented Hungarian competitive swimmer Ari Boeck in his hotel room. Boeck pulls Beck's hand between her legs to feel her "swollen and open" sex, but Beck withdraws his hand, opens the door to the hotel corridor, and commands Boeck in his schoolroom German to dress herself.[17] Duty first! It is not until he moves into a flat in the city center after divorcing his wife and is seriously injured by a gunshot in *The Abominable Man* that he opens up to the joy of simultaneous orgasms while falling in love with the much younger Maoist Rhea Nielsen.

So Beck, in all his deficiency and gloom, represents us all—a twentieth-century everyman. And as such his perspective on the sociopsychological dimensions and contexts of crime in Sweden in the highly popular and internationally influential decalogy *The Story of a Crime* becomes intertwined with a more collective outlook and mood. The focus on Beck's persona outside his police work is typical of characterization in the police procedural genre, where private life is interwoven with public life and the personal is political. When Beck commits his midsummer fraud he relates this to police work: "There is nothing to indicate that policemen in general lie any less than anyone else. . . . Available data, in fact, suggests the opposite."[18] These novels thus not only echo the social concerns and political events of a transitional period in Sweden, as is typical for police procedurals, but also become increasingly critical of the failing social democratic project of the welfare state, the nationalization of the police, and the corruption of old institutions.

In the early novels, sexually active females and children are victimized in a highly misogynistic and unequal society, while their murderers represent male alienation in postwar Sweden. From *Murder at the Savoy* (1970 [1971]) onward, however, the "dispatched" characters instead represent the malice of society, while the assassins are portrayed as sensitive victims of the failed welfare state. This increasing politicization is evident when comparing the different descriptions of Christmas in *Roseanna* and *The Laughing Policeman* (1968 [1970]). If the former depicts a slushy, grey Stockholm, the latter reinforces the gloom and political agenda by referring to Christmas as an "advertising orgy" with "buying hysteria" spreading like the "Black Death."[19]

The decalogy, however, is not purely a Beck mystery series as the typical English cover blurb "A Martin Beck Novel" suggests. Even if he can be considered a protagonist, the detective work here is always collective. Despite Beck's patience and deductive strengths, he never solves a crime on his own. Colleagues Kollberg, Rönn, Larsson, Skacke, and Melander are a microcosm of Sjöwall and Wahlöö's vision of a utopian society where collaboration is essential and individualism is regarded as a contemporary plague. This is palpable in *The Laughing Policeman* when Detective Stenström is murdered because of his ambition to solve a cold case by himself. No wonder the last word in the last book of the series is "Marx."

Selected Bibliography

Roseanna (1965 [1967])
The Man Who Went Up in Smoke (1966 [1969])
The Man on the Balcony (1967 [1968])
The Laughing Policeman (1968 [1970])
The Fire Engine That Disappeared (1969 [1970])
Murder at the Savoy (1970 [1971])
The Abominable Man (1971 [1972])
The Locked Room (1972 [1973])
Cop Killer (1974 [1975])
The Terrorists (1975 [1976])

—Niklas Salmose

HÉCTOR BELASCOARÁN SHAYNE

Paco Ignacio Taibo II
(1949–)

Detective Héctor Belascoarán Shayne reigns as the longest-running gumshoe in Mexican fiction. Appearing in ten novels between 1975 and 2004, the quirky detective has captivated readers around the world, making his creator one of the most widely read Mexican writers ever. In fact, so popular is Taibo's character, that like Sherlock Holmes, Shayne had to be magically resurrected in the fifth installment of the series to appease the public outcry over his death.

Actively involved in leftist politics, Taibo decided to write a detective novel as a way to address social issues without the prescriptive commentary of the social novel. He recognized, though, that not all of the conventions of the detective genre applied to the Mexican—and, by extension, Latin American—context. In the traditional detective novel, the always highly moral detective, even if officially unaffiliated with the state, acts as its agent and helps restore order and implement justice. However, the long history of undemocratic rule and repressive political and economic practices in Latin America mean that the state is commonly seen as a *perpetrator* of crime and social injustice. Taibo thus looked to a different genre, the hard-boiled, in which the state and its powerful allies are often ultimately to blame.

The publication of Taibo's *Días de combate* (Days of combat; 1975), the first installment of the Belascoarán Shayne saga, marks the beginning of the widely popular *neopolicial* movement, a term coined by the writer himself to describe contemporary detective novels rooted in a violence-ridden Latin America. As Shayne notes, "Like so many Mexicans he was thoroughly fed up with the gratuitous violence that made it almost impossible for a guy to simply finish an honest day's work and come home to some chorizo and provolone for dinner."[5] Although Shayne always suspects that he will have to contend with forces more powerful than he is, he does not hesitate to take up cases that will endanger his life.

The Mexican gumshoe gets his colorful last names from his Basque sailor father and Irish folk-singer mother. When readers meet Shayne for the first time in *Días de combate,* he has just thrown away a coveted middle-class life in his beloved but frustrating Mexico City, deciding in his thirties to give up everything to become a private investigator. Driven by curiosity and stubbornness, he sets off to catch a strangler known as "El Cerevro." He quits his job as a mechanical engineer for General Electric, separates from his wife, and obtains his detective license by completing a correspondence course. Shayne sets up his base of operations in an office he shares with an entertaining ensemble of *chilangos,* or people from Mexico City, that includes first a plumber and later an upholsterer and a sewage engineer. The investigator also meets Taibo's literary alter ego in several of the novels.

Shayne's newly found purpose in life turns into a quixotic pursuit of justice against the forces of evil (the state, power, and money). The detective's new line of work is in line with his college years, when he was active in the antiestablishment movements of the 1960s, and his investigations often bring up uncomfortable episodes of Mexico's history. Even if criminals go unpunished, Shayne seeks to unveil the truth for himself and, even more importantly, to validate the victims' story. Justice may not be served, but at least the reader knows who the criminals are. In *Easy Thing* (1977 [1990]), Shayne sets out to prove the innocence of labor union workers accused of murdering an engineer during a strike. In *No Happy Ending* (1989 [2003]), he investigates the existence of a government-sanctioned paramilitary group sent to repress student protests that is responsible for the Corpus Christi Massacre of 1971. In *The Uncomfortable Dead* (2004 [2006]), his investigation uncovers a plot to privatize and sell off valuable land seized from an indigenous community in southern Mexico. In the final showdown of *Días de combate,* "El Cerevro" challenges Shayne to identify the real criminal in their country. The detective points, inevitably, to the government. Even so Shayne kills the strangler as punishment for his murder spree.

Taibo succeeds in interweaving these grave cases with lighter ones that send his protagonist on a journey through unusual social worlds, such as Mexican wrestling or soap operas. In *Easy Thing,* for instance, Shayne investigates if Emiliano Zapata, one of the national heroes of the Mexican Revolution, is still alive. The diversity of characters, the liveliness of the action, and the rich descriptions of Mexican culture that emerge throughout the series produce a vivid image of contemporary Mexico.

But it is Shayne's characterization that steals the show. The sleuth comically indulges in the guilty pleasure of cigarettes and cola. He is obsessed with the possibility of being poisoned. Owner of a sharp tongue, Shayne possesses a dark humor that perfectly captures the frustrations of the trade and of living in Mexico. His cocky attitude and quixotic ventures have left him with only one eye and a limp. Yet in spite of the powerful forces opposed to him, Héctor Belascoarán Shayne is a relentless optimist. He takes chances on love and does not give up on his countrymen, or humanity for that matter. And at the end of the day, the Mexican detective always has the last laugh.

Selected Bibliography

Días de combate (Days of combat; 1975)
An Easy Thing (1977 [1990])
Some Clouds (1985 [1993])
No Happy Ending (1989 [2003])
Return to the Same City (1989 [2007])
Frontera Dreams (1990 [2002])
Adiós Madrid (Goodbye Madrid; 1993)
The Uncomfortable Dead (2004 [2006])

—Patricia Catoira

DETECTIVE INSPECTOR NAPOLEON BONAPARTE

Arthur W. Upfield
(1890–1964)

Australia's half-caste detective Napoleon Bonaparte solved twenty-nine cases from *The Barrakee Mystery* (1929) to *The Lake Frome Monster* (1966), including missing persons, murders, and other crimes. Bony, as he instructs his friends to call him, appears to be almost ageless in spite of his feats of detection and narrow escapes from an assortment of criminals. The only visible change in his appearance is a touch of silver at the temples, although he occasionally observes that he is not as fit and tireless as he used to be. His intensely blue, almost mesmerizing, eyes remain the same.

Different layers of Bony's personality and character are revealed throughout the series, and sometimes discussed repeatedly. He is often conflicted because of his mixed racial heritage (half aboriginal and half white). He has deep insecurities arising from the contrast between his background (unknown father, dead mother, and name assigned because as an orphan he was discovered gnawing on a biography of the emperor) and his continually evolving life (mission school education, university degree, happy marriage, three sons, and successful career). Bony's achievements are many, yet he is looked down upon by many. He knows that a "touch of color" is the first thing in people's minds when they meet him.

This is certainly true in Bony's work. Tension is caused by his mixed race, and members of both groups, white and aboriginal, often view him with initial distrust. To allay this suspicion, he frequently appears under a variety of aliases, changing both his name and occupation as he believes people will talk to him more freely if they do not see him as a representative of the law. Bony describes his occupation variously as a stockman, a pastoralist, a horsebreaker, a Rabbitoh (worker on the Rabbit Fence), and a station roustabout, demonstrating further versatility while expertly shearing a sheep and stitching up an ugly wound in a man's scalp.

Bony deals with cases all over Australia, from the stations of Queensland to the pearling community of Broome, from the emptiness of the Nullarbor Plain to the beautiful Kimberleys. This not only allows Bony to encounter many different people and subcultures but also allows for the depictions of novel environments and uniquely Australian phenomena: the long periods of drought that alternate with floods (*Death of a Lake*, 1954), the sneakers or king waves on the southern coast (*The White Savage*, 1961), and the frenzy of rabbits suffering from myxomatosis (*The Bone Is Pointed*, 1938).

The exoticism of scenes like these and the correlation of the outback to the American West have made the "Bony books" more popular in the United States than they have been in Australia, where a common point of criticism has been their lack of literary value. Although Upfield was well read, as evidenced by the number of literary allusions in his novels, his prose is straightforward rather than poetic. Another criticism is the privileging of white culture over Bony's aboriginal heritage. Some find his claim to have received logic and reason from the former, and patience and the ability to read the land from the latter, reductive. However, although many characters in the novels demonstrate racism, Bony himself does not dismiss one culture at the expense of the other. He does find miscegenation problematic, citing his own uneasy situation as evidence of the problems it can cause. In what is arguably the most melodramatic (but also the most moving) scene in the Bony series, a mixed couple commits suicide; they feel inextricably bound to each other but believe it is impossible to be together in Australia's racist society. Bony's status as a mixed-race detective continues to fascinate readers while at the same time inviting potential criticism.

"When engaged on a murder hunt, I have no scruples and no ethics," Bony says, and it is quickly apparent that he has his own ideas of what justice is and how it should be administered.[20] He does not believe that punishment should be left to God but has no qualms about protecting the perpetrator if he feels the crime was unintentional or morally justified. On one occasion, he even instructs a young woman on how to word her statement to the police, resulting in a narrative that hardly mirrors the facts. It is Bony's dedication to justice—sometimes his own version of it—however, that wins over the communities he seeks to aid. Those who at first distrust him come to recognize Bony for the unique and admirable individual that he is. They see his total commitment to his assignments, and his care for others, and come to esteem him for his determination to move beyond his humble beginnings to become a successful man who enjoys the respect of all who truly know him. Bony himself takes great pride in his record—"I locate a killer once I start on his tracks."[21] And the cases he is assigned—cold cases, given to him because others have failed to read the clues and solve the crimes—are never simple.

Bony repeatedly mentions the assistance he receives from the natural world, the Book of the Bush, as he calls it. Instead of fingerprinting and blood typing, he gains information from the flora and fauna, and from the tracks he follows across the dusty outback. More important than these, however, may be time itself. A criminal can try to bury his crime, but in time the sands that covered it will blow away, and Detective Inspector Napoleon Bonaparte will be waiting to exact justice.

Selected Bibliography

Mr. Jelly's Business (1937)
The Bone Is Pointed (1938)
Death of a Lake (1954)
Bony and the Black Virgin (1959)
The Will of the Tribe (1962)

—Winona Howe

INSPECTOR TYADOR BORLÚ

China Miéville
(1972–)

China Miéville's work frequently integrates elements of fantasy, science fiction, and many other genres. *The City and the City* (2009), however, is clearly—even enthusiastically—a crime novel, and is thus an excellent example of the way the form has begun to cross literary borders. And despite the fact that Miéville is not primarily a crime writer, he has created in this novel an extraordinary investigative figure, Inspector Tyador Borlú, who embodies many of the key features of fictional detectives: their flexibility, their inherent liminality, and their frequently complex relationship to crime and justice. What is important here is not Borlú's character per se but the multiple roles he plays.

The City and the City is narrated in the first-person voice often associated with the hard-boiled novels, and its opening scenes are very much in line with the gritty traditions of the police procedural. The laconic Borlú fits perfectly into a milieu of run-down housing estates and delinquent youth, and as he begins to investigate the murder of an unidentified young woman with Constable Lizbyet Corwi, readers are immersed in a fictional system that is deeply familiar (although in a setting that is unfamiliar). Borlú's interaction with Corwi follows the pattern of an older, experienced, world-weary detective working alongside a younger, starry-eyed sidekick. A comparison might be made, for instance, to Henning Mankell's Kurt Wallander and his partner Ann-Britt Höglund, or to any number of police TV shows and movies. As the investigation continues, Borlú teams up with Senior Detective Qussim Dhatt to pursue the investigation outside of his own jurisdiction, and we encounter another well-known structure: the mismatched but nonetheless effective police partnership. The differences between the two police officers are both cultural and procedural, with Dhatt favoring a more direct, and at times brutal, approach to interrogation than Borlú is comfortable with, but they eventually develop a respect for and reliance on each other—again, a common trope. Finally, the last section of the novel is a murky political conspiracy thriller, in which Borlú works alongside yet another investigator, Ashil, to link the seemingly random murder with which the novel opens to deep structures of corporate and political malfeasance. These fugue-like transformations are an intentional act of homage on Miéville's part, a way of celebrating the crime genre and its traditions, but they are also a virtuoso demonstration of the flexibility of the fictional detective.[22]

In all of his various roles, however, Borlú remains stable. In part, this is due to his relative anonymity. He lives alone, spends little time on anything but the investigation, and offers readers very little in the way of personal information. He is completely immersed in his investigation and in noting and describing his environment. This is important because his environment is the key to Borlú's liminality. To some extent all fictional investigators are borderline figures, existing somewhere between crime and punishment, freedom and order, and revenge and justice, but Borlú's world is a startlingly literal representation of this condition.

He is a citizen of Besźel, which exists alongside, or superimposed over, its so-called doppler-city Ul Qoma, with which it shares a physical, but not administrative or cognitive, space. In a way that can be read as fantastic, metaphorical, or literal, the two cities represent one *space* split into two *places* through a radical act of collective will and social organization. One street, or house, or even tree is in one city, the next in the other, and the inhabitants of both go about their lives without acknowledging or interacting with each other through an internalized process of "unseeing."[23] Borlú's investigation, however, takes him back and forth between Ul Qoma and Besźel, linking the two zones. Ultimately, it takes him to a third place located in both—or is it neither?—of the two cities. This use of the investigator to connect seemingly disparate worlds (social, economic, racial, etc.) is a common hard-boiled trope, but Miéville's extreme development of it lays bare one of the key features of the genre, and of its central figure.

When Borlú's investigation takes him beyond the border of the two cities, he enters something known as "Breach."[24] This is a place, a legal state, and the term used to describe the security apparatus that enforces the separation between Besźel and Ul Qoma. Borlú commits Breach—and thus transgresses his society's most deeply held value—in pursuit of his investigation. Many investigative figures operate along the line that separates legal from illegal, and here Borlú steps across this boundary. He is only able to continue his investigation by cooperating with Ashil, who is an agent of Breach, in the investigation of his own crime. By the end of the novel, Borlú, too, has been recruited into Breach, one more radical shift in position for this protean investigator. Rather than solving murders and risking his own life to bring the culprits to justice as he does in *The City and the City*, he will in future be investigating crimes of perception, of orientation, and of attitude. As Borlú puts it, his new task "is not to uphold the law" but to "maintain the skin that keeps law in place."[25] This is in many ways a troubling situation, and one that is representative of the tension that exists throughout much crime fiction between the need to enforce the law and the sense that the law itself may at times be as problematic as the crimes it exists to control.

Selected Bibliography

Perdido Street Station (2000)
The Scar (2002)

The Tain (2002)
Iron Council (2004)
Kraken (2010)
Three Moments of an Explosion: Stories (2015)
This Census-Taker (2016)
The Last Days of New Paris (2016)

—Eric Sandberg

LIEUTENANT BORUVKA

Josef Skvorecky
(1924–2012)

Like a melancholic thought bubble in both mind and appearance, senior Prague police homicide detective Lieutenant Josef Boruvka first delighted Czech readers in 1960 with a series of short stories ultimately collected in 1966 as *The Mournful Demeanour of Lieutenant Boruvka* (1966 [1973]). He is a modest criminologist who solves complex crime puzzles in a drab society under Communist Party control. "Joe" Boruvka, whose Czech surname means "blueberry," is known as "Comrade Bubble" by his police team for his portly appearance, balding round head (which signifies cerebral detachment), and almost supernatural ability to solve crimes. His crack scientific and commonsense mind is often at odds with young Sergeant Pavel Malek, whose Slovak surname, meaning "small," is suggestive of his mental stature, or perhaps even the apparatchik mentality of Slovaks within a bicultural Czechoslovakia. Czech-language readers familiar with the flamboyant 1920s European literary tradition of eccentric detectives would have readily identified Karel Capek's folksy, unpretentious Dr. Mejzlik as Boruvka's predecessor.

Boruvka, born just after the end of World War I, is an old-fashioned reactionary who finds himself trapped between an imposed communism and a nascent 1960s liberalism. He is very much a product of the classical Catholic education he received at the Kostelac Gymnasia in eastern Bohemia, well before the Nazi occupation of 1938, when Czechoslovakia was a democratic republic. Caught in a loveless marriage to an Italian dressmaker, Josef has a romantic, guilt-ridden weakness for intelligent blonde women, including a junior sergeant who pleases him with her towering chignon when not irritating him with her leaps of logic. His male chauvinism extends to a futile concern for the moral education of his teenage daughter, Zuzana ("Sue"), who is caught up in the antiauthoritarian identity crisis that would lead to the short-lived Prague Spring in 1968. Boruvka has a suppressed, anachronistic persona that allows him to function under communist scrutiny while remaining a member of the hapless Catholic People's Party, a protective outward mien acquired while serving in the Czech tank corps alongside the occupying Germans, when he excelled as a physical trainer and sax player in the army band.

Boruvka abhors the loose ends typically found in Capek's stories, seeing them as arising from a nonmaterialistic philosophy tending toward mysticism. Given that both Capek and Skvorecky studied philosophy and aesthetics at Charles University in Prague, one can see why the lieutenant "liked mysteries, but only solved ones."[26] Boruvka, having lectured in criminology under Soviet rule, is theoretically an exponent of *diamat* or materialist investigation and brings mechanical, physical, biological, chemical, and social skills to his work. His proceduralism is also a criticism of aesthetic detection, thus *Sins for Father Knox* (1973 [1988]), wherein we find both Boruvka and his female alter ego, singer-sleuth Eve Adam, breaking the ten commandments of literary detection proclaimed by Ronald Knox in 1929. Boruvka's respect for logical method is eroded when he realizes he has had Eve wrongly convicted and imprisoned for a poisoning murder. He is so soft-hearted that at the precise moment he uncovers the actual murderer we find, as always, an "expression of inexpressible sadness on Lieutenant Boruvka's round face."[27]

In *The End of Lieutenant Boruvka* (1975 [1990]), Skvorecky depicts Boruvka in a hard-boiled series of retrospective cases set in a gritty landscape of Warsaw Pact social realism, peopled with informants against alleged revisionists and Zionists and individuals desperate to escape. Headstrong Zuzana is pregnant by an irresponsible psychiatrist but loved nevertheless by a flakey American, Mack, destined to be deported. Boruvka is increasingly under pressure from Orwellian forces undermining just outcomes, "counterespionage" collaborators who regard murder as a less important crime than an illegal exit to the West. The decadent party elite is protected, such as Major Kautsky who hijacks the investigation in "Miss Peskova Regrets" to whitewash the overdosing of a young dancer on LSD. Victims, like the two teenagers found shot in a field that both the Soviet and Czech armies patrol, receive no justice from Boruvka's elegant solution. At the end, in "Pirates" Boruvka faces characters for whom defection, people smuggling, and escape to America offer the only existential hope. In an endgame act of defiance and empathy, he betrays his fellow officers and helps a six-year-old girl take flight to her parents in Pittsburgh, knowing he faces an endless prison sentence.

A thinning Joe Boruvka reappears in the late 1970s as a parking lot attendant in Toronto and becomes a peripheral but defining advisor in the satirical novel *The Return of Lieutenant Boruvka* (1980 [1991]). Eve Adam has helped him escape prison in Prague and ended up inside herself. Zuzana has moved up from the United States to Toronto to take care of him and taken a secretarial position with the Watchful Sisters, a one-woman detective agency. A female friend has been found shot dead, and the list of suspects is a who's who of the Czech émigré factions. Fraudulent Austrian royals, exiled anticommunists, Nazi sympathizers, former collaborators, and Soviet spies offer a microcosm of European angst and vengeful grudges misunderstood by naïve and apathetic Canadians. Boruvka, an outsider in a novel narrated by Canadian Neil Donby, the victim's brother, provides the logical questions that solve the crime. In the epilogue Eve is reunited in marriage with Boruvka in Memphis, and Neil has caught Boruvka's "oppressive disease, the European virus. A melancholy that sometimes knocks me off my feet and eats away at the very substance of optimism."[28] Boruvka is thus the only literary detective at the geographic, political, and ideological center of twentieth-century European angst who bridges the Atlantic, carrying the burden and hope of displaced identity.

Selected Bibliography

The Mournful Demeanour of Lieutenant Boruvka (1966 [1973])
Sins for Father Knox (1973 [1988])
The End of Lieutenant Boruvka (1975 [1990])
The Return of Lieutenant Boruvka (1980 [1991])

—Chad A. Evans

DAME BEATRICE ADELA LESTRANGE BRADLEY

Gladys Mitchell
(1901–1983)

In 1929, Gladys Mitchell, an enthusiastic Freudian, teacher, and feminist, introduced the mystery-devouring interwar readership to Mrs. Bradley. A far cry from the domestically astute detectives often associated with the Golden Age, Mitchell's irrepressible detective is a Home Office psychiatric consultant and psychoanalyst. Between 1929 and 1984, Mitchell published sixty-six Bradley novels. Remarkable for their macabre humor, occasional pathos, and surreal undertones, Mitchell's novels have frequently been neglected by critics. The modest attention that Mitchell has received, in comparison with her innovative creation of the genre's first psychoanalytic detective, is quite disproportionate, but Bradley remains an irreverent and unforgettable character in interwar detection.

Many Golden Age detectives occupied both marginalized and privileged social positions: the fashionable Hercule Poirot is a refugee; Peter Wimsey is both an aristocrat and a PTSD survivor; Miss Marple, a pillar of her community, is mocked for her age. Even Dorothy L. Sayers's Oxford-educated female detective, Harriet Vane, is trapped between marriage, with a potential loss of intellectual, financial, and legal autonomy, and remaining independent and facing misogynist accusations of sexual frustration and mental pathology. In contrast, Bradley is not troubled by the many contradictions of her position. As both detective and analyst, she occupies two of the era's leading "savant" roles. Both figures are invested with the power to uncover the secrets of the past and the mind, and these skills make her a delight in an era of detection defined by its interest in the "why" rather than the "how" of crime.[29]

As an empowered woman and gifted intellectual, Bradley offers an original take on psychoanalysis. While pseudo-Freud inspires fear of sexually "thwarted" women in Sayers's *Gaudy Night*, Bradley eschews misogynist stereotypes to tell more complex stories of women's psychological, intellectual, and sexual lives. Many of her novels center on women-led institutions, including convents, training colleges, and schools, rather than the country house settings often associated with the era. In *St Peter's Finger* (1938), for example, the convent is shown to offer opportunities for female friendship, self-development, and rewarding work, which are an antidote to the restrictions of traditional women's roles.

As a female detective, too, Bradley can be defined against the roles presented by contemporary writers. She is not comfortingly asexual, like Marple, but neither does she combine romance with sleuthing like Agatha Christie's chipper heroine Tuppence Beresford. Instead, Bradley has been married three times and given birth to innumerable children, including her barrister son, Sir Ferdinand, with whom she consults on legal matters and unashamedly flirts, while he plays "off the Freudian Oedipus complex against her with a delicate and admirable wit."[30] Although an elderly woman, she is a far cry from "soothing"; she "leers" rather than looks, scoffs at incest taboos, and discusses nymphomania over tea at the vicarage.[31]

Desire and subversion play below the surface of many Golden Age novels, but Bradley speaks the unspeakable, going so far as to describe murder as perfectly sensible, in the right circumstances. Clearly, her unconventional theory of crime distinguishes her from detectives who pursue justice for its own sake. She allows one murderer to escape, convinced that the person will never offend again, and shocks another to death so the murderer avoids legal punishment. Most outrageously, she admits to killing her first husband: "I was tried for it and acquitted, but I did it boys and girls, I did it."[32] Her ability to manipulate the law is connected with her insider/outsider role. She has authored books on criminology, provides expert testimony in trials, advises the government on medico-legal policy, and is a respected public figure, who later in life will be made a dame. Rather than scoffing at her age and gender, the police welcome her into investigations and treat her with awe. This must have been a rare pleasure for interwar female readers used to seeing their heroines mocked by the authorities until the novels' final pages.

Bradley, then, is a dynamic contradiction, merrily transgressing the norms of feminine physique, psyche, and behavior. "A small, shrivelled, bird-like woman, who might have been thirty-five and who might have been ninety," she is at once terrifying and "superlatively attractive," despite seeming at times not quite certifiably human; as Patricia Craig and Mary Cadogan have put it, she "looks like a reconstituted pterodactyl and behaves like the Cumaean Sibyl."[33] Giving little thought to growing old, she shows no signs of doing so gracefully, dressing hideously in "sage-green, purple and yellow" combinations.[34] Blessed with a rich and powerful voice, she also emits "eldritch" shrieks and cackles from a "saurian" mouth located in a yellow, chameleon-like countenance.[35] To many, she is wholly disconcerting. Perhaps this is rightly so: Bradley's clawlike hands are extraordinarily strong, enabling her to overpower "homicidal maniacs" and strike fear into the hearts of Borstal boys, who become well behaved and respectful under her guidance.[36] Like her readers, all are ultimately won over, sometimes by her wit, generosity, and insight; others are simply won over, without ever understanding why.

Selected Bibliography

Speedy Death (1929)
The Saltmarsh Murders (1932)

Death at the Opera (1934)
Dead Men's Morris (1936)
St Peter's Finger (1938)
When Last I Died (1941)
Laurels Are Poison (1942)
Tom Brown's Body (1949)

—Samantha Walton

SIMON BRENNER

Wolf Haas
(1960–)

Conceived in defiance of a literary establishment that had for fifteen years refused to publish Haas's novels, the quirky ex-policeman turned private investigator Simon Brenner is now celebrated by literary critics and readers alike. Cranky, ambitionless, and often underestimated, Brenner (whose name translates as "Burner") is a reluctant hero who embodies many stereotypical Austrian traits while at the same time undermining traditional images of Austria as an unspoiled tourist destination with a rich cultural heritage, traditional values, and wholesome inhabitants.

At the beginning of the series, the forty-four-year-old Brenner has just quit the police force after nineteen years of service. Without any real prospects, he begins freelancing for an insurance agency that asks him to investigate an unsolved case from his police career. This is the first of many temporary jobs that take him all over Austria. Investigating crime in ski resorts, beautiful provincial towns, and the capital Vienna, Brenner uncovers the ugly underbelly of idyllic tourist destinations. He not only implicates many of Austria's institutions and traditions, such as the police force, the Catholic Church, and the Salzburg Festival, but also challenges conventional images of Austria as a safe and orderly place.

Haas conceived the underdog sleuth with a wry sense of humor as a poor relative of respectable society. Although he often rebels against authority, Brenner is a normal man. There is nothing special about his physical appearance, and he is not particularly gifted in any way (he has no talent for music, languages, math, or even sports). He is often grumpy, and he tries to use the system to his advantage—for example, trying to stay in his government-subsidized flat even after quitting his government job. Needless to say, the system usually proves even more corrupt than he is, thwarting his attempts at subterfuge and trickery. Brenner thus embodies independence and, despite his unsuccessful attempts to game the system, by refusing to be beholden to anybody, a sort of stubborn integrity. His general lack of ambition allows him to expose people and institutions without regard for personal consequences. The price he pays is perpetual financial instability and a lack of permanent relationships.

Brenner's cases quite often turn out to be about something different than initial appearances suggest. They include a variety of subplots and supporting characters and tend to draw Brenner in, even when he is working in seemingly unrelated jobs as, for instance, an ambulance driver or chauffeur. Typically, having just found an ordinary job, a routine, a salary, an apartment, and a pension, he is reluctant to take on the investigation. This is true of the most recent novel in the series, *Brennerova* (2014), in which he declares himself officially retired before once again getting sucked into a case and a fake marriage with a Russian client, neither of which he is eager to pursue.

One of Brenner's most distinctive features is his tendency to ruminate instead of concentrate. While he gets frustrated by his inability to tell the essential from the inessential, this method allows him to solve cases by unconsciously noticing minor details and making mental leaps that defy linear reasoning: "Because that's the advantage that brooding has over thinking. That you can brood over everything simultaneously."[37] Clearly not the fastest approach—brooding offers no control over outcomes—it nevertheless permits him to make associations between seemingly unrelated events and ideas. Brenner's investigative detours are mirrored by the novels' digressive storytelling that exposes readers to more details than are strictly necessary for the solution of the crime. This allows for a wider examination of Austrian culture and mores.

A defining characteristic of the Brenner novels is the unusual perspective from which they are told. A nameless narrator speaks in a distinct Austrian German full of idiomatic expressions, grammatically incorrect sentences, fillers, and other attributes of speech. The irreverent narrator often addresses readers directly, urging them to pay attention and alluding to events about to happen. He not only knows Brenner's thoughts, feelings, and motives but also comments on them and evaluates them from his perspective—one that often proves sexist and ethnocentrist. In *Das ewige Leben* (2003; Eternal life), originally planned as the last installment in the series, the narrator is killed—but defying the inherent realism of the genre, this does not stop him from relating the subsequent installments of Brenner's adventures. This ploy allows for a further exploration of Austrian identity as the deceased narrator's darkly witty comments and wry observations accentuate the series' scathing critique.

Brenner has some similarities to the lonely hero of the hard-boiled novel. He occasionally drinks too much (which causes his migraines to flare up) and, despite his reluctance to engage in physical altercations, gets repeatedly beaten up. At times he is willing to bend the law and cover for perpetrators whose crimes he considers justified or insignificant, following his own sense of justice rather than laws and social norms. Determined to protect the innocent, Brenner's cranky demeanor belies a soft spot for all of humanity.

Selected Bibliography

Resurrection (1996 [2013])
The Bone Man (1997 [2012])
Come, Sweet Death! (1998 [2014])
Silentium! (Silence! 1999)
Wie die Tiere (Like animals; 2001)
Das ewige Leben (Eternal life; 2003)
Brenner and God (2009 [2012])
Brennerova (2014)

—Heike Henderson

VALERIA BRINTON (WOODVILLE/MACALLAN)

Wilkie Collins
(1824–1889)

Wilkie Collins was instrumental in the creation of the Victorian sensation novel. In these unsettling domestic dramas, plots twist and turn on a knife-edge as readers are taken on breathless, and on occasion outlandish, journeys that could terrify any respectable member of the nineteenth-century middle class. Collins is best known for his early novels *The Woman in White* and *The Moonstone*, which stand as touchstones for the genre, but some of his less well-known works are home to his truly radical arguments and characters.

One such character is the intrepid Valeria Macallan, or Woodville, née Brinton. The uncertainty over this young woman's married name arises from the trouble she finds herself in at the start of her marriage, a difficulty that compels her to ignore the gendered rules of Victorian propriety and turn sleuth to clear her husband's name and, in turn, her own, in Collins's *The Law and the Lady*. The novel was originally serialized in the *Graphic* newspaper between 1874 and 1875, with the reader left in suspense from episode to episode, as Valeria struggles to find out the truth about the man she loves.

Valeria's troubles begin with a portentous mistake when she signs her maiden name instead of her new name in the marriage register. Following this "bad beginning," her rather hopeless bridegroom, Eustace, realizes that he is unworthy of his blushing bride and that this is the perfect moment to reflect upon his first marriage and the resulting murder trial.[38] Eustace, it transpires, has been living under the purgatorial Scottish sentence of "Not Proven" for the murder of his first wife. He does not see fit to share all of this with Valeria and instead chooses to leave her to discover the full truth for herself. This is where the question of names comes in, and with the uncertainty over whether Valeria is a Woodville or a Macallan also comes uncertainty over whether she is a wife or a mistress. Of course, in a strict, moralizing Victorian society, to be a mistress is to be fallen, and to be fallen is to have your name reviled, your position in society revoked, and your future condemned. Collins's brave protagonist is thus highly motivated to transgress the limitations placed upon her sex by Victorian society, and in doing so, Valeria enters the active sphere of male deduction and reason in order to defend her feminized husband's honor. As she declares with ferocious determination, "What the Law has failed to do for you, your Wife must do for you."[39]

The novel is populated with eccentric characters, as was typical for the genre, and during her attempt to free her husband from the onus of the unfair verdict, Valeria must spend time with the bizarrely named Messerimus Dexter. Dexter is a peculiar mix of man and machine; his half body blends indistinguishably into his wheelchair as he speeds about shouting absurd exclamations. He likens himself to Napoleon, a rather dubious and threating figure in Victorian England, and to Shakespeare writing Lear. He is a confusing and threatening mix of physical and verbal difference, and is possessed of a dangerous sexuality that is directed at both Ariel, his devoted "slave," and Valeria in a scene that was later modified by the editor of the *Graphic* so as not to offend readers. It is a testament to Valeria's strength of character and determination that she takes all of this aberrant and devious behavior in her stride.

Collins was deeply concerned with the position of women within the confines of Victorian marital laws, as is clear from earlier novels like the 1862 *No Name*, and by using Valeria as an investigator in her attempts to save her husband and herself, he is making a strong comment about both women's abilities and their vulnerability within a society that places such a value on "respectability." Collins utilizes sensation fiction's creation of domestic disorder to question societal norms. Valeria's capitalized declaration "And there they [Eustace and his friends] would have remained, for all time—but for Me" demonstrates her powerful sense of self and the certainty of her mission.[40]

At one point, Valeria needs to consult a trial document in her quest to find the truth. Here Collins is exploiting the public's unquenchable interest in legal matters, as contemporary cases were frequently reported to sensational effect in the press. The Victorians were fascinated by private domestic lives laid bare for cannibalistic public consumption. However, Valeria's integrity remains intact as she takes us through this domestic drama, because while clearing Eustace's name it is his first marriage that lies exposed. So, while she arguably transcends the boundaries of Victorian female respectability, Valeria is still able to remain a moral figure, as her fight for the truth is inspired by marital love and fidelity.

This novel is often wrongfully understood to feature the first "lady detective," although this honor belongs to Catherine Crowe's *Susan Hopley; or, The Adventures of a Maidservant* (1841) and its protagonist. But while she might not be the first female sleuth, and even if she only takes up detection out of love, Valeria has still earned her place in crime's hall of fame with her astonishing tenacity, which enables her to break the boundaries of Victorian expectations and become a radical and indomitable investigative force.

Selected Bibliography

The Dead Secret (1856)
The Woman in White (1860)
No Name (1862)
Armadale (1866)
The Moonstone (1868)

—Joanne Ella Parsons

FATHER BROWN

G. K. Chesterton
(1874–1936)

Father Brown, a humble, bumbling Roman Catholic priest, without even a first name to distinguish him from other clergymen, represents a paradoxical fusion of innocence and wisdom in his persistent pursuit of the truth. He combines religion and crime-fighting in a surprising twist on the whodunit: the theological thriller. Each of his fifty-three short stories published between 1910 and 1936 serves as a vehicle for both G. K. Chesterton's religious apologetics and his intellectual adroitness; the unassuming priest leads his readers through a wonderland of philosophical discussions, acute observation of human nature, and humorous wordplay. Never mind that his innocuous appearance and childlike personality make policemen and murderers alike question his competency (or even his sanity); "the stumpy little *curé* of Essex" observes the human and material world around him, considers the supernatural implications of his observations, and identifies the perpetrators before they even know they are suspected.[41]

From the very first Father Brown story, "The Blue Cross" (1910), we are aware of the priest's obscurity. The tale doesn't even begin with Father Brown. Rather, it starts with Valentin, head of the Paris police, and the criminal he pursues, Flambeau. Only after an extensive explanation of this notorious criminal's modus operandi do we hear of a "little priest" from Essex with "a face as round and dull as a Norfolk dumpling" and "eyes as empty as the North Sea."[42] His experience as a parish priest and confessor gives him a depth and breadth of knowledge of every kind of person—and every kind of crime. Ultimately, Father Brown not only stops the world's greatest criminal in his tracks but also converts him and makes him his sidekick.

How does a man with a face of a cherub thus conquer the world? When he first encounters Flambeau, Father Brown is not fooled by his disguise; when Flambeau, dressed as a priest, attacks reason, Father Brown knows "it is bad theology."[43] When they meet again three adventures later, with Flambeau still pursuing his life of crime, the priest tells him, "I am a priest, Monsieur Flambeau, . . . and I am ready to hear your confession."[44] Flambeau repents, and in a startling character rebirth, the suave and swashbuckling Frenchman becomes the childlike disciple of the dull-eyed but sharp-witted priest. What a contrast between the phlegmatic priest and his fiery sidekick! Brown: the color of earth, of brown sauce, and of dullness, plainness, and mud, a name of anonymity as well as universality. Flambeau: a torch, a fire, a flame, and an energy all his own. Like any dynamic detective duo, they play to each other's strengths and complement each other's weaknesses. Yet as Flambeau doggedly applies his firsthand knowledge of criminology to each case, Father Brown keeps three steps ahead of him by relying on his knowledge of human nature and the supernatural.

This spiritual psychology is his key to the human soul. Any intelligent detective can solve a crime using his powers of deduction and "little grey cells," but it takes a curé and a confessor to see the world through a moral lens and parse its mysteries from a supernatural perspective. This conflation of the natural and supernatural is a typical example of Chestertonian paradox, juxtaposing conflicting perspectives in order to view reality more clearly. When not administering the last rites or attending priestly conferences, Father Brown participates in a corpse-filled Christmas pageant ("The Flying Stars," 1911), helps a married women elope ("The Scandal of Father Brown," 1933), and pays for a window before he has broken it ("The Blue Cross," 1910). "The Oracle of the Dog" (1923) is not merely a puzzle of a missing weapon, or a display of supernatural powers, but a study in the nature of mankind—and the nature of dogkind. In "The Hammer of God" (1910), instead of grappling with the physical impossibility of matching suspects with means and opportunity, Father Brown identifies the human motive first. This leads him to understand the physical simplicity of the murder, and with perfect gravity, he expounds the solution and induces the culprit to confess—to the police. All such unorthodox adventures end—to Flambeau's bewildered relief—in perfectly orthodox explanations, while readers are left shaking their heads over the simplicity of it all.

Unlike some of the other great detectives of the Golden Age, Father Brown is not primarily concerned with the devious complexities of ingenious murder plots. Instead, his adventures illuminate the fundamental simplicity of crime—anything that contravenes the laws of God or man—and the inescapable complexity of its punishment, for as we know, justice without mercy is a cruel thing. For those "whose creed require[s] them to be cloistered and ignorant of the world," detection work is a matter of wisdom over knowledge, of deeper comprehension over superficial observation.[45] In an unstable world, the spiritual sleuth Father Brown offers his readers both the certainty of fact and the simplicity of faith, as he dispenses justice and mercy in equal measure.

Selected Bibliography

The Innocence of Father Brown (1911)
The Wisdom of Father Brown (1914)
The Incredulity of Father Brown (1926)
The Secret of Father Brown (1927)
The Scandal of Father Brown (1935)

—Catherine Simmerer

INSPECTOR BUCKET

Charles Dickens
(1812–1870)

Inspector Bucket appeared in Charles Dickens's *Bleak House* (1852) less than a decade after the publication of Edgar Allan Poe's "The Murders in the Rue Morgue," which many claim as the first-ever detective story. However, Dickens and his creation tend to be overshadowed by their American ancestors in accounts of the history of detective fiction, despite the fact that they played a crucial role of their own. Bucket was a formative influence on the evolution of the literary detective and had an important role in changing public attitudes toward law enforcement in England by showing policemen and detectives in a positive light at a time when they were often viewed with suspicion and hostility.

Dickens based Bucket on a friend, Inspector Charles Frederick Field (1805–1874) of the Metropolitan Police, a fact acknowledged in his article "A Detective Police Party." The real-life basis of the character was transposed from Dickens's nonfiction writings, such as "On Duty with Inspector Field," into the Bucket of *Bleak House*, a "stoutly built, steady-looking, sharp-eyed man in black, of about the middle-age."[46] But with the writer's craft he added to this authentic foundation an enigmatic, out-of-the-ordinary quality. Bucket is "a person with a hat and stick in his hand who was not there when he [Snagsby] himself came in and has not since entered by the door or by either of the windows."[47] This introduction of a mysterious, but also complex and nuanced, personality within the context of apparent normality was Dickens's contribution to the emerging template of the fictional detective. Bucket is able to mix with and relate to the masses whilst ultimately remaining separate from them. And all the while he manages to remain a decent, generous-spirited man who sits at the moral center of a novel he doesn't even appear in until chapter 22; he refuses to sneak around in the shadows as do characters such as Tulkinghorn or Snagsby, or to act deceitfully like Smallwood or Crook. He shows compassion and understanding toward people of all social classes and is throughout viewed as a conscientious family man, even allowing his wife ("a woman in fifty thousand—in a hundred and fifty thousand!") to assist him with his investigations.[48]

The choice of the inspector's surname is a characteristic Dickensian aptronym. "Bucket" suggests a capacity to retain or hold large amounts of material (in this case information), a vessel for all of the results of his attentive observation of details, often gleaned while inconspicuously blending into the background. Yet this studied observation of the world around him belies "the velocity and certainty" of his mind and his resultant capacity to leap into action when required.[49] And because he is evidently so capable, the reader is less perturbed when he makes mistakes or wrong assumptions. Bucket is tricked by suspects including Lady Dedlock and Mademoiselle Hortense, and yet notwithstanding these slipups the detective's dogged perseverance and compassionate humanity remain impressively reassuring, establishing a general feeling that whilst errors might be made along the way, eventually the detective is likely to get his man (or woman) and restore the social equilibrium.

In addition to the way Inspector Bucket extends the richness and range of the Victorian literary detective figure, the character also has a much broader cultural significance as a barometer of changing popular attitudes toward law enforcement during this nineteenth century. The fact that Dickens, the most popular novelist of his time, was so positive in his portrayal of the character of Bucket, at times almost raising him to the level of the hero, meant that his literary creation could not help but contribute toward the reshaping of public attitudes toward policing in England. No more than a decade or two earlier, the pervading view had been overwhelmingly negative, as was illustrated by the public response to the deaths-in-action of a number of real-life policemen. In 1830, after PC Joseph Grantham was kicked to death as he tried to break up a fight (the first Metropolitan Police officer to be killed in the line of duty in England), and in 1833, after the death of PC Robert Culley, stabbed whilst policing a political rally that turned into a riot, the inquest juries returned verdicts of justifiable homicide.[50] These verdicts were illustrations of a general uneasiness with the very existence of police or detective forces, meaning that Dickens's entirely positive representation of Bucket must be seen as a counterpoint, designed to encourage a view of the detective as a necessary and desirable feature of any functioning modern society.

The effectiveness of Dickens's renovation of the reputation of those involved in law enforcement is evident in the lofty status achieved by the detective figure by the end of the nineteenth century. Arthur Conan Doyle's Sherlock Holmes had by then taken on an almost mythical status, becoming the first popular superhero, with Dickens's writings, such as *Oliver Twist* (1838), "The Modern Science of Thief-Taking," "On Duty with Inspector Field," "Three Detective Anecdotes," and "A Detective Police Party" doing much to prepare the ground for such hero worship. He had shown readers that police officers and detectives were on their side, not working against them, and associated them with ideas of professionalism, extraordinary talent, and fascinating personality. Inspector Bucket in *Bleak House* in particular helped turn the tide in the favor of the detective, conjuring up an image of a man who could be trusted wholeheartedly, rather than necessarily feared or reviled.

Selected Bibliography

Oliver Twist (1838)
Martin Chuzzlewit (1844)
Dombey and Son (1848)
David Copperfield (1850)
Great Expectations (1861)
A Tale of Two Cities (1861)
The Mystery of Edwin Drood (1870)

—Neil McCaw

BROTHER CADFAEL

Ellis Peters (Edith Pargeter)
(1913–1995)

Brother Cadfael is an unusual detective. Indeed, according to Ellis Peters, his name was chosen because it was so rare it appeared "only once in Welsh history."[1] He practices an early form of forensic science in the medieval setting of mid-twelfth-century England, against the backdrop of King Stephen and his cousin Empress Maud's struggle for the crown. After having spent many years as a soldier and a seaman, the Welsh Cadfael left the world behind for the life of a monk, exchanging his sword and shield for a garden spade and robes. When he first appeared in *A Morbid Taste for Bones* (1977), the fifty-seven-year-old had been a Benedictine for seventeen peaceful years. But over the course of twenty novels and three short stories, the Cadfael Chronicles present the detective as a contemplative healer whose wide experience of the world of men—and women—makes him a careful observer and an empathetic listener able to navigate the politics of a nation violently divided by class and faction.

As a military man, Cadfael followed the orders of his superiors. As a monk in the Abbey of St. Peter and St. Paul at Shrewsbury in Shropshire, Cadfael has a similar responsibility to his superiors and in particular to his abbot. Precisely because of his worldly experience, he is often sent out into the world to carry out missions, solve crimes, and explain mysteries, especially those affecting the religious world of the abbey. In *A Morbid Taste for Bones*, for example, Prior Robert insists the abbey needs the relics of a saint to encourage pilgrimages. As a Welshman, Cadfael is assigned to a party sent to retrieve the bones of St. Winifred from Gwytherin, Wales. When a murder ensues, he both solves the crime and maneuvers across cultures and beliefs. By deftly placing the body of the murderer in St. Winifred's reliquary, while placing the victim's body with the saint's bones into the saint's original tomb, he pleases both the Welsh, who get to keep their saint, and the prior's party, which is delighted to have obtained their "saint." During the investigation, Cadfael's careful study of the body, seemingly felled by an arrow but actually stabbed to death first, and his observation of the crime scene help to exonerate the Englishman first suspected. A similar pattern emerges throughout the chronicles: the obvious suspect, often a young man in love with a young woman, is not guilty, and Cadfael's intuition and forensic science help both prove him innocent and eventually identify the culprit.

As an herbalist with knowledge of both Western and Eastern medicine, which he studied while living in Syria after the First Crusade, Cadfael ministers to the medical needs of the monks of the abbey, as well as the townspeople and the lepers of nearby St. Giles. This position gives him great freedom of movement within and beyond the confines of the abbey. His knowledge of herbs and plants also serves him well in his investigations. In *The Leper of St. Giles* (1981), for instance, Cadfael finds traces of three different plants on the body and realizes that the crime could only have occurred where all three plants grow near each other. In *Monk's Hood* (1980), Cadfael smells the eponymous deadly plant on Gervase Bonel's breath. Bonel's illegitimate son Meurig is the perpetrator; he had hoped to prevent his father from deeding lands to the abbey. After he confesses, Cadfael encourages him to escape to live a long life doing only good henceforth.

Indeed, many of the guilty in the chronicles are spared the rope of justice. Though Sheriff Beringar—a representative of the legal, secular world with whom Cadfael develops a close relationship—must bring criminals to justice, even if their crimes may seem justified, he sometimes looks the other way while Cadfael works his practical magic. To take one example of this sort of thoughtful justice, Cadfael allows the culprit in *The Leper of St. Giles* to vanish because he killed to save his granddaughter from exploitation and is suffering from incurable, late-stage leprosy.

While the Cadfael stories are thus often concerned with questions of investigation and morality, they also offer a strong personal narrative. In *The Virgin in the Ice* (1982), Cadfael discovers that he has a son from a liaison with the Saracen Miriam. Olivier de Bretagne has taken his father's religion and a Christian name, and serves Empress Maud. Cadfael meets him again in *The Pilgrim of Hate* (1984) but once again does not confess that he is Olivier's father. Finally, in the twentieth chronicle, *Brother Cadfael's Penance* (1994), Cadfael leaves the abbey to rescue his son from King Stephen's men. Olivier, soon to be a father himself, now learns that Cadfael is his father. Returning to the abbey, Cadfael is accepted as an errant brother. On this quiet note end the chronicles of one of the earliest and most influential detectives in historical fiction.

Selected Bibliography

One Corpse Too Many (1979)
Saint Peter's Fair (1981)
The Devil's Novice (1983)
The Sanctuary Sparrow (1983)
Dead Man's Ransom (1984)
An Excellent Mystery (1985)
The Raven in the Foregate (1986)
The Rose Rent (1986)
The Hermit of Eyton Forest (1987)
The Confession of Brother Haluin (1988)
A Rare Benedictine: The Advent of Brother Cadfael (short stories, 1988)
The Heretic's Apprentice (1989)

The Potter's Field (1989)
The Summer of the Danes (1991)
The Holy Thief (1992)

—Linda Ledford-Miller

INSPECTOR CADIN

Didier Daeninckx
(1949–)

France has an important tradition of politically committed crime fiction that delivers a severe critique of both the authorities and the social order. This social criticism is associated in particular with the *roman noir*, which grew out of the American hard-boiled after World War II but soon developed into a genre of its own. The 1970s saw the rise of a specific kind of *romans noir* called *néo-polars*. This short-lived but influential movement professed a stark leftist ideology and was highly critical of capitalism, consumerism, French society, and the state. Didier Daeninckx's five books (four novels and a collection of short stories) about Inspector Cadin are representative of such politically denunciatory crime fiction, or what Andrew Pepper calls "radical crime fiction."[2]

The Cadin novels dig into affairs that have been concealed by the authorities, such as the deportation of Jews during the Occupation and the 1961 massacre of Algerians in Paris. These two events are at the heart of *Murder in Memoriam* (1984 [1991]), which brought many sordid details into the open, discussing events that had until then been largely unknown, or willfully ignored, by the public. The novel's epigraph, which claims we are condemned to relive the past if we forget it, reveals the importance Daeninckx attaches to history and historical knowledge. The historical events unveiled by Cadin are, nonetheless, adapted to the ideological framework of the narratives and also serve as indicators of present "dysfunctions," as Dominique Jeannerod argues.[3] This kind of denunciatory crime fiction is antiestablishment, and the author presents a well-documented vision of the past that emphasizes dubious elements left out of the official historiography, forms of oppression, corruption, and dominance conducted or endorsed by the authorities.

Inspector Cadin was introduced in *Mort au premier tour* (Murder in the first round), which was written in 1977 but only published in 1982. He gained notoriety in 1984 with the publication of *Murder in Memoriam*, the only Cadin novel translated into English to date. Cadin is a meticulous and able investigator whose refusal to comply with corruption to protect the state or the police force tends to get him into trouble. His behavior often surprises ordinary people who expect the police to be against them, as when Cadin offers to negotiate on behalf of striking gravediggers with enraged families who object to the strike and threaten to attack them. It is unheard of that a policeman should offer to act as a spokesperson for strikers making demands on local authorities. Indeed, several secondary characters comment upon the police's complicity with a corrupt system. As Cadin is still intent on doing proper police work, he is often confronted with the conundrum of defending the police while acknowledging its corruption or indifference to the troubles of ordinary people, especially the poor and the underprivileged.

In consequence of his unruly professional behavior, Cadin frequently gets transferred from one post to another. A former friend cries out in desperation at Cadin's insistence on digging up "explosive" files from the state archives: "I understand why you don't manage to stay long in the same posting. Getting rid of a big mouth like you is a security measure!"[4] Hence, the four novels are set in different places: Cadin works in Strasbourg in 1977 (*Mort au premier tour*), then in Hazebrouck (*Le géant inachevé*, 1984 [The unfinished giant]), Courvilliers (*Le bourreau et son double*, 1986 [The executioner and his double]), and finally, Toulouse in *Murder in Memoriam*. Each novel ends with Cadin's transfer to a different city. Sometimes he is demoted, and sometimes the transfer is masked as a promotion, but the authorities always want to move this troublemaker along.

It is thus unsurprising that Cadin is a lonely figure whose only close companion throughout the series is a cat, which has been abandoned by a former tenant in the inspector's new apartment in Courvilliers (*Le bourreau et son double*). When Cadin in turn leaves the apartment, because of yet another transfer resulting from his obstinate refusal to run investigations according to the wishes of his superiors, he leaves the animal behind. Nevertheless, he is careful to leave a note of its name for the next tenant. Occasionally, the inspector picks up prostitutes in shady areas close to the railway station to obtain carnal pleasure and a brief moment of release from growing frustrations. No girlfriends or other close personal relationships appear in the stories. Still, the inspector is far from insensitive to the charms of the opposite sex and is attracted to women involved in his investigations: "In my brief career I had twice before fallen in love with witnesses or victims. And to think some people see the police as heartless!"[5]

The short stories collected in *Le facteur fatal* (1990 [The fatal factor]) return to the investigations presented in the four previous novels and give crucial information about Cadin's personal background. His disillusionment and distress gradually grow until the last short story, which takes place in Aubervilliers during the final minutes of the 1980s. At the exact moment the world enters the 1990s, ex-Inspector Cadin exits with a bang, thereby marking the end of an era. This tragic conclusion to the series allowed Daeninckx the freedom to develop his writing in new directions, but these radical crime novels about a courageous, sensitive, and tormented detective continue to offer important insights into recent French history.

Selected Bibliography

Mort au premier tour (Murder in the first round; 1982)
Le géant inachevé (The unfinished giant; 1984)
Murder in Memoriam (1984 [1991])
A Very Profitable War (1984 [2013])
Le bourreau et son double (The executioner and his double; 1986)
Le facteur fatal (The fatal factor; 1990)
Nazis in the Metro (1996 [2014])

—Andrea Hynynen

ALBERT CAMPION

Margery Allingham
(1904–1966)

Margery Allingham's Albert Campion, one of the most ambiguous and secretive detectives of the British Golden Age, leaves no reader indifferent. When she introduced Campion in *The Crime at Black Dudley* in 1929, Allingham did not know that this groundbreaking character would become the archetypal gentleman detective, and make her internationally recognized as a leading crime writer. Although this first novel does not feature the well-known aristocratic sleuth as its hero, it outlines Campion's basic characteristics, such as his misleading insanity and the "tow-coloured hair and the foolish pale-blue eyes behind the tortoiseshell-rimmed spectacles."[6] But most importantly, Campion is a mysterious figure who, despite his illustrious social background, mingles with criminals rather than with the respectable classes.

The fact that Campion was originally intended by Allingham to be a minor criminal with good underworld connections is important, as it is exactly this peculiarity that contributes to his metamorphosis into a full-fledged detective in *Mystery Mile* (1930). His fishy character is intensified by his relationship with his comic manservant, ex-burglar Magersfontein Lugg, who makes his appearance in this second novel. Allingham's detective is ready to use his fists if necessary but is also willing to cooperate with the police. Despite his suspect associates and habits, his hidden qualities elevate him to heroic heights, as an embodiment of the medieval knight forever saving young women from danger.

From the beginning, there is a puzzling obscurity about Campion's real profession. We are intrigued by his dual personality—either a lunatic or "a man of action"—but our imaginations are also captured by the mystery surrounding his name and identity.[7] Campion's family name is described as being highly "aristocratic," and as he claims in *The Fashion in Shrouds* (1938), while "Albert" is used publicly, he has quite a few "other noms-de-guerre," like Mornington Dodd or the Honourable Tootles Ash.[8] His use of a variety of names and his connections with most social classes undoubtedly contribute to his success as an amateur sleuth, while his idiotic looks not only are convincing but also prove to be the most valuable asset in his investigations. In *Traitor's Purse* (1941), however, Campion is revealed as genuinely intelligent when his amnesia causes him to lose his "stock-in-trade" investigative technique of misleading foolishness.

Campion changes and develops with each novel, which is unsurprising considering that Allingham was always more interested in characterization than in reproducing a formula. After his marriage with his ideal partner, the female "gentleman" Lady Amanda Fitton, Campion becomes less courageous but more responsible. They fall in love in *Sweet Danger* (1933), become partners in crime in *The Fashion in Shrouds* (1938), decide to get married in *Traitor's Purse* (1941), and have a son in *The Tiger in the Smoke* (1952). Their relationship is situated at the intersection of tradition and modernity: while they both believe in honor and virtue, they are equal partners.

Campion is also a bridge figure in other ways, a time traveller between the pre- and the postwar world. Like Dorothy L. Sayers or Agatha Christie, Allingham was preoccupied with portraying post–Great War social and cultural changes. By maintaining a belief in the traditional values of her society, she re-creates a myth of Englishness, which is then dissolved by the traumatized amateur detective antihero and the crime itself. Campion's thoroughly ambiguous position as a gentleman and a detective is due to a general feature of Golden Age crime fiction: his presence in the modern world sustains the illusion of the continuity of the past, yet his involvement in the investigation at the side of the police is largely inconsistent with aristocratic, gentlemanly virtues. *Police at the Funeral* (1931) and *Hide My Eyes* (1958), for instance, are both effective representations of this constructed memory world in which Campion mediates between the police and the closed circle of upper-middle-class society. As a detective, his career requires him to be highly competent and flexible, able to navigate the postwar era, while his intellect, conservatism, and distinguished background make him seem like "an island of wisdom in a sea of fools, cowards, and comic foils."[9]

Although no one has ever been able to tell who Campion is, the past decades have seen numerous attempts, by literary critics and lovers of crime fiction, to establish his long-overdue and well-deserved position within the genre, and to reinvent his legacy in the history of crime fiction. A film adaptation, a BBC adaptation of eight novels, and the ceaseless reissue of his books are all evidence that it is still the Golden Age for Albert Campion.

Selected Bibliography

The Crime at Black Dudley (1929)
Mystery Mile (1930)
Police at the Funeral (1931)
Sweet Danger (1933)
The Fashion in Shrouds (1938)
Traitor's Purse (1941)
The Tiger in the Smoke (1952)
Hide My Eyes (1958)

—Renata Zsamba

STEVE CARELLA

Ed McBain (Evan Hunter)
(1926–2005)

Steve Carella was not supposed to be the hero of the 87th Precinct novels. As McBain explained in the introduction to *Cop Hater* (1956), "It seemed to me that a single cop did not a series make, and it further seemed to me that something new in the annals of police procedurals . . . would be a squadroom *full* of cops, each with different traits, who—when put together—would form a *conglomerate* hero."[10] Thinking that this ensemble approach to crime fiction made individual cops disposable, McBain had Carella shot and killed at the ending of *The Pusher* (1956), the third novel in the series. This death did not make it past the novel's first draft: the editor protested that Carella was the "star" of the series, and the fatal shooting was rewritten as a severe injury. After this near-death experience, Carella went on to have one of the longest and most significant careers in American crime fiction, appearing in a total of fifty-five novels published over a period of fifty years.

Ed McBain was born Salvatore A. Lombino but changed his name to Evan Hunter on the advice of an editor who thought it would help him sell more books. He adopted the pseudonym McBain for the 87th Precinct series but also continued to work as Hunter, and under this name (and other pseudonyms), wrote several novels as well as the screenplay for Hitchcock's *The Birds* (1963). However, it is as the author of the 87th Precinct novels that he will be best remembered. Inspired by the popular American radio and television show *Dragnet*, McBain wanted to infuse his own series with grit and realism. To this end, he spent time riding with real cops in New York City. While not the inventor of the police procedural, McBain's combination of fast-paced and realistic crime plots with authentic procedures and an impressive level of forensic detail popularized the genre for a wide audience.

The novels' investigative work is carried out by a diverse collection of detectives and uniformed officers in addition to Carella, including Jewish Meyer Meyer, and the upper-class Cotton Hawes. Other important characters include Bert Kling, the rookie who develops into a competent officer, the black Arthur Brown, the short but martial Hal Willis, female Eileen Burk, and Japanese American "Tack" Fujiwara. These individuals arguably make up, as LeRoy Panek has observed, "the first ethnically diverse group of cops" in American fiction.[11] Less palatable is the racist and bigoted Roger Havilland, succeeded after his death by the similarly unsympathetic Andy Parker. The presence of corrupt, racist, and misogynist cops is crucial to the series and to its aspiration to realistically portray police work in an American megacity.

While this diverse collective is what truly makes the 87th Precinct series, Carella is arguably the moral center of the group. On streets haunted by violent crime, where poverty, racial tension, greed, desire, and stupidity motivate the criminal, Carella is the very archetype of the hardworking, relentless professional detective who desires to protect the weak and bring order. Carella is described as a "big man, but not a heavy one. He gave an impression of great power, but the power was not a meaty one. It was, instead, a fine-honed muscular power."[12] This attractive exterior combined with his dogged determination is one key to his stardom. These qualities make him the character that the intended white, male reader is most likely to identify with, yet Carella does not revel in his whiteness. Of Italian descent, like McBain himself, Carella is sometimes torn between worlds and becomes increasingly sensitive to racial and gender injustice as the series progresses.

After accepting the idea that Carella was vital to the success of the series, McBain appears to have grown increasingly fond of him and eventually furnished a nemesis in the form of the Deaf Man. This character features in six of the 87th Precinct novels, and while he is investigated by other detectives, he functions primarily as Carella's evil counterpart. Not actually deaf, he is a master criminal who sends clues that frustrate rather than help Carella in his investigations. Carella and the 87th Precinct team have little to oppose to the Deaf Man's otherworldly brilliance and strange schemes but their grit and hard work, and even when Carella and his fellow detectives manage to disrupt the Deaf Man's plans, it is often due to chance rather than deduction.

This model is used in countless 87th Precinct novels, and it emphasizes how McBain thought of Carella not primarily as a cop but as "a decent man in a job that required extreme patience and a strong stomach."[13] It is this strong sense of general humanity that is Carella's enduring legacy. None of the many novels, series, and television shows that have followed in the wake of the 87th Precinct books lack a Carella character who strives honestly and persistently to square his demanding profession with both the challenges of his private life and with the limits of his own capacities as a human being. McBain's series has had a profound influence outside of America, most notably on Maj Sjöwall and Per Wahlöö's novels about Martin Beck and the National Murder Squad. In this way, Carella can be said to have left his mark on Scandinavian crime writing and, due to its global popularity, beyond.

Selected Bibliography

Cop Hater (1956)
Killer's Wedge (1959)
King's Ransom (1959)
The Heckler (1960)
Lady, Lady, I Did It! (1961)
Doll (1965)
Sadie When She Died (1972)
Blood Relatives (1975)
Long Time No See (1977)
Eight Black Horses (1985)
Tricks (1987)
Widows (1991)
The Big Bad City (1999)

—Johan Höglund

THOMAS CARNACKI, THE GHOST FINDER

William Hope Hodgson
(1877–1918)

Sherlock Holmes may now be the world's most famous detective, but he faced keen competition from many Edwardian investigators. Few, however, are as fascinating as psychic investigator Thomas Carnacki of 472 Cheyne Walk, Chelsea, who combines logic and technology with an open-minded appreciation of pagan ritual and the occult to solve hauntings throughout the British Isles. Featured in six short stories in the illustrated monthly the *Idler* from 1910 to 1912, with three others appearing after Hodgson's death in World War I, Carnacki, the Ghost Finder says that of all his cases, only those involving a particularly vicious haunting or inexplicable phenomenon are worth relating to his engrossed guests over an after-dinner pipe. Carnacki's narration holds his listeners, and readers, in suspense until the end of each tale, when he reveals whether the haunting was indeed real. Sometimes criticized as underdeveloped and lacking warmth, Carnacki is nevertheless a contemplative character, who reflects deeply on the mysteries of life and death without the encumbrance of religious dogma.

Carnacki reveals little of his background or his beginnings as a detective except to relate how he became the eponymous "Searcher of the End House," during his first experience of a haunted house when he was still living with his mother. Afterward, his helpful nature motivated him to aid other families in restoring their own houses to order. There are few hints regarding Carnacki's appearance, and the accompanying black-and-white sketches are inconsistent. Artist Florence Briscoe first illustrated Carnacki in the typical Edwardian style as a man in a dinner jacket, his black hair slicked and parted down the middle, and sporting a small, fashionable moustache; other illustrators have depicted him as lean and balding, reminiscent of Holmes. Generally, faces and figures are rendered in profile, obscured by shadows in an atmosphere heavy with gloom and doom.

As an investigator, Carnacki shares Holmes's attention to detail, but crime writer Ellery Queen preferred Carnacki's methods of detection to his supernatural subjects.[14] Indeed, much of Carnacki's narrative is spent in examining the haunted house, sounding walls, securing doors and windows, and then keeping watch with his flash camera. Meticulous about equipment, he uses trip wires and sealing wax against human intruders as well as holy water and herbal amulets, such as garlic and hyssop brooms, against spirit invaders. His most important tool is the Electric Pentacle, outlined on the floor in chalk, the points connected with colored lasers. This diagram serves as a portal to, and a containment device for, "monstrosities of the Outer Circle," a concept that has been favored by later writers of weird tales.[15] The most complete descriptions of Carnacki's rituals as well as his theory about these Outer Monsters appear in "The Hog," a long story published after Hodgson's death.

Though half of his cases turn out to be frauds, Carnacki's descriptions of strange sounds and smells in the dark are among the most terrifying in Edwardian detective fiction, and his encounters with gigantic hands and porcine monsters are unique, resonating with later writers of weird tales such as Clark Ashton Smith and August Derleth. If Carnacki lacks depth, it is perhaps because Hodgson sacrifices characterization in favor of developing this mythos. Although H. P. Lovecraft was a fan of Hodgson's work, he disliked Carnacki, describing him as "a more or less conventional stock figure of the 'infallible detective' type—the progeny of M. Dupin and Sherlock Holmes, . . . moving through scenes and events badly marred by an atmosphere of professional 'occultism.'"[16]

On the contrary, Carnacki is all too human. He often runs screaming into the night, and he is injured in most of his stories, whether by hurling himself from a second-story window to escape a demon or by getting knocked down by a spring-loaded dagger. He carries a revolver, not just to protect himself from malicious humans, but also to dispatch himself rather than risk being taken bodily to hell. Unashamed of his cowardice, he is conscious not only of his stewardship of souls but also of his responsibilities as a narrator, interrupting his tales to insert commentary and questions, frustrated that he is not describing his terror well enough to convince his audience of the "realism of the unreal."[17]

Though Carnacki inevitably manages to dispel the mystery, dispatch the monsters, or neutralize the evil, he stresses that investigating life's mysteries is a lonely endeavor, an internal quest to find one's true character and to overcome fear with courage. Carnacki cannot explain every phenomenon, suggesting that inexplicable evil exists no matter how civilized the world becomes. Perhaps this is why these stories resonated with readers who faced indescribable suffering in the First and Second World Wars. Still in print today, Carnacki continues to appeal to many readers, and especially to writers of fan fiction, who have borrowed the titles of further adventures mentioned in his casebook—a sure sign of this investigator's continuing relevance.

Selected Bibliography

The House on the Borderland (1908)
The Ghost Pirates (1909)
The Night Land (1912)
Carnacki, the Ghost Finder (1913)

—Beth Walker

PEPE CARVALHO

Manuel Vázquez Montalbán
(1939–2003)

Ex-cop, ex-Marxist, but above all gourmand, Pepe Carvalho debuted in 1972 in *Yo maté a Kennedy* (I killed Kennedy). Created by prolific poet, journalist, and scriptwriter Manuel Vázquez Montalbán, the Barcelona-based Carvalho features in twenty-two novels. His companion and cook Biscuter assists him in his investigations, while call girl Charo, his long-term girlfriend, comes and goes between his many other amorous pursuits. A self-described staunchly apolitical private eye, who paradoxically always has an opinion on regional and national politics, he devotes his free time to chasing women and good food, and burning the canonical books he loves to hate (he sets one ablaze almost every night in his fireplace).[18] At work, he prefers to be paid in advance for cleaning up the "dirty laundry" of the wealthy: "Who says you know my rates? I don't have fixed rates. How about you pay me what you pay your centre forward," he defiantly demands of the Barcelona FC public relations representative; after all, "I'm the 'Golden Boot' of my profession."[19]

Throughout his detecting career, Carvalho is concerned with the interaction of the present and the past: during his investigations he usually reflects on Spanish and Catalan anxieties over the post–civil war, postdictatorship recuperation of historical memory, and the general state of political, social, and cultural affairs in Catalonia and Spain. Likewise, the development and gentrification of Barcelona's Raval and Barri Xino districts is always a concern. While the Carvalho series presents a panoramic view of Catalan politics, history, and culture, the detective's alliances defy any rigid interpretation of regional belonging. He is, after all, a Galician who was born in Barcelona, a Catalan who cannot speak the language, and a cosmopolitan urbanite who remains faithful to his home turf, the Chinese Quarter.

Murder in the Central Committee (1981) takes Carvalho "abroad" (to Madrid), where the General Secretary of the Communist Party has been killed. Vázquez Montalbán exploits this "foreign" locale to discuss questions of identity and loyalty, highlighting issues of political and historical importance, such as the enquiry into the murder of a man whose political association was, not that long ago under the Franco regime, illegal. The fact that Carvalho is cruising the unfamiliar landscape of Madrid enhances the detective's cultural and geographical dislocation, something he typically translates into a gastronomic preoccupation: "I'll miss your cooking, Biscuter. I'm going to a town which has given no more than a stew, an omelette and a dish of tripe to the gastronomic culture of the country."[20]

His obsession with good cuisine is a recurrent, and at times contentious, topic in the series, which Carvalho always presents with his trademark caustic humor and cynicism. In *Angst-Ridden Executive* (1977), Carvalho confesses that "it was only women and good food that saved us all from going mad under Franco."[21] Food is used not only as a marker of personal, regional, and national identity but also as a metaphor for the decline of the country's morals. In *Southern Seas* (1979), for example, Carvalho protests almost melancholically that "this Salamanca ham isn't what it used to be"; he is equally skeptical about his own profession: "Do you realise that we private eyes are the barometers of established morality? I tell you society is rotten."[22] For Carvalho, the state of Spanish politics is, like the ham, deteriorating. In *An Olympic Death* (1993), for instance, he is a disillusioned witness to the decline of a socialist dream during the 1990s pre-Olympic makeover of Barcelona. Rife with scandals, bribes, and corruption, the city is a stage for the farce of modernity.

Reflecting Vázquez Montalbán's own epicurean preoccupations (he published his own recipe book, *Recetas inmorales* [Immoral recipes] in 1981), Carvalho's passionate relationship with food transcended the PI's saga and outlived his creator: in 1989, a compilation of Carvalho's recipes was published (*Las recetas de Carvalho*) and between 2002 and 2003, a ten-volume encyclopedia called *Carvalho gastronómico* (Gastronomic Carvalho) came out. This series is no mere compendium of recipes, as it focuses on issues of regional identity, such as Mediterranean food and "Mediterraneanness," *mestizaje* food, and the cuisine of *finisterre*, a region on the west coast of Galicia.

By being cynical, and often politically incorrect, about some very sensitive topics, Vázquez Montalbán presents a middle path between Spanish and regional identities that highlights the difficulty of establishing clear-cut boundaries between the two. At times parodic, fusing high-culture literary references with popular culture forms, the Pepe Carvalho novels successfully raise, but do not resolve, concerns about Catalonia's struggle to reaffirm itself culturally and politically. Carvalho is certainly Spain's most enduring and iconic PI, and through him Vázquez Montalbán presents his unique views on issues ranging from the media to football, from Spain's recent turbulent political history to its ambiguous place in European politics, and of course on the dialectics, and pleasures, of food.

Selected Bibliography

Tattoo (1974 [2008])
Angst-Ridden Executive (1977 [2012])
Southern Seas (1979 [2012])
Murder in the Central Committee (1981 [1984])
Off Side (1988 [2012])
An Olympic Death (1993 [2010])
The Buenos Aires Quintet (1997 [2012])
The Man of my Life (2000 [2005])

—Carolina Miranda

MARIO CONDE

Leonardo Padura Fuentes
(1955–)

When Leonardo Padura published his first Mario Conde novel in 1991, Cuban crime fiction was in a sorry state. It had become a stilted exercise in politics with negligible literary value, attracting little critical attention and a meager readership. Today, the recipient of significant national and international prizes, Leonardo Padura is Cuba's best-selling author outside the island, and Mario Conde is perhaps Cuba's most beloved literary character of the last two decades.

Policial revolucionario (revolutionary crime fiction) developed in Cuba in the 1970s with a clear didactic aim. Investigators were staunch supporters of the revolution. They were prepared to work 24/7, all crimes were perceived as an attack on the revolution, sex was strictly excluded, and scenes of violent confrontations between police officers and criminals all but disappeared. Furthermore, to avoid the worst of sins, individualism, readers were given scant information about the protagonists (for whom it was virtually impossible to feel any empathy). The result was a long list of mostly dreary pamphlets that at times had little to do with literature. Mario Conde gave Cuban readers everything *policial revolucionario* lacked.

In the opening paragraphs of the first novel of the series, *Havana Blue* (1991 [2007]), the reader finds a hung-over and lonely lieutenant Mario Conde, angry at being asked to report for work on a Saturday, and struggling to get out of bed. Immediately, a flashback takes us to 1972, with a young Conde starting *preuniversitario* (the last year of secondary school) meeting a group of friends who become staple characters in the series, mostly as victims of the revolution, symbols of the broken dreams of a generation. Thus, in barely five pages, Padura introduces his protagonist, sets the scene, and breaks almost every rule in the "How to Write Crime Fiction in Revolutionary Cuba" handbook.

The first four novels of the series (known as the *Havana Quartet* or the *Four Seasons*) take place in 1989, the year the Berlin Wall fell and Cuba lost almost every international ally and trading partner. The ensuing crisis plays a crucial part in the tone of the series, in which numerous characters, struggling to make ends meet, reflect at length upon the clash between the utopian revolutionary dream and the reality of everyday life. Conde himself wonders time and again how he became a police officer, when his dream was to be a writer. In time we learn that his first (and only) literary attempt was cut short by a school principal who considered it insufficiently revolutionary. Instead, he joined the force because he dislikes "bastards going unpunished."[23] Of course, who the bastards are for Conde has been quite controversial in some (official) Cuban quarters, as each novel focuses on issues previously unmentioned in Cuban crime fiction: corruption at the deputy minister level (*Havana Blue*), the expropriation of art immediately after the revolution (*Havana Blue*), drug trafficking in schools (*Havana Gold*, 1994 [2008]), and institutional homophobia (*Havana Red*, 1997 [2005]).

After *Havana Blue*, Mario Conde leaves the police force, thus becoming the first private detective in revolutionary crime fiction since Juglar Ares, who in Cardenas Acuña's *Enigma for a Sunday* (1971) had to step aside so the revolutionary police could complete the investigation. This major departure from the norm is not only a sign of the times (the liberalization permitting some forms of small-scale capitalism on which Cuba embarked in the late 1990s) but also a clear statement of the failings of Cuba's police force and the lack of trust toward it felt by many, including Mario Conde.

In *Havana Gold* the ex-lieutenant is a secondhand book dealer who through a number of coincidences ends up investigating a suicide. In the most recent novel of the series, *Herejes* (Heretics; as yet unpublished in English translation), Mario Conde is fifty-four years old and still lives alone but has a steady partner (Tamara, the ex-wife of the corrupt officer of the first book of the series). While he still struggles to make any money selling books, Conde is a far more contented individual who enjoys the freedom and self-respect he has gained after leaving the police force. It is this satisfaction that allows him to discuss with depth and at length a topic that had surfaced but could not be developed in previous novels of the series: the gap between dreams and reality, the way other people (or indeed the Cuban Revolution) can limit choices in life, and the extent to which free will exists. This is done through two seemingly unrelated investigations within the Jewish community and the emo subculture in Havana.

The character of Mario Conde has grown with every new novel in the series. In his latest iteration it is evident that Leonardo Padura feels somehow constrained by the genre for which he created Mario Conde, to the extent that some critics wonder whether *Herejes* is crime fiction at all. It is, but it is crime fiction with no fixed boundaries, always ready to expand and to use the investigative framework to reflect upon the paths we take in life and the extent to which we can control them. Twenty-five years after *Havana Blue*, Mario Conde has become a more developed, nuanced, and fascinating character who Padura has promised will continue to explore Cuba's contradictions.

Selected Bibliography

Havana Blue (1991 [2007])
Havana Gold (1994 [2008])
Havana Red (1997 [2005])
Havana Black (1998 [2006])
La cola de la serpiente (2003, revised edition 2011)
Adiós Hemingway (2005)
Havana Fever (2005 [2009])
Herejes (2013)

—Carlos Uxó

SERGEANT CUFF

Wilkie Collins
(1824–1889)

The inclusion of the character of Sergeant Cuff from Wilkie Collins's novel *The Moonstone* (1868) in a list of the most significant literary detectives may at first seem questionable. Cuff appears in a single medium-sized Victorian novel that most people no longer read, is jettisoned from the narrative at a relatively early stage, does not play any significant role in the solution of the central crime, and at the conclusion is nowhere to be seen. And yet, despite this, when considering the historical development of English detective fiction and the detectives within it, Cuff is an important landmark, rather than just a supporting character in what T. S. Eliot labeled "the first, the longest, and the best of English detective novels in a genre invented by Collins and not Poe."[24]

Nonetheless, to some extent Cuff's importance is due to the novel in which he features and the author who created him. For many critics, including Eliot, in one way or another all subsequent detective fiction can be traced back to Collins. He wrote the earliest English example of the detective story, "A Stolen Letter" (1854); created the first English female detective, in "The Diary of Anne Rodway" (1856); and in *The Moonstone*, first published in serial form in Charles Dickens's journal *All the Year Round*, produced a seminal example of the genre. Even its very narrative form, consisting of the first-person witness statements of those connected to the case, is an important innovation. Collins took the epistolary form he first piloted in *The Woman in White* (1860) and moved yet further away from the Victorian convention of the third-person omniscient narrator in an attempt to tell the story in a way that placed the readers themselves in the role of the detective, having to figure out things for themselves and judge the reliability of each individual witness.

Beyond this innovation in narrative form, *The Moonstone* is notable for helping to establish a number of stock elements of the emerging genre: it is a country-house locked-room mystery, featuring a limited range of potential suspects, a number of red herrings, and inept and unskilled official police officers. And key to its success is Collins's addition of the character of Sergeant Cuff, a recasting of the role of the literary detective that built on those, such as Inspector Bucket, created by his friend Dickens a decade or more earlier. Cuff is a skilled and insightful personality, a man who blends into the background while observing the world around him, and who conducts himself with tolerance and sensitivity in his dealings with people of all classes.

Collins's particular extension of the detective archetype features a more explicit focus on the method of detection, along with a more nuanced sense of the eccentricity central to the personality of the detective. Cuff's method acknowledges the importance of detailed forensic investigation: "At one end of the inquiry there was a murder, and at the other end there was a spot of ink on a tablecloth that nobody could account for. In all my experience along the dirtiest ways of this dirty little world, I have never met with such a thing as a trifle yet."[25] And his recognition of the need for a more systematic, close evaluation of each crime scene is contrasted with the often shambolic, bungling efforts of the local police. The more impressive, coherent sense of detective methodology displayed by Cuff is coupled to a more nuanced, charismatic personality; here is someone at home with the natural world, passionate, for example, about cultivating his much-loved roses: "I found Sergeant Cuff and the gardener, with a bottle of Scotch whisky between them, head over ears in an argument on the growing of roses."[26]

The richness of his personality makes Cuff, as the central detective figure, more engaging to the reader; he is not simply a means to bring about the narrative conclusion. As such even his fallibility is tolerated, giving him the added reality and humanity that one might expect from a character based so evidently on a real person. Collins's friend Inspector Jonathan Whicher, who despite a largely successful career was best known in the nineteenth century for failing to solve the infamous "Road Hill murders" (a case with many similarities to that of *The Moonstone* including the English country-house setting), provides an admirable, real-life model. Cuff, like Whicher, does not always have the answer. He leaves the narrative without having solved the case, although there are moments when he displays great insight and his three departing predictions do all come true. But what seemingly matters more to Collins is that it is possible to be a great detective *and* show the sort of human fallibility that characterizes Cuff; within the novel, Cuff retains his reputation even after he has left the scene and retired to a cottage in Dorking, because his professionalism, observational skill, and investigative technique mark him out as exceptional. Collins's success in creating him relies on skillfully balancing all of these elements; Cuff has reality, professionalism, and detective skill, allied with the sort of personal eccentricity and charisma that readers have since come to expect from their fictional detectives.

Selected Bibliography

"A Stolen Letter" (1854)
"The Diary of Anne Rodway" (1856)
The Woman in White (1860)
The Moonstone (1868)

—Neil McCaw

D

COMMANDER ADAM DALGLIESH

P. D. James
(1920–2014)

It is his keen understanding of words that makes P. D. James's Adam Dalgliesh both a remarkable detective and a well-respected poet. Some describe this character as Byronic, and this is an accurate portrayal, if one-sided, as Dalgliesh is also unmistakably modern in his multiplicity. Throughout the series, which spans fourteen novels published between 1962 and 2008, Dalgliesh embodies a separation of selves: poet and policeman, romantic but solitary, and gentlemanly in appearance but not in tact. His ability to look beyond the obvious answer is the result of his specialized attention to the language of those around him, thus making him one of the best of New Scotland Yard's literary coterie.

A classic example of the gentleman detective, Dalgliesh is described by women as tall and handsome, even though he often possesses a look of "stern withdrawn self-absorption as if he were stoically enduring a private pain."[1] Subordinates and superiors are as irked by Dalgliesh's record of solving high-profile cases—he's often referred to as the Yard's "Wonder Boy"—as they are by his intellect, demeanor, and attire. His appreciation for high art, literature, architecture, religious texts, classical music, and good wine, a trait shared with fictional detectives such as Dorothy L. Sayers's Lord Peter Wimsey and Colin Dexter's Inspector Morse, affords him a range of understanding beyond that of the common inspector. However, he truly excels at piecing together obscure details by scrutinizing the subtle nuances of words.

Dalgliesh's uncanny hunches help him to identify those with key information, and he instantly knows when they are lying. In *A Taste for Death* (1986), he realizes that the maid is providing a false alibi the second she speaks; he notes the subtlety of word choices and turns of phrase lost on the common ear, never missing an accidental slipup. Similarly, he exposes each of the Larksoken headland residents in *Devices and Desires* (1989) in this way. Dalgliesh can even assess a suspect's knowledge (or lack of knowledge) based on a single line of a letter, as is the case with the poison-pen letters written by a nursing home patient in *The Black Tower* (1975) and within the personal missives of the students at a nursing school in *Shroud for a Nightingale* (1971). We are constantly reminded that Dalgliesh also possesses an unnerving level of recall: he can recite the words of others as readily as he can lines of verse and scripture. But most importantly, his writerly relationship with language dictates that the commander's breakthroughs in his investigations only come when "something important ha[s] been said."[2]

Interestingly, in a time when poets are no longer household names, Dalgliesh's own poetry is somehow widely read *and* understood. He frequently finds his own books on the shelves of victims and suspects alike, and because of this literary notoriety, others sensationalize his abilities as an inspector. Still, he never indulges in the vanity of the literati and prefers not to discuss or even acknowledge his verse or personal life while on the job, except in those moments when absolutely necessary. This compartmentalization is an outward expression of a larger internal friction, as the commander is constantly on the verge of throwing in the towel, regularly vacillating between the importance of his job and the desire to write full time. He inevitably returns to detecting, in part because it serves as his poetic inspiration.

Dalgliesh's dichotomous existence is a source of admiration and irritation among those closest to him. His colleagues declare that "at times he's cold enough to be barely human," a sentiment that seems to carry into his personal life because, by his own admission, although he is "good with the words," he lacks "the willingness to touch and be touched."[3] Long after the death of his wife and infant son during childbirth, he either seeks the affections of the unavailable or, as is the case with Deborah Riscoe whom he begins to date at the end of *Cover Her Face* (1962), emotionally and physically distances himself via his work. Even the passing of his aunt (his only living relative) in *Devices and Desires* is met with what can only be described as a dignified reticence. This need to smother his feelings at times borders on the absurd, for when he summons the fortitude near the series' end to foster a relationship with Cambridge professor Emma Lavenham in *The Murder Room* (2003), he proposes marriage by shoving a handwritten note into her palm as he flees to watch her reaction from a distance.

Nonetheless, his solitary, poetic disposition makes Dalgliesh hypersensitive to the reality that successful detecting greatly hinges on a need to violate the privacy of others, and this trait has been adroitly depicted in on-screen portrayals of the character. Most of the Adam Dalgliesh novels have been adapted for British television as a miniseries in which Roy Marsden played Dalgliesh from 1983 to 1998. Martin Shaw took on the role in subsequent renditions of *Death in Holy Orders* (2001) and *The Murder Room*. And while the last Dalgliesh novel was published in 2008, he made later appearances in James's crossover novels with Cordelia Gray. Dalgliesh will remain an important part of the mystery canon, as he is not only the anchor of P. D. James's remarkable writing career but also a timeless representation of the cultured detective who grudgingly navigates between worlds.

Selected Bibliography

Unnatural Causes (1967)
Shroud for a Nightingale (1971)
Death of an Expert Witness (1977)
A Taste for Death (1986)

Devices and Desires (1989)
Original Sin (1994)
The Murder Room (2003)

—Meghan P. Nolan

DETECTIVE SUPERINTENDENT ANDREW DALZIEL AND DCI PETER PASCOE

Reginald Hill
(1936–2012)

Detecting duos are an established feature of crime fiction, as old as the genre itself. Few, however, are as remarkable as Reginald Hill's Mid-Yorkshire CID's Andrew Dalziel and DCI Peter Pascoe, who add a distinctly novel twist to the trope, breaking with the traditional hero-sidekick pairing in favor of a more evenly matched collaboration. At a first glance it would appear that the detectives, while undoubtedly equal in aptitude, have absolutely nothing else in common, and this juxtaposition of personalities creates an almost comic pairing, not unlike Laurel and Hardy, who need each other to exist. Both, however, are hardworking, good policemen who care deeply about justice, and this allows them to stomach each other until their initial mutual disdain turns to grudging admiration and finally blossoms into friendship.

Dalziel, affectionately referred to as "Fat Andy," whose very name strikes terror into the hearts of villains and police officers alike, is a larger-than-life Rabelaisian figure. A Yorkshire man of Scots origins—thus a true northerner—he is a lover of ale, whisky, food, and rugby; sneers at formal education and modern technology; and is "given to scratching himself brazenly in the most unseemly places."[4] He appears vulgar, blunt, uncouth, coarse, and bullying, and is not averse to occasional intimidation or violence. This is a distinctly non-PC character. By contrast, Pascoe is a southerner and an intellectual with a degree in social science, a liberal outlook, and a well-developed conscience. Respectful and sensitive, he is quietly pedantic, fastidiously proper, refined, and cultured—presenting the immaculately tailored, soft-spoken, boyish, and charming face of modern policing.

This formula of "opposites attract" certainly seems to have attracted a wide readership, but it would not work as well if the pair were utterly disparate, overblown stereotypes. Hill's strength in characterization lies in subtly but unmistakably developing degrees and shadings of behavior, so that over the course of the twenty-four books in the series, the many similarities shared by the detectives become visible, giving rise to more nuanced, interesting, and "human" personalities.

It quickly becomes apparent that just like his name—a pronunciation trap for the unwary (Dee-ell)—Dalziel is not quite what he seems. His exaggerated asinine offensiveness is, in part at least, a clever ruse, employed in order to mystify his opponents (be they criminals, witnesses, or fellow police officers), so that, lulled into a false sense of security, they underestimate the considerable mental capabilities of the superintendent. Although constantly cracking jokes at the expense of his long-suffering subordinates (DS Shirley Novello is addressed exclusively as "Ivor" and DC Ethelbert Bowler, as "Hat"), Dalziel is fiercely protective and loyal, fighting to push Pascoe through the ranks and making sure that the gay DS Wield is sheltered from homophobic attacks. If "being on Dalziel's team meant you often had to put up with being treated like a personal slave," it also implies that "if anyone tried to mess with one of his cubs, they found themselves messing with Daddy Bear too."[5] Notwithstanding his great bulk, Dalziel is unexpectedly agile and graceful, and can be charming, sensitive, and kind, revealing a great sense of humor—his deadpan quips are one of the greatest joys of the series. Despite his professed dislike of all things academic, he is also erudite and well read, frequently surprising his learned DCI with high-culture references.

By the same token, Pascoe possesses character traits at odds with his golden-boy status, often becoming more Dalzielesque than the "Fat Man" himself. There is a hand of iron inside his velvet glove, and he is not above occasional bullying, harassment, or even violence, on many occasions letting himself be driven by obsessive idées fixes, displaying an irrational stubbornness and lack of insight (he doesn't notice Wield's homosexuality), mixed with impatience, self-importance, and a certain vanity—not helped by Ellie, his rather difficult to like, "holier-than-thou," liberal academic wife.

Apart from this interesting characterization, the books are also noteworthy for Hill's irreverent and playful take on the very genre of detective fiction. Departing from the dictum that crime stories should be stylistically undemanding, he habitually introduces complex structural devices, changing narrative viewpoints, voices, and styles, thus enlarging and altering the form of the novels; *The Wood Beyond* (1995) features a parallel story about Pascoe's ancestor, set during World War I; "One Small Step" (published in *Asking for the Moon*, 1996) is a science-fiction investigation in space; large parts of *Death's Jest Book* (2003) are presented as a series of letters, while *A Cure for All Diseases* (2008) comprises transcripts of an audio-diary. Perhaps most unusual in a police procedural are Hill's dizzying allusions to other literary works that, far from merely serving as an easy source of quotations, greatly influence both the structure and plot of the narratives. They range from Shakespeare (*A Killing Kindness* [1980]) to Edgar Allan Poe ("Pascoe's Ghost" and "Dalziel's Ghost" from *Asking for the Moon*) and Jane Austen (*A Cure for All Diseases*). These formal innovations, coupled with humor, a distinct use of language—especially Yorkshire dialect—virtuoso plotting, and a memorable cast of supporting characters, ensure that Dalziel and Pascoe remain one of the most brilliant and surprising sleuthing partnerships in British detective fiction.

Selected Bibliography

A Clubbable Woman (1970)
An April Shroud (1975)
A Killing Kindness (1980)
Deadheads (1983)
Under World (1988)
Pictures of Perfection (1994)

Asking for the Moon (1996)
On Beulah Height (1998)
Death's Jest-Book (2003)
The Death of Dalziel (2007)
A Cure for All Diseases (2008)
Midnight Fugue (2009)

—Agnieszka Jasnowska

STEPHANIE DELACOUR

Julia Kristeva
(1941–)

The growing fascination with crime fiction as a reflection of the contemporary globalized world has proved attractive not just to writers and readers but also to academics. It is perhaps for this reason that the renowned French scholar, practicing psychoanalyst, and cultural critic Julia Kristeva employs the character of a female investigative journalist, Stephanie Delacour, as her fictional double in three novels, *The Old Man and the Wolves* (1991 [1994]), *Possessions* (1996 [1998]), and *Murder in Byzantium* (2004 [2006]). Kristeva's detective novels have aroused some controversy due to the fact that they embody her theoretical concepts and their vicissitudes, but Stephanie Delacour is a delightful and intriguing character with enormous appetite for life, who "could also be a detective when she felt like it."[6]

Delacour, a native of France, is a journalist for the newspaper *Événement de Paris*. She is repeatedly sent as a special correspondent to Santa Varvara, an imaginary state that displays characteristics of both the United States and various postcommunist countries, in order to report on violations of human rights, political corruption, the drug trade, human trafficking, and other problems engendered by the globalized economy and mass migration. In *Murder in Byzantium* Delacour juxtaposes Santa Varvara with both France as a European cradle of cultural sophistication and an imaginary Byzantium. Investigating a murder committed by a professor of Byzantine history, who is fascinated with the princess Anna Comnena's account of her father's reign in the twelfth century, Delacour conceives of the mythical place in terms of crime writing by women: "[Byzantium] is a detective story written long before Agatha Christie, Patricia Cornwell, and other Mary Higgins Clarks came on the scene!"[7]

Always elegant, the cultivated Delacour gradually becomes romantically involved with Santa Varvara's chief detective Northrop Rilsky and moves in with him in *Murder in Byzantium*. Rilsky is a classical music lover who plays the violin, has excellent, if conservative, taste in fashion—he is fond of suits à la Cary Grant—and is a wine connoisseur. He also prides himself on his knowledge of psychology and psychoanalysis. Nimbly moving in the corrupt political circles of Santa Varvara, he vainly seeks to reconcile his love for what is just and right with the corruption of Santa Varvaran society; he is a "saint fallen among rogues, yet able to live with their villainy," secretly enjoying his "inadmissible similarity" to his rather brutal and dumb assistant, Andrew Popov.[8] Yet, only when Delacour cooperates with Rilsky and Popov do they solve crimes successfully.

Delacour speaks Santavarvaran because as an ambassador's child she spent a few years there. However, she keeps reminding the reader that existing between two languages and cultures amounts to being a perennial traveler, and compares the transit between them to gender transformation: "As I put on another language I practice a kind of transsexualism."[9] By declaring detection a "surgical passion," she breaks out of the opposition between the rational and irrational, thus resolutely following in the footsteps of her eminent male predecessor, Edgar Allan Poe's C. Auguste Dupin, adopting a theory about crime that "bring[s] us closer to something like *The Murders in the Rue Morgue*."[10] Yet, she is also certain that as a woman journalist-detective she has "two advantages: intuition and perseverance."[11] Indeed, aware that access to other people's experience is fragmentary, and manifests itself in "the vestiges they leave in colors, sounds, or words," Delacour is capable of empathically identifying with victims and perpetrators because the detective "may turn out to be quite a chameleon."[12] She works by building up files on murder victims and perpetrators, thus reconstructing their lives and characters. Even if Delacour does not always help bring criminals to justice, she is capable of understanding the bigger picture—the circumstances, passions, and calculations that brought about the crime in the first place. Yet the search for the identity of the murderer turns into the investigator's quest for her own identity. As she declares, "I investigate, therefore I am."[13] Furthermore, her last name—Delacour—connects her to the law. Thus, Kristeva's woman detective mediates between the juridical order and art, irony and affect, language and the nonverbal, as well as between a Westernized global world order and Eastern Europe.[14]

Selected Bibliography

The Old Man and the Wolves (1991 [1994])
Possessions (1996 [1998])
Murder in Byzantium (2004 [2006])

—Zofia Kolbuszewska

C. AUGUSTE DUPIN

Edgar Allan Poe
(1809–1849)

Edgar Allan Poe's famed inspector, often described as the first fictional detective, had an impact far beyond the traditional boundaries of genre fiction. Not only was C. Auguste Dupin a prototype for two of the most famous literary investigators, Sherlock Holmes and Hercule Poirot, whose cultural significance extends even further beyond the written page than their literary ancestor's, but he has also been recognized as a key figure in psychoanalysis, a highly specialized form of detective work in its own right. Examined thoroughly in Jacques Lacan's "Seminar on the Purloined Letter," Dupin's idiosyncratic mannerisms, methods, and semiprofessional status came to influence psychoanalysis as a discipline of (extremely) private investigation, and thus in a subtle way the broader "inward turn" of the twentieth century. Any extended analysis of Dupin's significance must involve, therefore, some interpretive ingenuity, some channeling of his expansive imagination to avoid repeating the standard error of reducing him solely to a proto-Holmes.

In "The Murders at the Rue Morgue" (1841), Dupin opines to his unnamed companion about the sort of games men with particular analytic skills excel at. The great inspector, he claims, is like the great whist player who notes and remembers variations in the dispositions and countenances, the glances and gestures, of his partner and opponents, signs that bypass the observation of others entirely. Dupin, most impressively, is a reader of thoughts, though not in any particularly mysterious or occult way; instead, he is carefully attuned to the emergence of thought out of itself, the way it unfolds dialectically in the mind as it takes in and processes the concrete stimuli of an environment. His understanding of the way thought *moves*—demonstrated to his friend through "the extraordinary manner in which [he] had chimed in with my [own] meditations"—provides Dupin with the main advantage he has over the Paris Prefecture (the police), who impair their vision "by holding the object too close" and losing sight of the matter of the whole.[19] This is to say that Dupin proceeds by glances rather than gazes, possessing a dynamic investigative vision that follows a winding dialectical path through the thicket of others' errors, seeing where their attention was too concentrated, sustained, or direct, and feeling his way along the peculiar "deviations from the plane of the ordinary" that every case affords.[20]

These deviations are like Epicurean swerves in a subatomic material universe—those random movements the pre-Socratic materialists offered as an explanation for chance encounters in an otherwise determined world—and Dupin prides himself on his ability to operate on a different scale of observation than the professionals, bringing inquiry to bear on otherwise baffling chance intersections (as when a frightened, escaped orangutan meets a jerry-rigged casement only he could swing himself through). While attempting to retrieve a compromising letter "purloined" from the boudoir of a member of the royal family, Dupin further demonstrates his ability to think from the perspective of other minds, mimicking the logic of a schoolboy by forming "an identification of the reasoner's intellect with that of his opponent," a game theory approach that *alters* one's original principles of investigation to account for the strange and unusual motivations of other people (rather than, as the police are wont to do, merely *extending* those principles).[21] Dupin's training—which is always self-training—certainly accords with Enlightenment assumptions about the necessity of "honing" one's reason, but it goes beyond simple exercises in repeatable logic, for he has taught himself to switch between modes of dynamic, engaged vision and abstraction as necessary, as when his glance turns inward and his eyes, "vacant in expression, [regard] only the wall" in front of him.[22]

Dupin's mental dexterity has been emulated and rewritten in characters like Holmes (who explicitly insults his forerunner's supposed genius in *A Study in*

Scarlet), Poirot, Dostoevsky's Petrovich, and Borges's Lönrott, and has been revived across various media, notably by Alan Moore in *The League of Extraordinary Gentlemen*. But as has been already suggested, his encounter with psychoanalysis and twentieth-century philosophy more generally is perhaps the most fascinating of the many "adaptations" of Dupin. Before Lacan gave his famous reading in *Ecrits*, Dupin was analyzed by Marie Bonaparte and would be the subject of subsequent commentary by Jacques Derrida. However, Dupin does not quite fit the traditional model of the Freudian psychoanalyst digging into the basement of his patient's unconscious; rather, it is the police who fruitlessly scour the depths of the minister's hiding places, leaving no dark spot uncovered in their pursuit of the stolen letter. Dupin's brilliance, then, lies in his ability to glide along the *surfaces* of thought as it unfolds, to occupy new subject-positions like a dexterous post-Freudian analyst. Rather than imposing and reimposing a monolithic analytic logic, he *reacts* to the police and the minister's cat-and-mouse act, noting each player's transforming relationship to the object of desire. Because he is attentive to the surfaces that conceal inner depths, because he knows that many of the best-trained minds can no longer see what is in plain sight, Dupin became a model for the intricate turns of twentieth-century theory that called into question traditional models of the subject, as well as the police logics of versions of human psychology that would fail again and again to uncover the real motivations behind the most peculiar events.

Selected Bibliography

The Murders in the Rue Morgue (1841)
The Mystery of Marie Rogêt (1842)
The Purloined Letter (1844)

—Zachary Tavlin

INSPECTOR "BENEDITO" ESPINOSA

Luiz Alfredo Garcia-Roza
(1936–)

Named after the Dutch philosopher Baruch Spinoza (the Portuguese version of his name is Benedito, or Bento, de Espinosa), Inspector Espinosa is a rare honest Brazilian police officer in a force known for corruption. Police corruption is in fact so common in Rio de Janeiro that the victim in Espinosa's first case, *The Silence of the Rain* (1996 [2003]), leaves a note "TO THE POLICE" and an envelope with twenty thousand dollars in it as a bribe to ignore his suicide.[15] However, when the wife of the "murder" victim offers to send Espinosa some mangoes from her garden, he replies, "Thanks, but not to the station—policemen can't always be trusted."[16] As an honest man among dishonest colleagues, Espinosa suffers from an isolation that is both self-imposed and a professional hazard. When he puts together an elite squad of trustworthy officers to investigate the killings of three police officers and their mistresses in *A Window in Copacabana* (2001 [2006])—no doubt related to their corruption—his colleagues distrust him even more than usual. Most officers think of being on the take as "just part of their pay. They look at bribes like a legitimate bonus that can double their salary," and Espinosa is the anomaly.[17]

Espinosa is a unique detective in other ways as well. Divorced, in his early forties, and with an ex-wife and a son living in the United States (and never named), he lives alone in the quiet Peixoto District of the Copacabana neighborhood of Rio de Janeiro. He has lived in the same apartment since the age of nine, inheriting it as an adolescent after his parents' death in a car crash. His grandmother stayed with him until he turned nineteen and then left him on his own in the family apartment. His idiosyncrasies abound. An avid reader, he has no bookshelves but rather creates a living "shelf in its purest state" by alternating books in vertical and horizontal "shelves" until they are as tall as the doorway.[18] His principal investigative method is thinking, an act as solitary as reading. Yet he is also a deeply sensual man. He has an attractive, younger girlfriend, Irene, a professional designer who often travels to São Paulo for work. Though they enjoy an active sexual relationship, they have no expectations of monogamy or marriage. In each novel Espinosa finds another woman at least temporarily attractive and often consummates the attraction, agonizing all the while about their age difference, physicality, and his inexorable march toward death. Alba in *The Silence of the Rain*, for example, owns a gym, while Kika in *December Heat* (1998 [2004]) is a beautiful young artist; both succumb to Espinosa's mysterious charms despite his graying hair and existential doubts.

Of course his colleagues find him strange. No one ever knows his first name for certain, though during an undercover operation he uses "Benedito" for his code name, telling a colleague that it is close to his real name. Like his namesake, author of *Ethics* (1677), Espinosa is a deeply ethical man. He respects everyone, whether street urchin or wealthy widow, treating each individual as his moral compass demands and investigating the death of the prostitute with the same seriousness as the death of the executive. This moral code places Espinosa in conversation with other downtrodden moral detectives such as Philip Marlowe, trading the mean streets of Los Angeles for the *becos* (alleyways) of Rio. Unlike other hard-boiled or noir detectives, however, Espinosa solves cases by imagining various scenarios, however improbable, eliminating those that do not work, and creating new ones throughout the course of an investigation. In short, he investigates by thinking, using reason, intuition, and psychological analysis, a method consistent with Garcia-Roza's career as a university teacher and scholar of philosophy and psychology.

Espinosa is chief of the First Precinct of Rio de Janeiro, but his dedication to reflection leads him to contemplate the creation of a new nonadministrative post for himself, with a single responsibility: thinking. For Espinosa, murder is more than the act itself, or the death itself: it is an event filled with ambiguity. He must apply his reason, his intuition, and even his imagination to discover not just the *who* but more importantly the *why* of crime. He delves deeply into aspects of his cases that go beyond forensic evidence, even doing a thorough investigation of a crime that has yet to occur, when Gabriel of *Southwesterly Wind* (1999 [2004]) confesses to a murder of an unknown person he has yet to commit. Espinosa's introspective approach even sends him back to his own childhood in *Alone in the Crowd* (2007 [2010]), to understand the apparently unmotivated murder, and to identify the killer, of a defenseless old woman. The process of contemplation and thinking leads him to wander the streets of his neighborhood, or sit on a bench in a nearby plaza, where he goes so often that the local demimonde accepts him as they accept the bench. He is the only police officer that inspires no fear, and perhaps even inspires trust, in the questionable characters that inhabit the shadows of the *cidade maravilhosa*, or "marvelous city," of Rio de Janeiro.

Selected Bibliography

The Silence of the Rain (1996 [2003])
December Heat (1998 [2004])
Southwesterly Wind (1999 [2004])
A Window in Copacabana (2001 [2006])
Pursuit (2003 [2006])
Blackout (2006 [2009])
Alone in the Crowd (2007 [2010])

—Linda Ledford-Miller

ERAST PETROVICH FANDORIN

Boris Akunin (Grigory Chkhartishvili)
(1956–)

Boris Akunin's Erast Fandorin stands out as one of the most extraordinary fictional detectives in terms of the variety, geographical scope, and historical impact of his investigations. In *The Winter Queen* (1998 [2003]) he starts his career as a young police officer in Moscow, revealing the conspiracy of an international terrorist organization striving to rule the world, while in *The Diamond Chariot* (2003 [2011]) he investigates a criminal political plot in Japan. Later, in *The Coronation* (2000 [2009]) and *The Death of Achilles* (1998 [2005]), Fandorin discloses multiple plots against the Russian royal family and high-ranking state authorities; in *Jade Rosary Beads* (2006) he works with Sherlock Holmes to track down Maurice Leblanc's famous fictional criminal Arsène Lupin and captures and kills Jack the Ripper; and in *The Planet Water* (2015) he even prevents the early onset of Nazism—to list only a few of his heroic deeds.

While Fandorin lives and acts between the 1860s and the 1910s, in a reality that is as much literary as it is historical, his creator Boris Akunin—the pen name of Grigory Chkhartishvili—is our contemporary. Russian mystery writer, scholar of Japanese culture, historian, and popular blogger, Akunin revived the tradition of writing entertaining fiction for intellectuals. Like Umberto Eco's postmodernist *The Name of Rose*, Akunin's literary project appeals to different audiences simultaneously: those who follow the plot and enjoy the stylized nineteenth-century narrative, as well as those who read the texts as literary riddles, recognizing their multiple allusions to crime fiction and world literature. Fandorin's televisual and literary origins are a good example of this dual appeal. Borrowing his protagonist's refined behavior from Lord Peter Wimsey, his deductive method from Sherlock Holmes, and his engineering skills and resourcefulness from Phileas Fogg, Akunin also acknowledged that he was inspired by the hero of David Lynch's television series *Twin Peaks*, FBI special agent Dale Cooper, from whom Fandorin inherited his habit of mental exercises.

Fandorin's image combines Western and Eastern features. This ironically reflects Russia's unique geopolitical location between West and East, a conceptual location that constitutes the core of her national identity. Raised by a British governess, Fandorin always remains a refined gentleman. He never forgets his manners, wears a perfect suit, and strives for enlightenment, reason, and progress. That is to say, he represents a perfect Westerner. However, he also possesses outstanding intuition, meditates, and practices Eastern combat techniques he learned from a ninja clan during his time in Japan. His loyal servant, bodyguard, and assistant Masa, a former Japanese bandit, also contributes to the Eastern side of the detective's image. Fandorin's personal code of honor brings together Confucian teachings based on the *Analects* with the principles of British gentlemanly behavior. In his investigations, the combination of both intuition and deduction helps Fandorin, although often it is his ability to resist the allure of mysticism and to follow the light of reason that saves the day, as in *Jade Rosary Beads*.

While Fandorin may sometimes seem to be an excessively literary construct, his nobility and courage, along with his minor flaws like stuttering, make him an endearing character. More importantly, he is a character built around paradox. He possesses uncanny luck in all games of chance and, knowing this, uses the gift only in exceptional circumstances. In love, he easily wins hearts, but he inevitably brings danger and death to the women he loves, and thus must stay away from any woman who may invoke a deep passion. This tragic curse starts with his mother who dies in childbirth and reappears in *The Winter Queen*, where his fiancée Lisa dies on their wedding day in an attack planned by the female "mother" of a terrorist organization in revenge for Fandorin's role in the demise of her "children."

Fandorin's investigations are often incomplete: while he manages to disclose numerous crimes, on a larger, historical scale his local victories turn out to be strategic losses. For example, in *The Black City* (2012), Fandorin manages to reveal a conspiracy against Franz Ferdinand but fails to prevent both his assassination and the beginning of World War I. This consistently paradoxical situation is determined by Akunin's agenda as a historian. In most of his novels the writer revisits pivotal moments of Russian and world history such as the Russo-Turkish War in the 1870s, the eve of the Russo-Japanese War in 1904, and World War I. Akunin places his protagonist at points of bifurcation when alternative historical paths were possible, and questions the inevitability of events. According to him, world wars and Russia's epic failures were not predetermined by social and economic factors but were rather the result of conspiracy, unfortunate coincidence, or mistake. Revealing the complexity of Russia's past through Fandorin's adventures, Akunin diverges from the post-Soviet trend of nostalgic idealization of "the Russia we have lost."[1]

Throughout the series, Fandorin tries to prevent these catastrophes and comes very close to fulfilling his task but inevitably fails. Of course, his failure is predetermined by the course of history as we know it—but still, for a while the reader's perception oscillates between the suspension of disbelief usual for a work of fiction and an extraordinary doubt in history as we know it.

Selected Bibliography

The Death of Achilles (1998 [2006])
Murder on the Leviathan (1998 [2005])
The Turkish Gambit (1998 [2006])

The Winter Queen (1998 [2003])
Special Assignments: The Further Adventures of Erast Fandorin (1999 [2007])
The State Counsellor (1999 [2008])
The Coronation (2000 [2009])

—Milla Fedorova

PROFESSOR KATE FANSLER

Amanda Cross (Carolyn Gold Heilbrun)
(1926–2003)

Shaped as a challenge to the pattern set by Agatha Christie's Miss Marple, and later emulated by numerous academic mystery writers, Amanda Cross's Kate Fansler offers a remarkable model of the erudite, feminist professor-sleuth. Fansler is a distinguished tenured professor of literature at one of New York's largest and most prestigious universities. Born into, yet early in life estranged from, a wealthy Wall Street family, she relishes her egotistic independence from traditional models of domestic bliss and openly scorns the idea of bearing and rearing children. Fetching herself a cigarette to go with her favorite Beefeater martini, befriending a number of brainy and gifted women, and romancing quite a few handsome men, Fansler remains single well into her forties, until Reed Amhearst, an assistant district attorney, succeeds in persuading her otherwise.

Fansler ingeniously takes advantage of her intimidating, "very professorish" looks—she is elegant and "attractive without being charming"—as well as her own and her eventual husband's expertise and influence within the two institutions they serve, academia and law enforcement.[2] In the first novel of the series, *In the Last Analysis* (1964), Fansler finds herself drawn, as a suspect, into the investigation of the murder of one of her students. Her penchant for asking probing questions and telling good stories unexpectedly turns to her advantage, as her apparently implausible crime narrative helps Amhearst and the police to catch the real culprit. The two subsequent novels, *The James Joyce Mysteries* (1967) and *Poetic Justice* (1970), show Fansler as Amhearst's interlocutor rather than partner in crime solving; her career as amateur detective, frequently contrasted with his professional dexterity, develops erratically. Although it is Fansler, not Amhearst, who identifies the perpetrators in *The Theban Mysteries* (1971) and *The Questions of Max* (1976), she is not fully acknowledged as an independent private eye until she solves the case of a staged murder in the Nero Award–winning *Death in a Tenured Position* (1981), which may be treated as a turning point in Kate Fansler's investigative career.

Starting from *Sweet Death, Kind Death* (1984), in which Amhearst decides to give up his occupation and Fansler is politely asked to look into the case of the supposed suicide of an eminent woman professor, Fansler's reputation grows steadily. In time Amhearst swaps his assistant DA position for an academic career, and Fansler becomes a renowned expert in "an abstruse field," who is "in demand for literary-type murders."[3] Her long-standing experience with the small world of tenured and untenured professors is found invaluable whenever an investigation requires an inside knowledge of academic circles. As Fansler has only indirect links with law enforcement, she does not always feel the necessity for sharing the results of her inquiries with the police. In *Poetic Justice*, *The Players Come Again* (1990), *Honest Doubt* (2000), or *The Edge of Doom* (2002), the very unraveling of mysteries appears to her sufficiently rewarding: "I happen to think seeking the truth is also the intelligent plan to pursue," she declares in *The Theban Mysteries* (1971), and acts accordingly.[4]

Distancing herself from Miss Marple's habit of seeing analogies in real-life incidents, Fansler looks for hints and assistance in the authors she has read. "Life isn't evidence," announces Fansler, a literature scholar, in retort to Amhearst's acerbic complaint that she does not distinguish between fact and fiction.[5] Life, she reckons, is a text—a good story someone narrates and decodes—but the stuff it is made of does not necessarily constitute material evidence in itself. Solving mysteries with the help of flights of fancy, intricate speculations, and literary criticism is for Cross's professor-detective a standard procedure. Although a specialist in the Victorian period, in her inquiries Fansler does not always resort to Charles Dickens or Alfred Tennyson; she finds Agatha Christie or John le Carré as helpful (or misleading) as the writers from the classical literary canon. Throughout the series, quoting literature is an established mode of communication between people from all walks of life. Therefore, Fansler—one of the very few professors considered both entertaining and profound—finds it easy to converse with her students and colleagues, as well as with nonacademic suspects and police investigators. In Cross's fictional world, the latter do read, drop quotations, and discuss literature as readily as the former, as if they realize what sort of fictional world they inhabit.

The author of the series, Professor Carolyn Heilbrun, was an eminent scholar who served as president of the Modern Language Association and was the first woman to receive tenure in Columbia University's English Department. Their subtle parody of academic discourse (literary sources are alluded to even when someone's life is at stake), metatextual commentaries concerning the poetics of detective fiction, and avid interest in gender-related problems make the Amanda Cross novels a fine example of self-reflexive academic mystery fiction that is nonetheless able to appeal to a wide readership.

Selected Bibliography

In the Last Analysis (1964)
The James Joyce Mysteries (1967)
Poetic Justice (1970)
The Theban Mysteries (1971)
The Question of Max (1976)
Death in a Tenured Position (1981)
Sweet Death, Kind Death (1984)
No Word from Winifred (1986)
A Trap for Fools (1989)
The Players Come Again (1990)
An Imperfect Spy (1995)

The Collected Stories of Amanda Cross (1997)
The Puzzled Heart (1998)
Honest Doubt (2000)
The Edge of Doom (2002)

—Ludmiła Gruszewska-Blaim

DR. GIDEON FELL

John Dickson Carr
(1906–1977)

The first appearance of Dr. Gideon Fell in 1933 let a breath of fresh air into the stale atmosphere of Golden Age detective fiction. At the time, the genre was largely populated by athletic, aristocratic detectives such as Dorothy L. Sayers's Lord Peter Wimsey and S. S. Van Dine's Philo Vance. Throughout a career spanning twenty-three novels, five short stories, and five radio-plays, Gideon Fell renewed the tradition of fictional sleuths by undermining the physical and physiological traits typically characterizing male Golden Age detectives. Physically modeled on Carr's literary idol, G. K. Chesterton, Fell is in many ways the converse of the prince of detectives, Sherlock Holmes. While Holmes is a gaunt, austere bachelor, who speaks the formal idiom of the late Victorian period, Fell is monstrously fat, married, devoted to alcohol, and speaks in the pompously overblown tones of Samuel Johnson, interspersed with loud interjections: "O Lord! O Bacchus! O my ancient hat!"[6] While Holmes writes treatises on the various types of tobacco ash, Fell studies the role of the supernatural in English fiction, and his magnum opus is *The Drinking Customs of England from the Earliest Days*. Nevertheless, Fell is presented as a serious lexicographer and historian, who loves lecturing on any topic that interests him: death traps, cryptography, the Spanish inquisition, and of course, locked-room mysteries.

Fell sweeps away much of the self-conscious vanity and pretentiousness characterizing of Golden Age detectives such as Wimsey and Vance. Unlike these sleuths, Fell does not have clear notions about the nature and practice of detection; although he helps Chief Inspector David Hadley in his most complicated cases, Fell is rarely interested in physical evidence such as fingerprints or footmarks and instead finds the solution through reasoning and by what he calls "woolgathering."[7] Fell sometimes suppresses evidence or allows the criminal to escape or commit suicide, which would be unthinkable for many detectives. However, Fell's lack of hypocrisy and freedom from pretentiousness may make him seem like "a childish old fool," as he sometimes calls himself.[8] In the second Fell novel, *The Mad Hatter Mystery* (1933), for instance, Fell's love of acting and his interest in children's toys are very clear: while he is playing the role of Hadley and interrogating a suspect with a dummy pistol and fake handcuffs, he accidentally scoots a toy mouse across the table in one of the most amusing passages of the book. This emphasis on Fell's childish eccentricity is most pronounced in the early novels. In fact, although Carr did not develop Fell's personality over the thirty-year span of novels, as, for example, Margery Allingham and Sayers did with Albert Campion and Wimsey, the early novels are experimental. *The Eight of Swords* (1934) and *The Blind Barber* (1934), for instance, are principally comedies, in which Fell acts as a slapstick detective.

Despite the light and mocking tone of his early novels, Fell is a great sleuth. His name is almost synonymous with the locked-room mystery, a subgenre in which a crime is committed under apparently impossible circumstances. Throughout his career, Fell rationally explained some of the most complicated and apparently unsolvable mysteries in the history of crime fiction, ranging from murders committed in a darkened house when the only three witnesses could vouch for one another (*Death Watch*, 1935) to defenestrations from within locked rooms (*The Case of the Constant Suicides*, 1941; *The Dead Man's Knock*, 1958) and crimes committed in prison while under constant observation (*Hag's Nook*, 1933), in guarded towers (*He Who Whispers*, 1946), and on tennis courts (*The Problem of the Wire Cage*, 1940). His most famous novel, however, is *The Hollow Man* (1935), which contains the celebrated locked-room lecture in which Fell outlines the seven types of explanation for a murder perpetrated in a sealed room.

In this chapter, Fell produces a strong defense of the locked-room mystery, which has often been charged with improbability, and suggests that the detective story in general belongs not to the domain of realism but to that of fantasy. It was after the publication of this novel that Fell became inextricably associated with locked-room mysteries. It is not a coincidence that Golden Age writers such as Clayton Rawson, Anthony Boucher, and Derek Smith paid homage to Fell by quoting his lecture in *Death from a Top Hat* (1938), *Nine Times Nine* (1942), and *Whistle up the Devil* (1953), respectively. Smith even presented Fell as a real person whose cases had merely been narrated by Carr.

In the world of contemporary crime fiction, Fell is still recognized as the doyen of the impossible crimes. In Maj Sjöwall and Per Wahlöö's *Locked Room* (1972), for instance, Martin Beck comes across a study of the sealed-room problem, which contains identical expressions to those Fell used in his famous lecture. Even though the locked-room mystery is a less popular subgenre now than during the Golden Age of detective fiction, many contemporary sleuths who have to deal with impossible murders, from Paul Halter's Alan Twist to Bill Pronzini's Nameless, would certainly love to ask the great Gideon Fell for a little advice.

Selected Bibliography

Hag's Nook (1933)
The Mad Hatter Mystery (1933)
The Blind Barber (1934)
The Eight of Swords (1934)
Death Watch (1935)
The Hollow Man (1935)
The Problem of the Wire Cage (1940)
The Case of the Constant Suicides (1941)
He Who Whispers (1946)
The Dead Man's Knock (1958)

—Stefano Serafini

GERVASE FEN

Edmund Crispin
(1921–1978)

The first half of the twentieth century saw the creation of many wonderfully eccentric fictional sleuths, but only Gervase Fen could have sent this telegram: "COME AND PLAY THE CATHEDRAL SERVICES ALL THE ORGANISTS HAVE BEEN SHOT UP DISMAL BUSINESS THE MUSIC WASN'T AS BAD AS ALL THAT EITHER . . . BRING ME A BUTTERFLY NET I NEED ONE."[9] This callously cheerful and self-interested demand that a friend travel across wartime England to face potential danger, with cumbersome luggage to boot, is typical of Fen's disregard for the comfort of others. Nonetheless, he is a complex character, capable of sensitivity and kindness when confronted by the victims of crime, especially when those victims are young and vulnerable.

At the start of his recorded adventures, Fen is in his early forties, "a tall, lean man with a ruddy, cheerful, clean-shaven face and brown hair which stood up mutinously in spikes at the crown of his head. . . . His eyes . . . showed charity and understanding as well as a taste for mischief."[10] Fen is professor of English language and literature at the fictional Oxford college of St. Christopher's and has many academic publications to his name. He is contentedly married, with children. Despite his conventional academic career, Fen is a man of restless and inquisitive intellect, with many idiosyncrasies, chief of which is his small, battered red racing car, whose name, Lily Christine III, is scrawled in white paint across her bonnet and who boasts an amply endowed, chromium nude, jutting dangerously from her radiator cap. Lily Christine III is the most flamboyant of Fen's many characteristic eccentricities, but he is frequently absorbed by other hobbies, ranging from etymology to playing the saxophone, which he approaches with typical gusto but little skill. His creator Edmund Crispin (the pseudonym used by Bruce Montgomery) was a successful composer, and it is natural that Fen has an enduring passion for music and opera.

Fen's chief hobby is detection, and in *Frequent Hearses* (1950) he admits to himself that this comes close to being an addiction. His interest lies in solving unusual murders in distinctive settings, not in mundane crimes involving the drudgery of routine inquiries. Fen ascribes his detective success to intuition. In reality, his achievements are due to his intelligence, moral courage, and ability to think and do things that his contemporaries are too hidebound or timorous to contemplate. He is not intimidated by rank or power and will boldly go where most policemen fear to tread. Nor is Fen concerned with preserving his dignity. This leads him into a number of crazy exploits, including many wild chases. The most notable of these occurs in *The Moving Toyshop* (1946) in which Fen leads a motley band of undergraduates, an aging academic on a bicycle, a poet, and a young lady called Sally in a mad pursuit through the sedate streets of Oxford, culminating in an interrogation in a punt. Despite his flippancy, Fen is a man of action, whose service in the Great War has honed his survival instincts. He is a natural detective, whose physical and mental attributes combine to create a remarkably successful investigator.

Three of Fen's earlier adventures take place in Oxford, where he is allowed access to police investigations by Sir Richard Freeman, the chief constable, who is as passionately interested in English literature as Fen is in detection. Further afield, Fen investigates murder in a cathedral close, a public school, a film studio, and even during a Parliamentary election. Fen has no problem in establishing himself wherever he goes; his self-confidence and wayward charm make him friends, even amongst the police officers who are officially investigating the crimes, such as Detective Inspector Humbleby of Scotland Yard who becomes a friend and sometimes asks for Fen's assistance.

Always a rebel, Fen transgresses the literary norms of his form by breaching the fourth wall that keeps fictional characters in their proper place. In *The Moving Toyshop* he makes up titles for his adventures in order to help Crispin with his work, and when deciding which direction to turn, his companion makes an impish reference to the original publisher's politics: "'Let's go left,' Cadogan suggested. 'After all, Gollancz is publishing this book.'"[11] Crispin's prose is elegant and erudite, which is lucky as Fen would have not just quietly transgressed but instead violently demolished the fourth wall to protest if the writing style used to narrate his adventures was inadequate. Fortunately, the spice of mischief and the liveliness of Fen's character keep any tendency toward pretentiousness in check.

Gervase Fen may be considered the enfant terrible of crime fiction. No other detective would use theatrical makeup to adorn his face like a clown in the dressing room of the singer whose death he is investigating. Nor would they play the fool while wearing a cow mask to infiltrate a black mass: "He mooed experimentally, and then, seeming pleased with the sound, did it again. He continued to moo all the way to their destination."[12] It is in keeping with Fen's character that he never swears but instead quotes Lewis Carroll's White Rabbit, "*Oh my fur and whiskers.*"[13]

Philip Larkin said of Edmund Crispin that beneath a formidable exterior he had unsuspected depths of frivolity. It could be said of Crispin's literary creation that beneath a frivolous exterior, Fen concealed unsuspected depths of compassion, courage, and integrity. The majority of the Gervase Fen novels have been recently republished, and the scene may be set for a long overdue revival.

Selected Bibliography

The Case of the Gilded Fly (1944)
Holy Disorders (1946)
The Moving Toyshop (1946)
Swan Song (1947)
Buried for Pleasure (1948)
Love Lies Bleeding (1948)
Frequent Hearses (1950)
The Long Divorce (1951)

—Carol Westron

G

MRS. GLADDEN

Andrew Forrester (James Redding Ware)
(1832–1909)

We learn very little about Mrs. Gladden in the tales contained within Andrew Forrester's *Female Detective* (1864). Her name is assumed, and while she generally refers to herself as Mrs. Gladden—qualifying it as her business name—she sometimes uses "Miss" and once refers to herself solely by the letter *G*. This is a mysterious figure who is at pains to keep her identity secret from both the reader and her friends and neighbors who, thanks to her dedication to concealment and artifice, assume she is a dressmaker. She thus refuses to reveal key defining attributes such as her age or marital status. We do not know what class she belongs to, although it is apparent that she can move with ease amongst all types of people, and the reader remains in the dark about her motivations for joining the police force. But whatever Mrs. Gladden's reasons, we do know that it is certainly not for the satisfaction of seeing justice served, as this is only rarely achieved in her stories.

When *The Female Detective* was first published in 1864, there were no women detectives in Britain, yet Mrs. Gladden serves as an independent enquiry agent who acts under the auspices of the Metropolitan Police. This is a complicated position, as she is often left to find her own cases, as in "Tenant for Life" in which she performs her detecting operations undercover, and this, alongside her assertive and critical stance toward the dominant structures of the police, indicates how progressive this text was for its time. However, while Mrs. Gladden clearly has some regrets about her work, her "profession has not led [her] towards hard-heartedness," and this ensures that she retains the compassion deemed essential to the Victorian notion of the "angel in the house," even if nothing else about her fits that restrictive category.[1]

In opposition to the dominant perspective of Victorian culture, which saw women as vulnerable, weak, and ineffective, the advantages of being a woman in detective work are made explicit in *The Female Detective*. Mrs. Gladden can, for example, get into places where a man would be denied access. She is also at times able to blur the distinct Victorian gender boundaries. For example, in "Tenant for Life" she shocks the degenerate heir, Sir Nathaniel, by donning a disguise that means she is mistaken for a man. Mrs. Gladden is keen to point out that criminality is not confined to the male sex; indeed, when a woman is a criminal, she is perceived as a worse fiend—more ruthless and dangerous—than her male counterparts. Therefore, it takes a woman to catch a woman. Equally, Mrs. Gladden is aware that her position as a female doing a man's job in a man's world means that she is an object of greater disgust than her male peers (who were themselves reviled as spies). So, while Forrester's collection is itself a fascinating piece of progressive literature that challenges gender norms and boundaries, it can at times reinforce them by presenting these attitudes as arising from the "natural" separation of the sexes and by accepting the idea that women, be they criminals or detectives, are always worse than their male equivalents.

Mrs. Gladden's methods of detection take many forms, and she is keen to apply scientific principles to her cases. In "Tenant for Life," the case rests on a quirk of pronunciation, and it is the science of phonology that helps to reveal the culprit. She is fond of using lists to determine the known and unknown aspects of a case, and she builds her evidence in an orderly fashion using methods of induction to assess information and seek the truth. In fact, she has what might be stereotypically described as a "masculine" approach to the collection, organization, and assessment of evidence. But, while she is able to piece together information with ease, she does have a rather varied level of involvement with the cases she recounts. In "Tenant for Life," she leads an unofficial investigation into the purchase of a child and is therefore instrumental in both creating the case and investigating the crime, whereas her only role in "A Child Found Dead: Murder or No Murder" is to introduce a doctor and his friend Hardal, who then proceed to solve the mystery.

Her retelling of criminal cases in which she does not lead the investigation allows Mrs. Gladden to reflect upon her fraught relationship with the Metropolitan Police force and the Victorian criminal justice system in general. Her tales frequently recount investigative failures and deal with the inability of both herself and the police to achieve justice in the face of sophisticated, and even not-so-sophisticated, criminal behavior. Mrs. Gladden is committed to the necessity and importance of detection and the need for a police agency, but at the same time she believes the organization itself is far from perfect. Her stories are therefore critical of the force's limitations. Accounts such as "The Unknown Weapon" are full of regret at her inability to prove what she knows to be true and the resulting lack of prosecution.

It is not really important who Mrs. Gladden is behind her deliberate disguises; she will always remain a mystery. What is significant is that she is an unusual Victorian sleuth, due to both her position as a professional female detective and her critical stance toward the limitations of justice. This, combined with her unwavering attempts to reveal the truth and uncover criminal activity, even if the deserved punishment never comes, offers an important early example of both the idealistic and critical tendencies frequently exhibited by crime fiction.

Selected Bibliography

The Female Detective (1864)

—Joanne Ella Parsons

INSPECTOR ALAN GRANT

Josephine Tey
(1896–1952)

Appearing in a handful of novels, Josephine Tey's Inspector Alan Grant has long been overlooked by critics, if not by readers. A dapper, haunted, poetry-loving police inspector, he was a natural successor to the satiric knights-errant of much Golden Age detective fiction. At the same time, he anticipated the complex protagonists of modern psychological crime writing. Grant's first appearance in *The Man in the Queue* (1929) established him as part of a rather dandified English police force. He commanded the envy and admiration of his peers because "the last thing he looked like was a police officer."[2] Alongside courage, intelligence, and energy, the man's elegant dress sense and enthusiasm for poetry marked him out to suspects as respectable but ultimately unthreatening. That rare thing among 1920s detectives, a professional police inspector, Grant also possessed the hallmarks of amateurs like Lord Peter Wimsey and Albert Campion, namely, a disposable income that enabled him to solve crimes for pleasure alone, and a degree of eccentric charisma.

Seven years passed between Grant's first appearance and his second, in *A Shilling for Candles* (1936). During that time, his creator, an unpretentious Scottish woman, focused on writing plays under the name Gordon Daviot, but finding that detective fiction paid better, she revived Grant under a fresh pseudonym, Josephine Tey. The Second World War intervened, and Grant's next case, *The Franchise Affair*, appeared in 1948, with him playing only a minor role. Each of Grant's exploits is unique in its scope and in the way it is investigated: he starts off as a man of action, chasing a criminal around London, but goes on to probe the psychology of transgendered living in *To Love and Be Wise* (1950) and solve from a hospital bed the historical mystery of King Richard III's alleged crimes in *The Daughter of Time* (1951). He investigates murder, missing persons, domestic violence, and the ethics of historical biography, in each case proposing a solution more psychologically in tune with twenty-first-century thought than that of his own time.

Grant is often assisted by the adoring Sergeant Williams. He introduces his colleague, Inspector Rodgers, to the fine arts, at one stage remarking on "how shocked the writers of slick detective stories would be if they could witness two police inspectors sitting on a willow tree swapping poems."[3] His network also includes an actress, Marta Hallard, who enables him to exchange ideas on a human, rather than professional, level, and to think about the communities he investigates as groups of performers. There is never a hint of sexual attraction on either side of the relationship—indeed, Hallard seems more interested in women than men—making Grant virtually unique among mid-twentieth-century detective heroes.

In his later cases, Grant's sensitivity becomes less a professional advantage than an obstacle to personal fulfillment, as he grows more psychologically invested in each case. In *The Singing Sands* (1952), his final investigation, he spends a great deal of time wondering whether he should find a wife and settle down. At the same time, his mental health begins to deteriorate, with claustrophobia and panic attacks accompanying a strong fixation with the unidentified corpse. His final three cases all begin with his obsessive interest in the faces of male victims. Troubled by the direction his thoughts are taking, Grant argues repeatedly with a voice in his head, which points out that if the dead man "had been a fat commercial traveller with a moustache like a badly kept hedge and a face like a boiled pudding," he would never have investigated the case.[4]

There is something subtle and understated about Alan Grant's masculinity. He never proves himself as a red-blooded male. His interest in male beauty, his half-scientific, half-superstitious belief in reading personality traits from people's faces, and his identification with victims mean that when he uncovers the truth things appear less clear-cut than they did before the investigation began. This may be why, when Alfred Hitchcock filmed *A Shilling for Candles* as *Young and Innocent* in 1937, the character was cut out altogether, in favor of a more conventional romantic hero. Unlike most major British detectives, Grant never became the hero of a television series, possibly because each novel occupies a distinct sphere and has a distinct style. However, the books themselves have never been out of print in Great Britain. In the twenty-first century, there has been a resurgence of interest in both Grant and his creator, evidenced by Nicola Upson's series of historical mysteries featuring Tey herself as a detective, beginning with *An Expert in Murder* (2008).

As a character, Grant stands for something between the neat artificiality of the Golden Age that predated his strongest cases and the psychological grit that characterizes later suspense novels. His influence is most directly felt in the figure of Adam Dalgliesh, P. D. James's poetry-loving senior police officer, who has difficulties sustaining relationships outside of work. However, the books have also inspired crime writers keen to explore the confusions and contradictions of gender, including Val McDermid, who has remarked on Tey's significance in "open[ing] up the possibility of unconventional secrets": "It is that fascination with who we really are and what actually shapes our relationships," McDermid writes, "that is the key to Tey's role as the bridge between the golden age and contemporary crime fiction."[5] Alan Grant is thus a major figure in the development of the British detective novel because he is a character out of his time.

Selected Bibliography

The Man in the Queue (1929)
A Shilling for Candles (1936)
The Franchise Affair (1948)
To Love and Be Wise (1950)
The Daughter of Time (1951)
The Singing Sands (1952)

—J. C. Bernthal

CORDELIA GRAY

P. D. James
(1920–2014)

P. D. James's Cordelia Gray is radically different to her detective predecessors, including both strongly masculine figures like Sherlock Holmes or Philip Marlowe, and also Agatha Christie's popular incarnation of the amateur female detective, the elderly Miss Jane Marple. First appearing in 1972, the independent and self-reliant Gray had powerful cultural resonance for a British society caught up in debates about the political and social status of women. This political atmosphere is evident in both of Gray's cases. In *An Unsuitable Job for a Woman* (1972), scientist Sir Ronald Callender employs Gray to investigate the apparent suicide of his son. In *The Skull beneath the Skin* (1982), set on an island owned by Victorian necrophilia collector Ambrose Gorringe, Gray investigates macabre poison-pen letters delivered to the leading actress in an amateur production of *The Duchess of Malfi*. In a clear statement of feminist intent, Gray contends in both mysteries against powerful masculine figures who threaten her with professional and personal ruin.

As a young woman, Gray must continually contest social and gender conventions to carry out her work as a private detective. At the start of *Unsuitable Job*, Gray's former employer (later business partner) Bernie Pryde commits suicide, and Gray becomes at twenty-two the sole proprietor of Pryde's Detective Agency. Learning of Pryde's demise, the landlady at his local pub remarks to Gray, "You'll be looking for a new job, I suppose? After all, you can hardly keep the Agency going on your own. It isn't a suitable job for a woman."[6] This opinion is reiterated throughout the narrative: the police imply that a detective agency is not an appropriate place for a woman; the pub landlady goes on to inform Gray that her mother would not approve; and even the "Snout," a police informer who, by nature of his occupation, also steps outside social rules, assumes that Gray will be in need of a new job. Nonetheless, Gray decides to defy the weight of public expectation and run the agency herself.

Gray's appearance seemingly belies her profession: she has "thick, light brown hair framing features which looked as if a giant had placed a hand on her head and the other under her chin and gently squeezed the face together; large eyes, browny-green under a deep fringe of hair; wide cheek bones; a gentle, childish mouth. A cat's face."[7] Gray's features convey a sense of soft femininity and child-like naïveté that disconcerts and distracts clients and suspects alike. In fact, Gray possesses many of the characteristics that crime fiction readers have come to associate with the successful detective. She is intelligent and intuitive, is concerned with order, is able to keep secrets, and has a keen sense of moral justice that does not always align with the law. She also has an impressive knowledge of literature and art that is pertinent in both of her cases: in *Unsuitable Job*, a William Blake quotation holds a clue to the mystery; in *Skull beneath the Skin*, the poison-pen letters draw on Renaissance tragedies. And most importantly, Gray possesses the curiosity that her "cat's face" suggests. However, rather than utilizing the masculine methods of the traditional detective, Gray's investigative techniques are focused on the personal, the emotional, and the empathic.

A 1977 review of P. D. James's detective novels in the *Times* describes Gray as "charming, practical and above all believable."[8] Indeed, it is the ability to believe in Gray that makes her such an appealing detective figure. There is nothing outlandish, otherworldly, or two-dimensional about her. The reader is privy to her very human emotions, fears, and foibles, and is given an insight into her unusual past. When her mother dies shortly after giving birth, Gray is left with only her father, a political revolutionary who privileges ideology over family and is thus effectively absent from her life. Gray is raised in foster care, before being accepted into a convent school. At age sixteen, her father demands that Gray join him in supporting his work, dashing her academic plans for A levels and university. As Gray notes in *Skull beneath the Skin*, her father believed in the theory of gender equality rather than its practice; during the six months before his death, Gray fulfills the various roles of cook, nurse, and seamstress. In her subsequent occupation as private detective, she is able to embrace the independence and freedom previously denied to her.

The realistic representation of Gray means that she cannot be immune to danger, and like the proverbial cat, her curiosity (and detective skills) lead her literally into dangerous waters. In *Unsuitable Job*, she is thrown to the bottom of a well; in *Skull beneath the Skin*, Gray faces another watery death, this time in a cave known ominously as the "Devil's Kettle." But as Gray herself recognizes, she is a survivor, and she overcomes adversity to succeed. At the close of *Skull beneath the Skin*, Gray refuses to be silenced in her quest to bring the criminal to justice. In the face of intense pressure to drop the case, she feels "inviolate," knowing that "she would tell the truth; and she would survive."[9]

Undoubtedly, Cordelia Gray asserts the place of the (young) female private investigator in the crime fiction canon, proving that the business of detection *is* entirely suitable for a woman. If Gray's appearance in fiction was relatively short lived (James penned only two Cordelia Gray novels), her influence was not. As one of the first female private eyes to appear in fiction, literary critics and readers continue to return to Gray, marking the significance of her position in the development of the crime fiction canon.

Selected Bibliography

An Unsuitable Job for a Woman (1972)
The Skull beneath the Skin (1982)
Talking About Detective Fiction (2009)

—Laura Foster

DETECTIVE BENNY GRIESSEL

Deon Meyer
(1958–)

South African author Deon Meyer's Benny "Benna" Griessel is worse off than most of the many downtrodden and damaged male protagonists of contemporary crime fiction. Griessel's alcoholism does not merely lead to hangovers, embarrassment, or general anxiety; he is known in the police force as the man "who had once arrived at a murder scene so drunk that they had to load him in the ambulance along with the victim's corpse."[10] In *Devil's Peak* (2005 [2012]), the first novel featuring Griessel, his wife has thrown him out of their house after seventeen years of marriage; he has been a miserable drunk for the majority of their time together, but she finally takes this step when he hits her for the first time. He has moreover alienated his two teenage children, who witnessed the abuse.

In subsequent novels, Griessel continues to struggle with his memories of this event and with his drinking, both of which have him in a firm grip. Griessel nevertheless manages to be a very good detective. Despite the fact that he has faced disciplinary hearings—he is always acquitted—he feels comfortable with his superiors, both because he can drink all of them under the table and, more importantly, because he has a very high case-solution rate, higher than anyone else in the police force. He remains as committed to his work as he is to his addiction, or perhaps to fighting his addiction, even though it is his work that has pushed him into alcohol abuse.

Despite the fact that Griessel feels comfortable with many of his colleagues, there is no one else he can be completely honest with, and his closest confidante in all of the novels is his Alcoholics Anonymous sponsor, Dr. Barkhuizen. The doctor understands his dependence and is someone he can talk to, as he is neither a colleague nor a family member. During their sometimes quite psychologically exhausting conversations, and occasionally at an AA meeting, Griessel's genuine emotions and thoughts are allowed to surface. During these parts of the novels, we learn how he abandoned his dream of becoming a professional bass player because he realized he had always really wanted to be a policeman. Yet the violence the job entails, the crime scenes he has to witness, never leave him in peace: "I hear it. I can't help it. I hear it when I walk in on a scene when they are lying there. The scream hangs there—waiting for someone to hear it. And when you hear it, it gets in your head and it stays there."[11] To protect them from this pain, and the cruelty people are capable of, it is not possible for Griessel to share his work with his family, or with Alexa, with whom he starts a relationship in *7 Days* (2011 [2012]). He instead turns to his best friend and worst enemy Jack Daniels: "It helps me get through the day."[12]

One side effect of his severe alcohol addiction is his talent in the art of deception; he can easily lie to anyone to conceal the fact that he has been drinking all night, or that he has spent the night at a murder victim's house because he did not know where else to go. However, this addiction-driven duplicity might also be the reason he is so good at what he does; he can trust his intuition when talking to witnesses and suspects, and can tell when they are hiding something. Despite the damage and chaos his drinking causes, he manages to advance in his career and eventually becomes detective captain in the Hawks, or South Africa's Directorate for Priority Crime Investigation. He is also appointed mentor to younger police officers. Even though he is called wise and trustworthy by his superiors, he worries that the responsibility is too much for him. This is another example of his almost constant self-loathing.

Beyond his troubles and his talents, Griessel is also distinguished from his colleagues by his surprisingly progressive racial and sexual politics. He is repeatedly described as Slavic-looking, even as resembling a Russian noble. One colleague thinks he looks like a young Khrushchev and refers to him as Nikita. Yet his whiteness is not always emphasized, while his tolerance of people of all colors is. This is not always the case with his white colleagues in postapartheid South Africa. He is, furthermore, tolerant of female police officers, even female superiors, something the novels make clear is far from a commonplace attitude in the South African police force.

However, in sharp contrast to this, Griessel's role as father and husband is very traditional. He automatically and quite conventionally hates his daughter's boyfriends, and when he is forced to find a new apartment, he is at a loss. He does not know how to iron his clothes, cook, or clean. This is an experienced detective, used to all kinds of demanding work, yet he is completely helpless at home without a woman: "He had fuck-all. He had less than when he went to police college. Jissis."[13]

This expletive, Jissis, is Griessel's most frequent way to comment on the events of his personal and professional life. Afrikaans for "Jesus" or "Jeez," for Griessel it entails much more than its literal meaning; it is disappointment, it is fear, shock, and anger, but perhaps most of all, it is self-loathing. This is what Benny Griessel struggles against more than any clever murderer or vicious criminal conspiracy, and it is only on rare occasions he can beat it.

Selected Bibliography

Devil's Peak (2005 [2012])
Thirteen Hours (2008 [2010])
7 Days (2011 [2012])
Cobra (2014 [2014])
Icarus (2015 [2015])

—Katarina Gregersdotter

EBENEZER GRYCE

Anna Katharine Green
(1846–1935)

Years before Sherlock had settled in Baker Street, and decades before Lord Peter peered through his monocle and cried for Bunter, another detective was unraveling perplexing and murderous events, not in London or even Paris, but in nineteenth-century New York City. Well into middle age, "a portly, comfortable personage" who is frequently laid up with "severe attack[s] of rheumatism" that cripple his hands and leave him hobbling on stout canes, New York Police detective Ebenezer Gryce seems, at first glance, the unlikeliest of crime solvers.[14] Yet over the nearly forty years that he appeared in Anna Katharine Green's mysteries, he proved himself to be a talented and unshakeable detective, able to restore order in the highest circles of Gilded Age society.

Ebenezer Gryce made his first appearance in Green's debut novel, *The Leavenworth Case*, in 1878. The book was a publishing phenomenon. Its financial and popular success secured Green's reputation as the preeminent American detective fiction writer of her generation, resuscitated the fortunes of the venerable publishing house G. P. Putnam's Sons, and in the decades to follow would inspire some of the most notable names in the genre as well: Arthur Conan Doyle, Mary Roberts Rinehart, Dorothy L. Sayers, and Agatha Christie all numbered among its readership.

Working in the days before advanced forensics, when "fingermarks" and blood typing were in their infancy, Gryce relies on two techniques to solve crimes: the thoughtful interpretation of physical clues and exhaustive interviews with suspects and witnesses. Although he's not above tricking a witness—his capture of Horatio Leavenworth's killer is a master class in misdirection—he is never brutal or vengeful. As he says modestly to his associate Q when asked about his methods, "I have come across nothing that was not in plain sight of anybody who had eyes to see it."[15] And in a genre that relies so often on the act of looking—think of the ubiquitous magnifying glass, monocle, and microscope—Gryce's most distinguishing mannerism is his reluctance to meet *anyone*'s eye. "If [his eye] rested anywhere, it was always on some insignificant object in your vicinity, some vase, inkstand, book or button. These things he would take into his confidence, make the repository of his conclusions, but you—you might as well be the steeple on Trinity Church for all the connection you ever appeared to have with him or his thoughts."[16]

In her writing, Green demonstrates an extensive knowledge of her era's crime fiction. Her characters and she make frequent mention of their investigative predecessors. These include Edgar Allan Poe's C. Auguste Dupin, Émile Gaboriau's *roman policiers*, Thomas de Quincey's notorious essay *Murder as a Fine Art*, and important British innovators such as Charles Dickens and Wilkie Collins, whose Sergeants Bucket and Cuff would play such an integral role in the genre's early development. She also reveals an intimate familiarity with the American legal system. Indeed, such knowledge is a hallmark of her intricately plotted fiction. Green's father, James Wilson Green, was a prominent lawyer who enjoyed strong connections within the legal community, including at least two New York Police chiefs. This carries over into her fiction, with Gryce calling on the expertise of many different professionals, including coroners, district attorneys, and other members of the legal community, to solve the crimes he faces. Gryce also frequently delegates inquiries to the various young officers he mentors, trusting them to execute them independently.

At the time that Green was writing, police forces had a reputation for thuggishness and corruption—a state of affairs that led to scandals and public inquiries, not only in New York, but also in Chicago, London, and even as far afield as Melbourne. But Gryce, with his innocuous demeanor, unwavering morality, and physical limitations that preclude investigation-by-fisticuffs, serves as an ideal depiction of what the police *could* be like, even if contemporary readers would have been hard pressed to find such virtues in his real-life counterparts.

He is also set apart from many of his fictional competitors by his class. "I cannot pass myself off for a gentleman," he mourns.[17] Readers' class prejudices meant that elegant amateurs, in the mold of Sherlock Holmes, would dominate detective fiction until the rise of the police procedural after the Second World War. Unlike a police officer, an amateur's gentlemanly interest in crime is rarely touched by burdensome legal obligations or the taint of salary. Yet Gryce takes his career seriously and never doubts his own worth, even in the face of considerable skepticism. Reflecting on the beginnings of his career with the police in the 1840s, he admits to having been "full of ambition" and hopeful that the resolution of a challenging case would be a boon to his career.[18] His quiet pride in his abilities and his delight in the recognition he has earned are a consistent feature of all of the stories he appears in—a delight that readers have shared for nearly 140 years.

Selected Bibliography

The Leavenworth Case (1878)
A Strange Disappearance (1879)
Hand and Ring (1883)
Behind Closed Doors (1887)
The Staircase at Heart's Delight (1895)
That Affair Next Door (1897)
Lost Man's Lane (1898)
The Circular Study (1900)
The Mystery of the Hasty Arrow (1917)

—Claire Meldrum

BERNIE GÜNTHER

Philip Kerr
(1956–)

Bernie Günther (or Gunther) is a Berlin policeman and private detective who appears in and narrates (to date) twelve novels. The conventions are *noir,* but the mean streets are not LA but (usually) Berlin. Günther served as a soldier in the Great War (he fought at Verdun, hence his abiding dislike of the French) and works as a policeman in Berlin investigating murders in the late Weimar Republic and the early years of the Nazi regime. Detesting Germany's new masters, he leaves the police force to become a private detective specializing in finding missing persons (of which, he bitterly remarks, there is no shortage in 1930s Berlin). However, his exceptional skills as a detective mean that he is employed, however reluctantly, by Nazi officials. He serves on the Eastern Front during the war with the Soviet Union and works for the Nazis in Prague. He spends time as a prisoner in a Soviet POW camp, and even here his detective skills are of use. His work after 1945 takes him to Munich and Vienna, and in 1950 he flees Europe for Argentina.

Günther works in very bad places and in very bad times. For example, sections of *Field Gray* (2010) are set in German-occupied Minsk in 1941, and the novel is filled with savage violence; in *A Man without Breath* (2013), Günther is involved in investigating Soviet massacres near Smolensk. The vileness of the history and places that surround him is supplemented by a variety of often brutal individual murders that he must or wishes to investigate. Günther is highly conscious of the paradox of police work in appalling times: what does the death of a single person matter, when hundreds are being butchered a few kilometers away? He also finds himself working for very bad people—for Heydrich, Nebe, Goebbels, and for other Nazis (fictional and nonfictional), as well as ruthless US, Peronist, and East German security officials after 1945. Günther himself is part of this world: he commands execution squads on the Eastern Front, he is prepared to kill a murderer, and he even shoots a witness (in *Field Gray*) who endangers his own life. It is little wonder, given where he is, what he does, and what he witnesses, that Günther sees the world in Gothic terms. Evil has been let loose on the world; Germany's Romantic nightmares have become real.

In this morass, Günther is an efficient and effective detective. He exhibits considerable forensic skill as well as intuition in solving crimes. He can penetrate intrigues of labyrinthine intricacy, or even solve a traditional locked-room murder. Sometimes criminals escape immediate punishment (Heydrich in *Prague Fatale* [2011]); sometimes they are brought to some kind of justice (Krivyenko in *A Man without Breath*); and sometimes the investigation just ends in official lies (*A Quiet Flame* [2008]). Günther's work takes him first into the dark complexities of the corrupt and vicious Nazi state and then of a violent and corrupt postwar world. He moves robustly through the menacing streets of 1930s Berlin, the bombed-out landscapes of postwar German cities, and the lovely villas that hide terrible secrets. He is beaten up and shot at by a host of thugs in uniform and out of uniform, gangsters, black marketeers, and war criminals, but he still pursues his investigations. He is understandably cynical and suspicious about almost everyone and everything. His talk is blunt and his wit, rapid and biting. (The novels' convention is that the characters mostly speak German. Their language is given color by German idioms translated directly into English. Thus, a cop is a "bull," a cigarette, a "nail," and a crazy person, a "spinner.") Günther is insubordinate and derisive of authority but knows enough to be scared of the terrifying people (like Heydrich) that he has to deal with. In all his operations, he does, however, have a sense of a traditional morality. In *The Pale Criminal* (1990), the child murders are too grotesque, the anti-Jewish plot that underlies them, too vile, and the people involved, too criminal for Günther not to put himself at risk to achieve some kind of punishment for the perpetrators. Similarly, he feels compelled to attempt to rescue a woman from rape by Russian deserters in Vienna in 1947 (*A German Requiem* [1991]) though the odds are not good. Indeed, throughout the series, Günther's relations with women are complex. They are usually short lived and end in death (the list is long). He admires intelligent, resourceful, and beautiful women but seems unable to save them from the evil of the world (notably in *A Quiet Flame*). He is also frequently betrayed by them (this list, too, is long).

Günther is a complex figure, an agent of some kind of justice, and a brave man who nonetheless commits major crimes and is implicated in even bigger ones. The circumstances of his collaboration with the Nazis (and other criminals) are always clear, but that collaboration must make the reader uneasy (as it is meant to). He is, however, a physically and mentally tortured man, whose bleak sense of his own evil is paralleled by the desolation of the wartime and postwar landscapes through which he moves. Günther derives from Raymond Chandler's Philip Marlowe, and the novels' historical settings echo work by Graham Greene and Alan Furst. But Kerr's Günther novels on their own demonstrate that crime fiction can grapple successfully with important issues.

Selected Bibliography

March Violets (1989)
The Pale Criminal (1990)
A German Requiem (1991)
The One from the Other (2006)
A Quiet Flame (2008)
If the Dead Rise Not (2009)
Field Grey (2010)
Prague Fatale (2011)
A Man without Breath (2013)
The Lady from Zagreb (2015)
The Other Side of Silence (2016)
Prussian Blue (2017)

—David Malcolm

H

MIKE HAMMER

Mickey Spillane
(1918–2006)

Mike Hammer, Mickey Spillane's detective, forever changed the formula of the hard-boiled detective. The "Spillane Phenomenon"—the author's popularity and the unprecedented sales of his books, which have been described as "a primitive right-wing diatribe against some of the central principles of American democracy and English law"—is partly due to the novel characterization of his detective, Mike Hammer.[1] Hammer's persona sums up the dramatic shifts in the sociocultural and political environment in the United States during the postwar period. In one novel after another, Spillane uses Hammer to explore the extremes that best describe the atmosphere of the time; his works crystalize the conspiracies theories, fear, and anxieties that dominated the McCarthy era. With his questionable morality and readiness to inflict violence, Hammer takes a vigilante approach to justice and welcomes revenge as his personal mission. Both crusader and avenger, Spillane's detective creates an alternative narrative of law and order, and navigates—albeit unconsciously—complex interconnections between gender, justice, and crime. Hammer faces communists, enemies from beyond the US borders, and dangerous women who threaten the peace and order not only of his individual clients but also of the country at large.

Mike Hammer also offers a platform from which to explore the new market for popular fiction and changing readership patterns in the postwar period, as well as the accompanying shifts in the crime genre itself. Appearing in cheap, mass-market paperbacks, Spillane's detective seems more at home in this new medium, with its darker and more pessimistic plots and characters (especially the detective), than in earlier pulp magazines. Hammer's unconventional—and often violent—methods are similarly suited to the postwar era.

Hammer deviates from the classical persona of the hard-boiled detective as embodied by Raymond Chandler's Philip Marlowe and Dashiell Hammett's Continental Op and Sam Spade. Unlike these earlier figures, Hammer's missions have nothing to do with fulfilling justice or solving mysteries; rather, he is "a one-man war machine" who creates his own bloody version of the fight against crime.[2] He represents the chasm between law and justice, as he goes far beyond any legal boundaries to achieve his goals. He often stands against the system that he is supposed to keep in order and challenges the moral and professional codes of the detective. Furthermore, Hammer's motives often stem from personal desires. For example, in Spillane's first novel *I, the Jury* (1947), he speaks of hate as the force that drives him: "There was so much hate welled up inside me I was ready to blow up."[3]

Moreover, Hammer operates within a complex and somewhat disturbing gender scheme. He often attacks women and inflicts pain and violence on the female body in an imitation of the criminals that he hunts, fights, and captures. Violence and sex intermingle in a way that adds to the ruthlessness of the detective's character. In his novels, Spillane "opened the floodgates of sadism," with his detective—shockingly—as the agent who carries out sadistic acts against women.[4] For example, in *I, the Jury,* Hammer leads a relentless campaign to avenge his brutally murdered friend Jack. When Hammer finally discovers that Charlotte, a beautiful woman he is involved with, is his friend's killer, he shoots her while she is naked in the dramatic and memorable final scene of the novel.

Instead of working with or in parallel to the criminal justice system to eliminate social threats and solve crimes, as is typical for the investigative figure, Hammer himself seems to be the primary source of danger to those around him. Appointing himself as judge, jury, and executioner, Hammer does not hesitate to beat and torture people to get the information he needs and most importantly to get revenge. This is again evident in *Kiss Me Deadly* (1952) when he sets the criminal Lily Carver on fire and burns her, in an act of annihilation of the female body, as well as when he shoots Juno (who is ultimately revealed to be a man) in *Vengeance Is Mine!* (1950).

The confluence of violence and sexuality allows Hammer to be celebrated as perhaps *the* macho masculine figure of the fifties. Indeed, the detective's character brings to the forefront the gender politics of the time, when the concept of "feminine mystique" was used to push women back into the prewar domestic order.[5] This cultural misogyny was accompanied by increasing anxieties revolving around masculinity and heroism. A returning GI himself, Hammer is indicative of the need to constantly reaffirm masculinity in the postwar era. He thus demonstrates that the "hero" of earlier detective fiction, with his professional and moral codes, was no longer a suitable representative of postwar America. If violence, ruthlessness, and vindictiveness are the new standards against which the detective's character is measured, Mike Hammer perfectly fits the bill.

Selected Bibliography

I, the Jury (1947)
My Gun Is Quick (1950)
Vengeance Is Mine! (1950)
The Big Kill (1951)

One Lonely Night (1951)
Kiss Me, Deadly (1952)
The Girl Hunters (1962)
The Snake (1964)
The Twisted Thing (1966)
The Body Lovers (1967)
The Delta Factor (1967)
Survival . . . Zero! (1970)

—Maysaa Husam Jaber

CLIFF HARDY

Peter Corris
(1980–)

Australian crime writing was revitalized in 1980 by the arrival of Sydney private investigator Cliff Hardy in *The Dying Trade*. A successor to the hard-boiled California private eye, but transplanted down under, Hardy is tough but essentially romantic and loathes "the greed and conservatism that are constantly threatening to undercut what he sees as the real Australia."[6] Over the last three decades Hardy has become a fixture of the Australian crime fiction scene, appearing in more than forty novels, countless short stories, and a film, earning his creator, Peter Corris, the well-deserved moniker "the godfather of modern Australian crime fiction."

Cliff Hardy got into the private investigation game via the army, a couple of years at university, and a short-lived career as an insurance investigator. He grew up in the beachside suburb of Maroubra when it was still working class, lives in a run-down terrace house in Glebe, and drives a second hand Ford Falcon that is nearly as battered as he is. Although a little rough around the edges, he is also intelligent, well read, and has a sardonic sense of humor that he puts to good use commenting on Australian society. Generally laconic and laid back, yet handy with his fists when threatened, he enjoys a drink or ten, a smoke (in the early books), a good Le Carré novel, and a roll in the hay with the women he meets during the course of his investigations. He is particularly attracted to educated, professional women and wealthy femmes fatales, the latter usually smelling of some floral perfume he cannot name. While he has had long-term relationships over the years, these do not end well, with many of his paramours ending up dead. He does, however, find his long-lost daughter in *The Other Side of Sorrow* (1999) and in later books has a close bond with her and his infant grandson.

Usually hired by the rich and powerful to protect their interests, he ends up exposing their crimes and the corruption of the state, while championing the underdog and the exploited. Essentially a realistic character, he does not use scientific knowledge or heavy weaponry to solve cases, instead relying on his intelligence, doggedness, knowledge of human nature, and information garnered from friends and contacts in the police, media, and underworld. Hardy is not the sort of superhero who can defeat a whole bar full of bikers with one hand tied behind his back; in fact, his smart mouth means he is regularly beaten into unconsciousness by various thugs and henchmen. Instead, he must use his wits and the skills he picked up as an amateur boxer to escape physical danger.

Over the course of his long career Hardy has tangled with fraudulent physicians, corrupt cops, crooked politicians, immoral media moguls, and dodgy property developers, to name but a few. He has been jailed and has lost and regained his investigator's license. He has investigated missing persons, murderers, and blackmailers and gone behind the scenes in just about every legal and illegal industry operating in Sydney. Whether Hardy's investigations lead him through suburban brothels, sporting clubs, or the hall of high finance, each milieu offers an opportunity to interrogate sociocultural mores.

Hardy's actual age is a closely guarded secret. His army service in Malaya would suggest that he is in his eighties. However, Corris follows the lead of John D. MacDonald, arguing that it is possible to age a series character at "one-third the natural rate and no one will mind."[7] This puts Hardy in his late fifties in *That Empty Feeling* (2016), and although he has slowed down a little due to a heart attack and quadruple bypass operation, taken up exercise, cut down on drinking, and started engaging in slightly less athletic sex, the essential Hardy remains intact. While the urban landscape of inner-city Sydney morphs and gentrifies, Hardy's old-school ethics, left-leaning politics, and willingness to give and take a punch stay the same.

Sue Turnbull puts it succinctly: "Through the unwavering gaze of Cliff Hardy, Corris has conducted a longitudinal investigation of Australian society over the past thirty-five years, providing a searing and wry commentary on social justice, corruption and urban development. Like Hammett and Chandler . . . Corris portrays society itself as the crime."[8] Corris has said that the next Hardy book is likely to be his last, and if that is indeed the case let us raise a glass or two of cheap white wine and toast Cliff Hardy for bringing Australian crime fiction back to the mean streets where it belongs.

Selected Bibliography

The Dying Trade (1980)
The Empty Beach (1983)
Casino (1994)
The Black Prince (1998)
The Other Side of Sorrow (1999)
Master's Mates (2003)
Saving Billie (2005)
Appeal Denied (2007)
Gun Control (2015)
That Empty Feeling (2016)

—Leigh Redhead

INSPECTOR COSTAS HARITOS

Petros Markaris
(1937–)

Petros Markaris's Inspector Costas Haritos series is a leading example of contemporary Greek noir in the tradition of the modern detective story introduced to Greece by Yannis Maris in the 1950s. It has gained popularity not only locally but also throughout Europe, particularly in Germany, Italy, and Spain. Haritos, who narrates the novels, is in his fifties and is head of homicide in the Athenian police force. He is not your typical, idealized crime-fighting hero. Instead he balances on the tricky edge between his splendid failings and redeeming virtues, managing at the same time to capture the spirit of the current political and social circumstances surrounding the crimes he investigates.

Haritos belongs to a particular brand of likable antihero. He is cynical, self-critical, almost misanthropic, and outwardly composed while frequently boiling on the inside. Although during one of the unbearable heat waves in Athens he toys with the idea of buying a new air-conditioned car (to be paid for, like everything in contemporary Greece, Markaris suggests, in installments), he is touchingly faithful to his thirty-year-old Fiat Mirafiori. Like his car, Haritos often exhibits a dogged quality that makes him follow both clues and his instincts no matter where they lead him. At times he appears to be opinionated, even prejudiced, difficult, and according to his immediate superior, the chief of security Ghikas, unbending. His apparently misogynist attitudes lead him to consider an ambitious female reporter a lesbian and extend, in his darkest moments, even to his TV-addicted wife—though never to his daughter, in whose hands he is mere putty. He also appears to share the all-too-common Greek xenophobia and dislike of immigrants, which appears in the subtext of all Markaris's novels as a mark of the times: "If they'd killed a Greek, one of ours, one of the fast-food and crepe-eating Greeks of today, that would be different."[9] Haritos's actions, his work ethic, and his conscience though paint an entirely different picture: his unrelenting search for truth will never suffer on account of, or yield to, his private preferences.

One of the quirks that contribute to the individualization of his character, giving him a novelistic catchiness and readerly appeal, is his love of dictionaries. Whenever faced with an impasse, Haritos begins to investigate the lexicographic formulation of his current situation, finding in his dictionaries both respite and hope. Another distinctive feature is his personal interpretation of life, in which all events, both private and professional, feature in a complex dance of perpetually negotiable positions: his marriage is played out through a game of "getting one's own back," while every intimation of professional success is an incentive for Haritos (and every other respectable Greek) to rush to his superior to gloat. Both in his family life and on the job—made even more difficult by the requirements of, and influence exerted by, the media—Haritos struggles to maintain the balance that gives his life structure. Hence when in *Che Committed Suicide* (2003) he finds himself on a three-month medical leave after being seriously injured during an act of heroism, all life seeps out of him.

The Greek national past is very much alive in Haritos's mind and in his cases: the student rising in the polytechnic school and the struggles during the junta, or military dictatorship of 1967–1974, provide a historical backdrop that is often important to both the victims and the suspects. Haritos's personal experience of the era, when he was a cell guard at security headquarters in 1971, makes him uneasy when dealing with (former) communists but also apprehensive when in contact with those who have turned over a new leaf and unashamedly acquired significant financial, political, and social success. Obviously, times are changing, when "we commies are legal and you fascists are all democrats."[10] At every step Haritos is reminded of the changes that have led to a world filled with anxiety, uncertainty, insecurity, and alienation. The wealthy families no longer take in poor girls from the country to be their servants, instead replacing them with an imported workforce; Greek coffee has been replaced with iced coffee, and although in this binary division between old and new he is marked as traditional, even Haritos himself has upgraded from biscuits to croissants for breakfast. In a world filled with numerous "others," Haritos is only too ready to define the true Greek spirit whenever he recognizes it in his social surroundings: "Any Greek who doesn't believe that the state is stealing from him and doesn't feel the need to get his own back is either mad or a communist."[11]

Haritos's grumpiness and penchant for truth and justice in their numerous (and not always legally acceptable) forms are evocative of Georges Simenon's Maigret. Markaris's portrayal of present-day Athens, with its cinematic rendering of traffic-congested streets, tourist-infested localities, and its weather conditions and their effect on the inspector, also evokes Simenon's Paris. Most importantly, however, like Simenon, Markaris believes that crime fiction is a suitable vehicle for the investigation of social issues. According to the author, the "detective novel becomes more and more social. . . . It's not going to be long before we define the detective novel as a social one with a detective plot."[12]

Selected Bibliography

Deadline in Athens/Late-Night News (1995 [2004])
Zone Defense (1998 [2006])
Che Committed Suicide (2003 [2009])

—Nina Muždeka

TIMO HARJUNPÄÄ

Matti Yrjänä Joensuu
(1948–2011)

In the 1960s and 1970s in Sweden, Detective Martin Beck was awakening the social conscience of Scandinavian crime fiction. Close on his heels, however, was an equally important if less well-known colleague to the east, Finland's Timo Harjunpää. Harjunpää began his exacting work as a detective sergeant in the Helsinki Violent Crimes Unit in 1976 in *Väkivallan virkamies* (*Official Violence*), and during a career that spanned eleven novels concluding with *Harjunpää ja rautahuone* (*Harjunpää and the Iron Room*) in 2010, he mapped the changing urban landscape of Helsinki, discovering in it one dark corner after another. As a member of a relatively small police force, Harjunpää does not limit his investigations to murders alone. Rather, a range of criminal behavior is depicted in Joensuu's novels, including "arson, rape, treachery, theft, fraud, oppression, nuisance and even domestic and family violence."[13] In the Harjunpää novels, crime of all types is present at all levels of Finnish society.

Harjunpää's first appearance is as a thin and veiny twenty-five-year-old. With his largish nose and less than prominent chin, lack of self-assertiveness, and compassionate demeanor, Harjunpää is certainly not the hard-boiled type. In his work, action—violent action in particular—is a tool curtailed not only by official rules but also by a sense of personal vulnerability. Smoking, for instance, does not make him seem a hard man; rather, in his own mind at least, it only serves to erode his defenses against a much harder world. His personal revulsion against violence limits his preparedness; early in his career, he loads his revolver with a single bullet, and when he must do so, he reluctantly wields the weapon with sweaty palms.

Harjunpää's strength is of the silent type. Demonstrating a particularly Finnish perception of masculinity, he employs tenacity as his main weapon against crime. Complaining or bragging does not figure in this kind of temperament, and Harjunpää's interactions with everyone but his closest family and friends are markedly terse. However, his internal dialogue and attempts to understand the crimes he is investigating bring him close to the perpetrators both physically and emotionally. This creates a tension between his placid, even cool, outward manner and the empathizing inward man, and sometimes—particularly in connection to the sufferings of crime victims—he feels "something hard inside, die a little."[14] This encrusting of his emotion is only alleviated by the presence of Harjunpää's wife and children, and as he ages he depends more and more on the regenerative power of family life to cope with the pressures of his work. Yet the role of women in the Harjunpää novels is not limited to the domestic sphere. One of the most prominent characters in the novels, Detective Onerva Nykänen, Harjunpää's colleague and a single mother, wields logic and reason to an extent unrivalled by her male colleagues, often maintaining professional and ethical standards in a predominantly male work community. Nykänen also provides Harjunpää with emotional support, which seems to be something that cannot be expected from his male peers and supervisors.

In the society depicted by Joensuu, all of these defenses, abilities, and alliances are vital for both detective work and survival. As Voitto Ruohonen puts it, this environment's "central elements consist of poverty, social isolation and the disappearance of any meaning in life."[15] In Joensuu's novels, most people are lost in something, their careers or their relationships, hounded by schoolyard bullies, or trapped in generations of family dysfunction. What makes this even more poignant is Joensuu's manner of presenting the subjective horizons of criminals who are often victims themselves. These portrayals vary from the disturbed (Tweety, a peeping Tom in *To Steal Her Love* [1993 (2008)]) to corrupt police officers (Detective Sergeant Piipponen in *Priest of Evil* [2003 (2006)]) and sometimes to the tragically innocent (Mikael in *The Stone Murders* [1986 (1983)]). Occasionally, the very representatives of law turn out to be the most chilling predators, as is the case with the sadistic detective Lampinen in *To Steal Her Love*. Curiously, the demise of a criminal is rarely a direct result of the efforts of law enforcement activities. Rather, they meet their fates through an unpredictable flow of events mostly outside of Harjunpää's control, who is forever wading knee-deep through seas of frustration, collegial bickering, and betrayal by self-serving supervisors.

As a whole, the Harjunpää novels form a history of a police officer who changes with the times, compensating for an aging body with accumulated skills, personal resilience, and the emotional support his growing family provides him. In Harjunpää, Joensuu portrays the toll exacted by the work of solving crimes; as the chinks in the armor of professional routine open wider and wider, the suffering and the dead begin to haunt the detective. In this, Joensuu's own career in the Helsinki Police Department seems to mirror his fiction: his work left him with so many unpleasant memories that, after retirement, he moved out of the city. His novels can be seen as attempts to humanize the figure of the detective, as the sociohistorical dimensions of crime are brought to light and the human circumstances in which the detective, too, must live and work are traced.

In Finland, Joensuu is regarded as a writer who has successfully dissolved the boundary between high art and entertainment; his way of rewriting the genre accommodates examinations of the technical details of crime, moments of intense suspense and action, careful structuring of drama, complex portrayals of human behavior, and also perceptive depictions of a changing social milieu.

Selected Bibliography

Harjunpaa and the Stone Murders (1983 [1986])
To Steal Her Love (1993 [2008])
The Priest of Evil (2003 [2006])

—Juha-Pekka Alarauhio

TONY HILL

Val McDermid
(1955–)

There is no other detective in crime fiction quite like Tony Hill, a fascinating character with a deep and complicated personality. Personally damaged and often failing in his endeavors, Tony Hill brings into question all conventions and expectations about the male detective. Hill is a gifted clinical psychologist who works in secure mental hospitals helping people with extreme mental health problems.

However, it is his criminal profiling for the police that highlights an unusual, intuitive talent for detection and, perhaps more importantly, enables him to begin to find himself.

Hill had a traumatic and abusive childhood. Val McDermid writes of Hill's mother, "Vanessa was not most mothers. Her son had been an inconvenience since even before he'd been born and she'd managed to sidestep anything approaching a maternal response to him. . . . She despised him and scorned what he did for a living."[16] Understandably, Hill's self-esteem and his sense of self were damaged. Yet it is this background and his constant questioning of himself that develops the empathy he needs to help others. His traumatic childhood and his difficulty in adapting to the "normal" world also means he is a truly gifted profiler, able to "get into the heads" of killers. In some ways Hill is not so different to the killers that he tracks down; as he tells the new national task force of profilers in *Wire in the Blood* (1997), "The best profilers have probably got more in common with serial killers than with the rest of the human race."[17] And although this is dangerous, it means he is able to have an insight into their methods and motivations, and predict their moves.

Hill is at the forefront of the detective/profiler subgenre of detective fiction. His methods, deductions, and insights allow the reader to gain access to the mindset and twisted logic of the ever-fascinating figure of the serial killer. These thrillers are both whodunits and whydunits: "For Tony, finding out why was at least as important as finding out who."[18] Hill's background means he can see much more clearly than any of the other characters and he does not shy away from the most terrible aspects of the human psyche. McDermid has been accused of being bloodthirsty, yet her novels are not gratuitously violent. As Lee Childs says, "She's honest. Crimes are usually sordid and disgusting, and to present them otherwise is disingenuous."[19]

Relationships are crucial to the series, and McDermid explores the difficulty of connecting with another person. This is most apparent in the tempestuous relationship Hill has with the love of his life, his Achilles' heel and sidekick Carol Jordan. To the reader it is apparent that Jordan and Hill love each other. However, even from the first novel, *The Mermaids Singing* (1995), although there is real attraction, both are reluctant to follow it through, largely due to fear of intimacy, rejection, and failure. Indeed, Hill is often impotent and does not trust himself to perform successfully in a sexual situation. Thus whilst he truly loves Jordan, he feels he cannot afford to let her get close, fearing he will let her down.

Jordan is a beautiful and successful career woman in the male-centered world of the police. Her intelligence and methodical approach to her work complements Hill's insightful, unusual way of seeing things. Passionately believing in Hill and the art of profiling, Jordan brings him into as many investigations as she can, often against the wishes of those in command. Hill and Jordan rely on each other in public and in private, and they begin to share a domestic space when Jordan moves into an annex in Hill's house. In a way these spaces define their relationship: connected but still separated, close but not quite intimate.

However, Jacko Vance nearly severs the emotional ties between Jordan and Hill in *The Retribution* (2011). When we first meet him, Vance is a beloved celebrity who has carefully hidden his psychopathic and murderous tendencies. McDermid based this character on the real-life British celebrity pedophile Jimmy Savile.[20]

In *The Retribution* Vance commits an act against Jordan that is so appalling she cannot comprehend that Hill, with his intuition and insight, did not see it coming. This is a devastating blow to a relationship that had been tentatively moving forward. Yet the rift is slowly being healed in the subsequent books, much to the relief of readers who have learned to care about them both. Their relationship remains the focus of the series, perhaps more so than the crimes they investigate together.

Hill's character and story have developed and deepened over the twenty years of the series. Well read, articulate, intelligent, and complicated, Tony Hill offers a rewarding—and all too often missing—depth of character to crime fiction, making him one of the most innovative, believable, and fascinating of all contemporary fictional detectives.

Selected Bibliography

The Mermaids Singing (1995)
The Wire in the Blood (1997)
The Torment of Others (2004)
The Fever of the Bone (2009)
Cross and Burn (2013)
Splinter the Silence (2015)

—Ruth Heholt

HARRY HOLE

Jo Nesbø
(1960–)

He has survived an avalanche, fallen from a ski jumping tower, had his cheek ripped open and his finger replaced by a titanium prosthesis, been handcuffed underwater to a swimming pool drain, been severely bitten by a black Metzner, almost drowned in an underground tunnel, survived an apartment explosion by hiding in a refrigerator, and been shot twice in the chest and once in the forehead. He compares one of his enemies to a cockroach "you flush down the toilet, that comes creeping back," a description that seems equally suitable to himself.[21] He is Harry Hole, inspector for the crime squad in Oslo, Norway, and an FBI-trained expert on serial killers, and his roller-coaster life exemplifies the splatter detective genre.

Hole lives in a small apartment at Sofie's Gate in the district of Bislett in Oslo. Besides his beloved sister, Sis, who, according to Hole, has a "touch" of Down syndrome, his father Olav, and his old schoolmate Øystein Eikeland, his best friend is Jim Beam. He usually meets this "friend" at his favorite pub, Schröder, close to his flat. His passion is music and his taste eclectic, ranging from Duke Ellington to the Sex Pistols.

His acquaintances and colleagues are repeatedly drawn into his investigations and often fall prey to either the perpetrator's torturous and fatal bloodlust or Hole's lack of commitment. He becomes emotionally involved with Birgitta Enquist in *The Bat* (1997 [2012]). She is murdered. In *Cockroaches* (1998 [2013]) his "friend," the Norwegian ambassador's daughter Runa, is kidnapped and murdered. Hole's reprise with former girlfriend Anna in *Nemesis* (2002 [2008]) ends in her mysterious suicide. His stint with Salvation Army gal Martine in *The Redeemer* (2005 [2009]) is brief, but at least she survives. The strong mutual attraction between Hole and new partner Katrine Bratt ends with her commitment to a mental hospital, and his friend, chief of the forensic team, Beate Lönn, is murdered in *Police* (2013 [2013]). In all honesty, these deaths are often a stroke of bad luck, and Hole is not always to blame. But one feels sorry for Hole, with the same sort of sympathy one entertains toward Donald Duck or Charlie Chaplin.

Having any sort of friendship with Hole is at first quite unimaginable. During his first investigation in *The Bat* into the death of a mediocre Norwegian celebrity in Sydney, who turns out to be one of numerous victims of an exceptionally brutal serial killer, we learn in flashbacks that his drunk driving is responsible for the death of a colleague and for permanently incapacitating a civilian. A periodic drunkard, Hole is temporarily on the wagon. His manners never change, though, and before he even arrives at his hotel he has managed to lose his visa, be rude to the customs officer, and offend the aboriginal police officer who picks him up by referring to him as an "Australian Negro."[22]

But his personal shortcomings are gradually balanced by an utter unselfishness and a profound sense of justice—when he is not insulting his brain by binge drinking. His exceptional deductive strengths, alert sensory and cognitive system, eye for detail (the murderer in *The Devil's Star* [2003 (2005)] is revealed through fennel seeds in his excrement), and stubbornness make him a brilliant detective. His general antipathy toward any form of institutional authority or ethical decadence yields a social pathos as well as creating an alliance with his readers. During his career he frowns at diplomacy, yuppies, the pedophilic sex scene in Thailand, the Salvation Army, neo-Nazis, royalty, imperialism in Congo, the art scene, the breakdown of Yugoslavia, the drug mafia, and even the police. The last of these is represented through the corrupt, sociopathic police officer Tom Waaler, responsible for the murder of Hole's colleague Ellen Gjelten in *The Redbreast* (2000 [2006]) and a main antagonist in the following two novels, *Nemesis* and *The Devil's Star*. In short, Hole is a true antihero—a partisan fighting a lonely war against all kinds of corruption.

His one true love, Rakel, survives the serial killer in *The Snowman* (2007 [2010]) with her son Oleg but abandons Hole since he cannot prioritize family over work (or Jim Beam, for that matter). After solving the Snowman case Hole escapes to Hong Kong but is forced back to Oslo to assist in the investigation of a series of potential serial killings in *The Leopard* (2009 [2011]). He meets Rakel at his father's funeral but decides on another sojourn in Hong Kong, from where he once again returns when Oleg is arrested for murder. At the end of *Police* he finally finds an inner peace and stands before the altar with Rakel. The book ends with a moment of contented introspection on Hole's part: "Feeling that everything was right with the world, at rest, in harmony. Knowing this was how things would end, like this."[23] But "darkness," as well as humanity, "has a *taste*" for evil. And as the novel ends, as Hole thinks his optimistic thoughts, the young daughter of a friend sits on the toilet in the girl's changing room during a handball game: "She looked down. In the big gap between the door and floor she saw a shadow. And the tips of a pair of long, pointed shoes. Like cowboy boots."[24] As we discover in *The Thirst* (2017), Hole's adventures are not over after all.

Selected Bibliography

The Bat (1997 [2012])
Cockroaches (1998 [2013])
The Redbreast (2000 [2006])
Nemesis (2002 [2008])
The Devil's Star (2003 [2005])
The Redeemer (2005 [2009])
The Snowman (2007 [2010])
The Leopard (2009 [2011])
Phantom (2011 [2012])
Police (2013 [2013])
The Thirst (2017 [2017])

—Niklas Salmose

SHERLOCK HOLMES

Sir Arthur Conan Doyle
(1859–1930)

Sherlock Holmes is the first of all literary detectives. Not first in terms of chronology, obviously, but rather in the sense of being preeminent, most influential, and archetypal. His image, words, and adventures have taken hold not just of English but also of global popular consciousness in a way that no other fictional character has ever done. Early on in *A Study in Scarlet* (1887), the first Holmes story, his soon-to-be roommate Dr. Watson asks for a description of the man; the reply he receives aptly conjures up the enigma of the Great Detective: "It is not easy to express the inexpressible."[25] A sense of enigmatic eccentricity thus becomes a key feature of the legend, and by the time of *The Sign of Four* (1890), the second Holmes novel, the detective's curious foibles had become widely recognizable to the reading public: "He thrust the sharp point home, pressed down the tiny piston, and sank back into the velvet-lined armchair with a long sigh of satisfaction."[26] The dubious morality of Holmes's drug use (such behavior was not illegal at this time but was nevertheless seen as questionable) simply added to the richness of Arthur Conan Doyle's depiction of genius, to the extent that with the publication of the first collection of short stories, *The Adventures of Sherlock Holmes*, which appeared serially in the *Strand Magazine* from 1891, close to half a million readers were captivated.

Holmes was the first truly scientific detective, referencing cutting-edge forensic techniques including blood-testing and fingerprinting within the context of his own version of crime-scene investigation and systematic detection methods before these were officially adopted by real-life police forces. His reading of murder scenes, from *A Study in Scarlet* onward, marks out his methods as unique; in the story "The Boscombe Valley Mystery," for instance, when dealing with a murder scene, he delivers a master class in forensics, attentively working his way around the landscape on hands and knees until he discovers a suggestive set of footprints. By insisting on the importance of such a science of crime detection, Conan Doyle established a model of the fictional detective that would influence all those that followed. Equally influential was the combination of these innovative methods with the profound eccentricities of the detective's personality. Holmes uses drugs, plays the violin erratically, and displays an uncanny knowledge of a bizarre array of subject matters, including, for instance, not just exotic wildlife and obscure cultural practices but also the many variations of cigar ash and international tattoo inks. The detective as embodied by Holmes is also a melancholy figure, displaying at times a behavioral pattern approaching what in twenty-first-century parlance is called bipolar disorder. Taken together, this profile of the character of Sherlock Holmes begins to suggest a new kind of fictional detective, someone who can uncannily diagnose society's ills despite—or perhaps by—placing themselves beyond many of its rules and conventions.

By the time of the second tranche of stories, *The Memoirs of Sherlock Holmes* (1894), Conan Doyle himself had become bored, feeling hemmed in by his creation. He had aspirations to become a literary novelist, producing historical novels set in the medieval period of English history. But despite his efforts the reading public was only really interested in Holmes. So, Conan Doyle took the extraordinary step of killing him off, pushing him over the edge of the Reichenbach Falls in Switzerland whilst locked in a deathly embrace with his archenemy Professor Moriarty in the story "The Final Problem." The public reaction was profound; Conan Doyle received letters of abuse, newspapers carried articles lamenting the detective's passing, and even Conan Doyle's own mother made impassioned entreaties to her son to bring his creation back to life. But he would not relent. Holmes remained dead for nearly a decade, until the colossal cash offers became too difficult to resist.

When the detective eventually came back to life, subsequent Holmes stories included perhaps his most well-known adventure, *The Hound of the Baskervilles* (1902), another full-length novel, *The Valley of Fear* (1915), and three more collections of short stories. Across the range of these, Conan Doyle piloted many of the features of the fictional detective contemporary readers would now recognize: the ongoing display of detective genius; the paradigm of the detective and a faithful assistant; the detective's troubling personal history and characteristics; a contentious relationship with the official police force; the existence of an archnemesis; and a fluid relationship with the established legal system in which the detective is just as likely to apply his own sense of natural justice as he is to rely on the official standards of the law.

However, the Sherlock Holmes phenomenon extends far beyond Conan Doyle's own writings. Indeed, few of the familiar features that we associate with Holmes (such as the deerstalker, the Inverness cape, the calabash pipe, and the "Elementary, My Dear Watson" catchphrase) come to us from the original writings. Rather, they are a legacy of the many adaptations of the Great Detective. This legacy consists of thousands of film, television, stage, and literary reimaginings, demonstrating the remarkable capacity of this fictional character to grip the global public consciousness in a more profound way than any other, either before or since.

Selected Bibliography

A Study in Scarlet (1887)
The Sign of Four (1890)
The Adventures of Sherlock Holmes (1892)
The Memoirs of Sherlock Holmes (1894)
The Hound of the Baskervilles (1902)
The Return of Sherlock Holmes (1905)
The Valley of Fear (1915)
His Final Problem (1917)
The Case-Book of Sherlock Holmes (1927)

—Neil McCaw

HONG JUN

He Jiahong
(1953–)

Crime writing in China has an ancient history preserved in *gong'an*, or crime-case tales, dating back to the eleventh century. Until recently, though, when asked about detective fiction, many Chinese readers would reply "Sherlock Holmes." Through the efforts of He Jiahong, however, contemporary China now has a homegrown investigator, attorney Hong Jun.[27] Unlike expatriate authors like Qiu Xiaolong (United States) and Diane Wei Liang (UK), He Jiahong lives and works in China. He has taught university in Beijing and practiced law since completing his doctorate in America, an accomplishment he shares with his creation. The Hong Jun series is set in the late twentieth century, a period of accelerated change in China. This is a significant choice, because rapid social and economic change stresses legal systems; the law changes more slowly than the culture surrounding it. Few characters in the novels are interested in the past, but ironically, the causes of current problems often lie in that neglected history.

In the 1990s, Hong Jun returned to China from America and set up a private legal practice, instead of following the more common route of becoming a prosecutor and employee of the state. Educated in both Chinese and American law and experienced in both cultures, he is an effective guide to how their legal and cultural practices and expectations differ. Mature and handsome, with a fondness for American blues music, Hong is only thirty when his career begins in *Hanging Devils* (2015). In this and the next novel, *Black Holes* (2014), his character—calm, fair-minded, and moral but not priggish—is consistent. He brings fresh ideas to the practice of law in China, but he is not above flirting with his competent, attractive secretary, Song Jia. When offered a men's night out, though, including a massage with "extras," Hong declines because the situation is morally and ethically questionable. His pursuit of justice stems from this moral and ethical sense, and with some difficulty, he holds himself to the standards he hopes will come to characterize the Chinese legal profession.

Much of the excitement of the books comes from the readers' discovery of a very different system of law, one in which assumptions taken for granted in many nations are simply not applicable. As part of a changing system, Hong must often explain his role to his clients; they express surprise that he is independent of the state and earns his living from clients' fees. As Hong explains, "The law requires the police, prosecutors and the courts to scrutinize each other, and provide checks and balances," but attorneys as defenders of the accused or of victims of legal errors are cautiously being introduced into a Chinese tradition that is "inquisitorial" rather than adversarial.[28] Take, for example, the question every case involves in some form: "Did the police beat you?"[29] While the answer is always no, the question signals underlying assumptions in the system. Before accepting any case, Hong investigates whether it is legitimate, because lawyers are expected to argue based on truth not on allegiance to their clients, and it is this process that aligns him with the detective tradition. He questions witnesses, examines records of prior interrogations, and accepts no physical evidence at face value. In *Hanging Devils*, he investigates a ten-year-old rape and murder conviction that may have been a miscarriage of justice. In *Black Holes*, he is hired to defend a young stock trader who is accused of fraud. In the process of investigating both cases, Hong is drawn back to the period of the Cultural Revolution and the Educated Youth movement that sent young people from urban areas into rural districts.

The resentments and crimes of the past may be the initial motives, but when joined with blind ambition or unthinking greed, they fuel present misdeeds. In each case, Hong takes the extra investigative steps that the police skipped, or examines evidence that, when approached with an open mind, yields contradictions and new interpretations. Given his modern education, he is also aware of new forensic techniques such as the analysis of blood types and DNA. He is cautious and sensitive to the implications of his findings, but generally he discovers human weakness—such as greed, ruthless ambition, sexual indiscretion, or errors based on emotion or immaturity—behind the crimes he investigates. He believes that any system based on human action will involve mistakes; for instance, he frequently finds civil servants asleep at their desks or otherwise inattentive to their duties.

Then there is the legal system itself, which Hong sometimes compares to American practices "where it was normal to challenge verdicts, and where procedural justice and the protection of individual rights were so revered. . . . Hong Jun knew that, under the prevailing Chinese legal system, it was far easier for the courts to allow a wrongful verdict to stand than to get it overturned. Righting past wrongs was a propaganda slogan, pretence being cheaper than practice."[30] Hong consciously tries to lead by example and model the ethical behavior and concern for justice that he believes will eventually be part of the Chinese legal system at all levels.

Hong Jun allows readers to look into the Chinese legal system, which may seem mysterious and remote. He, too, must navigate the system, and in order to do his job well, he must consider its basis in tradition and the pressure it is under in "new China." Hong's cases provide much-needed context for understanding the challenges faced by China in both the past and the present.

Selected Bibliography

Black Holes (2014)
Hanging Devils (2015)

—Rebecca Martin

HUO SANG

Cheng Xiaoqing
(1893–1976)

While the modern detective story may have begun with Edgar Allan Poe's C. Auguste Dupin, China has its own tradition of the fictional sleuth. The father of the Chinese detective story is Cheng Xiaoqing, who modeled his investigators Huo Sang and Bao Lang on Sherlock Holmes and Dr. Watson. Heavily derivative from the outset, Cheng's detectives have names that are transliterations of the English-sounding "Hawthorn" and "Brown." Huo's sidekick Bao Lang is no doctor of medicine, but he is just as faithful a chronicler of the Chinese detective as his English counterpart is of Holmes. Readers can easily identify with Bao and Watson, thus sharing their awe and wonder over the detectives' supreme intelligence and intuitive grasp of each case. Holmes's archenemy Professor Moriarty, that Satan incarnate, is absent from Cheng's cast of characters. Instead, Huo's recurring rival is South-China Swallow (*Jiangnan* Swallow), a traditional knight-errant or Arsène Lupin figure.

The modus operandi of Huo and Bao in 1920s and 1930s Shanghai resembles that of their European counterparts in Victorian London. Holmes's residence at 221B Baker Street and Huo's at 77 Aiwen Road are the fulcrums where clients introduce the terrible weight of urban crime and evil to the detectives, who then balance the scale of justice through, in Holmes's refrain, "the science of deduction," logical ratiocination, and a certain amount of intuition and guesswork. On one hand, in both worlds modernization and urbanization have caused socioeconomic disparities and the rise of crime. Criminals resort to modern technologies of communication and transportation—the postal system, telegrams, telephones, personal notes, photographs, and public transportation—for their insidious purposes. On the other hand, modernity and science contribute to solving crimes.

The larger contexts of Holmes and Huo reveal their fundamental differences. Arthur Conan Doyle composed his stories at the height of the British Empire, into which the colonies' wealth and subjects flowed. Conditioned by his times, Conan Doyle uses tropes of racial and cultural otherness without any postcolonial qualms. In contrast, Cheng found himself in a transitional period in which China's moribund traditions wrestled with the emerging novelty of the West. Throughout his career, from translating Conan Doyle in the 1910s to penning the Huo Sang stories from the 1920s on, China was buffeted by colonialism, civil war, and World War II. Colonial and elite powers converged in Shanghai, particularly its International Settlements; war refugees and the poverty stricken also gravitated there.

Secure in his belief in British imperial and cerebral superiority, Holmes devotes himself to criminal cases as a "game," neither sleeping nor eating until the guilty party is apprehended—very much like a privileged child obsessed with a new toy. Huo, however, is neither idiosyncratic nor egotistical; instead, he is a Confucian gentleman (*junzi*), so moralistic that he lectures young westernized dandies and so paternalistic that he protects his female clients' reputations. Huo criticizes Shanghai's corrupt officials, greedy businessmen, moral decrepitude, and general mercantilism, oblivious to the irony of his own privileged situation within the affluent British Concession. While Westernized in his lifestyle, playing the violin, receiving guests with calling cards, and attending parties where ladies wear diamond brooches, Huo remains staunchly Confucian in adhering to the ancient sage's code of conduct.

Cheng's stories thus reflect the entanglement of Chinese Confucian and Western cultures. Rational and pragmatic, Confucianism is not antithetical to a Western modernity based on reason and science. Yet the Confucian focus on ethics threatens to rob Huo Sang of Holmesian eccentricities and wry humor. In effect, Cheng appears to have cultivated a Holmes "with Chinese characteristics," upright and humane, ever concerned with the common good. Certain stories can even be seen as parables of time-honored Chinese sayings. "The Other Photograph" illustrates the maxim that "even as the mantis captures the cicada, the yellow sparrow is not far behind." "The Examination Paper" epitomizes the aphorism "good accrues to the good, evil befalls the evil." An affinity to Chinese philosophy is evident as well. In "At the Ball," for instance, South-China Swallow blackmails an unscrupulous businessman to help improve his "karma," and despite paying Confucian lip service to the needs of refugees, Huo embodies a traditional literati disdain for the working class and uncultured poor in "The Odd Tenant."

There is but one English translation of Cheng, *Sherlock in Shanghai*, by Timothy C. Wong.[31] Like many other contemporary translators of Chinese literature, Wong takes great liberties in condensing, and even rewriting, Cheng's works, owing perhaps to their popular culture rather than *belles-lettres* status. However, translators who reduce or excise "nonessential" parts of a story in favor of a simplified, plot-driven narrative can interfere with a more in-depth understanding of a foreign culture. For instance, the opening story in the collection, "The Shoe," skips Cheng's original paragraph that sets the stage of Shanghai's volatile stock market in the early decades of the twentieth century, thus foreshadowing part of the motive for the murder. More revealingly, the Chinese heading for chapter 1, "A Feminine-Style Male Shoe," is translated as "The Crime Scene." Here simplification has sacrificed the important theme of gender indeterminacy, for just as social class is destabilized by Shanghai's modernity, so too is traditional masculinity, rendered fluffy and extravagant by upper-class playboys. The murder victim turns out to be the chaste second wife of a banker who mistakes a rowdy, drunken dandy who threw one of his shoes up into her balcony for her lover and stabs her to death in his rage. The traditional virtuous, steadfast female is a sacrificial lamb in the urban jungle of male competition. Wong's translation has entirely forgone Cheng's Shanghainese; local specificities have given way to the global lingua franca. It appears that once detecting readers leave their Western comfort zone in search of detectives in other languages and cultures, the "case" immediately turns into a Zen *koan*, a "public case" that is so mystifying that no one but the initiated can comprehend it.

Selected Bibliography

Sherlock in Shanghai: Stories of Crime and Detection by Cheng Xiaoqing (2007)

—Sheng-mei Ma

I

INSPECTOR EITARO IMANISHI

Seicho Matsumoto
(1909–1992)

Eitaro Imanishi is the creation of Seicho Matsumoto, Japan's best-selling, highest-earning author in the 1960s and, with 450 books to his credit, one of its most prolific. Matsumoto had an astonishing range of interests. His publications include essays and nonfiction works exploring domestic and international issues, historical novels, and the detective stories he is best known for outside of Japan. Matsumoto's work as a mystery writer has been characterized as belonging to the *shakai-ha* or "social school" of the detective genre. In this sense, Matsumoto was a groundbreaking author in Japan, for unlike earlier Japanese mystery writers he produced crime fiction that offers a portrait of the society in which a murder is committed, rather than an ingenious puzzle to be solved by the detective. It is writing that emphasizes the minutiae of daily life.

The eponymous hero of the most famous of Matsumoto's books available in English, *Inspector Imanishi Investigates* (published in 1961 as *Suna no Utsuwa* or *Vessel of Sand*), is a forty-five-year-old police officer who lives in a tiny apartment in Tokyo with his wife Yoshiko and their young son Taro. Imanishi is an antihero somewhat in the style of Georges Simenon's Maigret. He is described as a country boy transplanted to the city, an unassuming but respected homicide detective with a knack for writing haiku and for solving crimes. Physically, he is unprepossessing. Professionally, he is discreet and diligent. The heels of his shoes quickly become worn down as he trudges from place to place following leads and interviewing suspects. He puts in long days but is pessimistic that his efforts will bear fruit. Apart from his habit of smoking Peace cigarettes, the only indulgences he allows himself are an occasional trip to a bar with a colleague or a glass or two of sake on getting home at night. In his limited free time, he likes gardening and cultivates bonsai.

Inspector Imanishi Investigates describes the inspector's absorption in a mysterious case. A body is found early one morning on railway tracks in the city. The victim has no personal effects, and his face is so badly battered that identification of the corpse initially proves impossible. Following the gruesome discovery,

Imanishi spends all day questioning people resident or working in the vicinity of the crime, returning home at midnight. A few days later he is sent to the north of Japan to investigate leads. In the months that follow, until he can finally identify both the victim and the culprit, Imanishi displays complete dedication to the investigation, rarely spending time with his wife and son. He is a policeman so driven by a sense of duty that he is hesitant even to allow himself the luxury of returning to headquarters to have a cup of tea.

Imanishi is not just conscientious; he is also conventional, and he unquestioningly observes traditional Japanese gender roles. He is the principal breadwinner, while his wife takes care of the house, and he is careful not to discuss his job with her. She, for her part, accepts her husband's frequent absences without complaint, manages the household and the family finances, and assumes all responsibilities related to raising their son. This rigid distinction between the sexes extends to the workplace. None of Imanishi's colleagues in the Tokyo police station is a woman, and indeed, there are few female characters in *Inspector Imanishi Investigates*. Those that do appear are mostly relegated to subordinate or peripheral roles in the action. They include not only the policeman's quiet, obedient wife and his sister but also the unnamed, undifferentiated individuals Imanishi encounters in the course of his investigation: waitresses in restaurants, maids at an inn, the madam of a bar, and the hostesses in her employ.

Inspector Imanishi Investigates not only reflects the sexism endemic in Japanese society in the 1960s but also addresses issues still topical in present-day Japan such as suicide, *karōshi* (or death through overwork), and the need to maintain a socially appropriate mask. Rieko, the only fully fleshed-out female character in the novel, decides to kill herself because her lover has made her an accessory to murder. She stole a raincoat for him; later she cut his bloodstained shirt into tiny fragments and tossed them from a train window. Although Rieko has committed no sin more serious than the theft of an overcoat and the disposal of a bloodstained shirt, she commits a peculiarly Japanese type of suicide; having always conformed meticulously to society's rules, she feels tremendous guilt about even "minor infractions" and would rather turn her aggression upon herself than against others.[1]

Inspector Imanishi in turn is susceptible to *karōshi*, highlighting another social problem in Japan. He and his colleagues are all exhausted, drained by the relentless demands placed upon them by their work. They feel unable to take time off when involved in a case and are reluctant to complain. Their sense of duty compels them to investigate any lead, however tenuous. While it is this sort of socially realistic detail that provides the main focus for Matsumoto's readers, even the solution to the mystery Imanishi investigates can be seen as a form of social critique. It transpires that the criminal battered his victim's face beyond recognition literally to "save face" by concealing the secret of his own disreputable birth, as its disclosure might have ruined his future prospects.

Matsumoto's socially conscious works depend not on plot twists but on character development and exposition of motive. They explore how ordinary people can be led to commit a crime because of the flawed or inequitable social structures around them, and how an ordinary person like Imanishi can come to give up so much in defense of these very structures.

Selected Bibliography

The Voice and Other Stories (1955)
Points and Lines (1958)
Inspector Imanishi Investigates (1961)
Pro Bono (1961)

—Wendy Jones Nakanishi

J

VENUS JOHNSON

Pauline Elizabeth Hopkins
(1859–1930)

Although the honor of being the first woman to publish crime fiction is generally attributed to her compatriot Metta Fuller Victor, who authored *The Dead Letter* as Seeley Register in 1864, Pauline Hopkins's contributions to the genre are notable: she was the earliest black American writer to take up the mode, and her sleuth, Venus Johnson, is the first known African American detective. That both Hopkins and her detective are women makes their achievements all the more exceptional.

Figuring only in *Hagar's Daughter: A Story of Southern Caste Prejudice*, originally published pseudonymously in serial form from March 1901 through March 1902 in *Colored American Magazine*, a periodical Pauline Hopkins edited, Venus Johnson plays a minor but significant role. Or put more accurately given her performative, linguistic, and gendered fluidity, she plays several essential *roles*. The granddaughter of formerly enslaved individuals, Johnson is a twenty-year-old woman employed as a maid. Nodding to her capabilities, Senator Bowen, the father of her charge Jewel, approves of Johnson. He states, "If the girl ain't too proud to go out as a servant to help herself along, there must be something in her."[1] Johnson ostensibly works for the Bowens to help her brother Oliver through college, but of course, as her mother's and grandmother's jobs doing laundry and cleaning show, there were few career options available to black women twenty years after the American Civil War.

Nonetheless, Johnson proves herself to be more than "just" a maid, instigating the search for Jewel after she is kidnapped, providing information vital to solving the case, and eventually saving the day. While Jewel and her stepmother react to most situations by fainting, Johnson's level head is a key to her success as a sleuth. As the narrator comments, "The brain of the little brown maid was busy. She had her own ideas about certain things, and was planning for the deliverance of her loved young mistress."[2] She acts on her own to watch the unscrupulous General Benson, making note of his threatening behavior toward the Bowen women just before Jewel disappears, as well as saving a letter he leaves in his wake, evidence of his perfidy.

Johnson's only ostensible sign of strain is to swing into vernacular speech, according to the famed investigator, Detective Henson, to whom she turns for help. But this "lapse," as the white male detective deems it, is less a marker of strain than a badge of Johnson's adaptability. By switching from standard English to linguistic forms inaccessible to her white interlocutors, Johnson asserts the strength she derives from her duality. Unlike Detective Henson and her employers, she crosses sociocultural boundaries on a daily basis. Indeed, it is her ability to do so that ultimately saves Jewel and Johnson's grandmother from the kidnapper Benson. When pressed later on her sagacity, Johnson's comments tellingly blur standard and vernacular English while underlining her investigative acumen: "Well, you know Mis' Bowen, I ain't a bit slow, no'm, if I do say it, and I jus' thought hard for a minute, an' *it struck me*!"[3] This "eureka" moment, typical of early detectives, highlights her fellowship in their ranks.

When working undercover, Johnson's transformations are even more pronounced: she poses as a young man while on her rescue mission, taking on the mien and manner of her alter ego, Billy. During the entirety of her investigation, Hopkins refers to the amateur sleuth only with masculine designations such as "the lad," "the boy," and "he." This complicity between Johnson's disguise and the narrative voice serves to emphasize Johnson's competent, confident fluidity. It also underlines the thematic centrality of the social construction of identity and authenticity to the novel.

Johnson is not the only one to pass: nearly every character in the novel embodies a facade in relation to race, class, sex, or motive. This profoundly destabilizes the borders between seeming and being. Both the villain, General Benson, and the perceived hero, Detective Henson, changed their identities to hide from their pasts. Jewel Bowen, the romantic heroine; her rival and friend, Aurelia Madison; and Jewel's stepmother (revealed to be her biological mother) all suffer tragically when their previously obscured lineages become known. The intentional and accidental passing with which the text is rife challenges its world as well as the foundations of stability on which both detective fiction and racial discrimination rest. As Stephen F. Soitos claims, Hopkins uses "the detective form to question the moral and cultural foundation that typical detective fiction supports through the reestablishment of the natural order."[4] In other words, Johnson investigates a kidnapping case and white patriarchal hegemony at once.

Although Detective Henson publically takes credit for Johnson's detective work while in reality doing little more than serving as a sounding board for her ideas, Johnson's active mastery of her milieu pays off. In the end, she is the only character whose story has a positive trajectory: she alone in the novel realizes unobstructed love and is on the cusp of a generative future. Largely forgotten for nearly a century, Hopkins's Venus Johnson has begun to receive critical accolades and recognition, finally reclaiming her place as a pioneering sleuth and social activist, and thus her long-deferred happy ending.

Selected Bibliography

Contending Forces (1900)
Hagar's Daughter: A Story of Southern Caste Prejudice (1901–1902)
Winona: A Tale of Negro Life in the South and Southwest (1902)
Of One Blood; or, The Hidden Self (1902–1903)
The Magazine Novels of Pauline Hopkins (1988)

—Katherine E. Bishop

K

KEMAL KAYANKAYA

Jakob Arjouni
(1964–2013)

Kemal Kayankaya, a lonely private detective created by Jakob Arjouni, is an unusual figure in many ways within the context of German literature. He is a private eye like many others, but his identity is highly unorthodox. The opening pages of the first book in the Kayankaya series, *Happy Birthday, Turk!* (1985 [1994]), offer a firsthand account of his early life. Born in Turkey as the son of a locksmith, Kayankaya was brought to Germany by his father after his mother's death in childbirth. Adversity continued when Kayankaya lost his father in an accident and was sent to foster care. The result of this series of unfortunate events is a conflicted identity. Although raised by his German foster family in a typically German milieu, he is an immigrant in the eyes of the society; a thorough command of German language and culture, and being officially a German citizen, do not count for much, and for many his appearance defines his identity. Arjouni's novel resonated widely when it was first published, as this sort of conflicted identity was not widely discussed in the 1980s in West Germany.

Bearing in mind that much crime fiction emerges from the need for social and personal security, there is a certain irony in the structure of the Kayankaya stories. Here, a man from the East helps uncover the mysteries of crime, although he himself is seen, due to his ethnic identity, as the very cause of criminality within society. Brutal murders, labyrinthine liaisons, and cases of official corruption are solved at the hands of an apparent foreigner who is socially constructed as their likely perpetrator. The well-organized, hardworking, and disciplined figure of the German police officer seems to be unable to balance the scales of justice, and instead a questionable man comes forward to soothe Lady Justice.

The wisecracking, back-talking Kayankaya is obviously a successor to the heroes of Dashiell Hammett and Raymond Chandler. Adopting a straightforward, analytical process of investigation, and in spite of the fact that he exists surrounded by morally eroded human relations, he creates his own moral values and lives accordingly as he focuses on solving crimes, without worrying too much about their motivations or results. In the Kayankaya series, a hard-boiled type of writing is entwined with a realistic, contemporary atmosphere. Putting all the miserable and wretched figures of society, including prostitutes, pimps, bodyguards, racists, bullies, and lost immigrants into the background of his stories, Arjouni creates a lifelike world, full of vivid depictions of the peculiarities of his protagonist and the society he lives in.

Many of Kayankaya's investigations are not only deeply concerned with organized crime and delve into the corruption surrounding German officialdom but also feature more traditional, less political motives. In *Happy Birthday, Turk!* for instance, Kayankaya is hired by a Turkish woman who is looking for a private investigator she can trust to investigate her husband's mysterious death. Kayankaya takes the case and gradually explores the life of a man who was forced into crime by high-ranking police officers (but was ultimately killed by his wife's brother). *More Beer* (1987 [1994]) concerns an alleged eco-terrorist attack. Again, Kayankaya uncovers a trail of corruption, involving both the police and politicians, alongside the case of the murdered Friedrich Böllig, accused of selling the basic ingredients of mustard gas to the Iraqi government. A group of green activists is accused of killing him, but it turns out to be a crime arising from a love affair, not politics. In *One Death to Die* (1991 [1997]), the case centers on the problem of immigration and illegal workers. A Thai woman, who is sold into the thriving German sex trade, is promised a residence permit after her visa has expired. She suddenly disappears, and once again Kayankaya finds himself in a world of corruption and vice. After almost a decade-long break he returned in his fourth adventure *Kismet* (2001 [2007]). Here, Kayankaya finds himself in a nebulous situation while protecting a restaurant manager from unknown racketeers extorting money for a secret organization called the "Army of Reason." Another decade passed before the publication of the last book of the Kayankaya series *Brother Kemal* (2012 [2013]), in which he deals with two cases at once: finding the missing daughter of a financier and protecting a controversial Muslim writer against extremists at the Frankfurt Book Fair. Rather than being solely a beacon for minority groups, Kayankaya gradually evolved into a character who dealt with issues of concern to all levels of society, and who appealed to a diverse readership.

Arjouni's untimely death in 2013 ended the Kayankaya series prematurely. While German crime writing has produced many notable works, and promises to produce many more, few of them have offered an investigator as influential, as daring, and as different as Kemal Kayankaya.

Selected Bibliography

Happy Birthday, Turk! (1985 [1994])
More Beer (1987 [1994])
One Man, One Murder (1991 [1997])
Kismet (2001 [2007])
Brother Kemal (2012 [2013])

—Selim Şimşek

KŌSUKE KINDAICHI

Seishi Yokomizo
(1902–1981)

Seishi Yokomizo's Kōsuke Kindaichi shifted postwar Japanese detective fiction into a new stage of development. Yokomizo observed Japan's defeat in World War II from the rural prefecture of Okayama, where he moved to escape US air raids on Tokyo. Wartime militarism, and then postwar devastation, convinced him that detective fiction, with its reliance on logic and reason, was exactly what was needed to help Japan build a modern, democratic nation. He embodied this idea in the private detective Kōsuke Kindaichi, whose clue-based investigations take place within the orthodox detective fiction format. But this was not just a formal decision: the ideal setting of the classical whodunit, the isolated village or remote island, offered a suitable venue for the author to challenge Japan's reactionary cultural conventions, such as dangerously close kinship bonds and regressive local customs. Kindaichi visits these isolated, hidebound places and applies proper reasoning to mysteries interpreted by locals as manifestations of mystical curses or terrifying legends.

Unlike Kogorō Akechi's cases, the best of which appeared as short stories, the majority of Kindaichi's cases were developed as novels, often involving the classical setup of an apparently impossible crime. Kindaichi's first case, *Honjin satsujin jiken* (The Honjin murders; 1946) was also Yokomizo's first postwar novel. Here Kindaichi appears as a plain-looking young man of about twenty-five or twenty-six, slightly built with an unruly mop of hair. Although he ages into his midthirties in his later cases, his trademark outfit—a worn and wrinkled kimono and *hakama* trousers—does not change in more than thirty years. A slight accent suggests he is from the northern part of Japan, and he stutters occasionally, especially when he is excited. On such occasions, he also tends to scratch "his tousle-haired head with frightful vigor."[1] This became his main idiosyncratic habit when the novels were adapted later for TV and film.

Before *Honjin satsujin jiken,* Japanese houses were often said to be inappropriate settings for classical detective fiction due to their open structure, partitioned only with paper sliding doors. This explains the inclination of the pioneering writers of the genre toward Western architecture and life styles. Yet Yokomizo uses Kindaichi to create a locked-room murder in a Japanese-style house. It is an added bonus for dedicated fans of the genre that one of the suspects makes a lecture on locked-room murders in detective fiction, referring of course to John Dickson Carr's *Hollow Man* (1935).

Kindaichi's second case *Gokumontō* (Gokumon Island; 1947) follows a similar structure but displays more sophistication. On his way home from his war service, Kindaichi was asked by his dying fellow-soldier Chimata Kitō to stop the murder of his three sisters. This ominous prediction brings Kindaichi to Kitō's hometown—a small island dominated by his clan through tradition and power. The news of Kitō's death disheartens the islanders and brings social turmoil surrounding the choice of the next heir. Kitō's three sisters are killed one after another, with each murder method referring to poems composed by their late grandfather Kaemon Kitō. While investigating the Kitō clan, Kindaichi falls in love with Kitō's beautiful niece Sanae Kitō. After all the schemes of the late tycoon have been revealed, and Kindaichi has pointed out the true perpetrator, he invites Sanae to come with him to Tokyo where she can be free from the island mentality that ultimately caused the tragedy. Sanae, however, decides to stay on the island; she finds meaning in the old way of life. Kindaichi leaves the island with a bitter feeling of regret; Sanae's beauty is that of a quickly vanishing old Japan, which Kindaichi himself is helping to destroy.

Kindaichi appeared in more than twenty cases before leaving for America at the end of his last case, *Byōinzaka no kubukukuri no ie* (The house of hanging on hospital slope; 1978). It is as if he felt he was out of place in the now modernized and economically prosperous Japan. Kindaichi wanders around America before coming back to Japan to start a detective job. In a sense he goes back to where he started, two decades after the US occupation army left Japan in 1952.

Kindaichi's formal disappearance with the author's death in 1981 did not let him retire, however, as he found new audiences through various adaptations, firstly in films in the late 1970s and later in cartoons in the 1990s. When publisher Kadokawa ventured into the media tie-in business in the late 1970s, it was Kindaichi, with his anachronistic attire and his investigations into bloody murders set in rural Japan, that nostalgically captivated Japanese audiences. These films cemented the images of Kindaichi in the minds of younger audiences, which led to the expansion of the Kindaichi world in *The Young Kindaichi Case Files* (1992–[2003–]), a cartoon series written by Yozaburo Kanari and Seimaru Amagi and illustrated by Fumiya Sato. Kanari and Amagi reconstruct Kindaichi's cases with all their Gothic elements from the perspective of Kindaichi's grandson, Hajime Kindaichi. This series, and its anime and film adaptations, has helped carry Kindaichi, or at least a version of him, into the wider world.

Selected Bibliography

Honjin satsujin jiken (The Honjin murders; 1946)
Gokumontō (Gokumon Island; 1947)
The Inugami Clan (1951 [2003])
Yatsuhakamura (Yatsuhaka Village; 1951)

—Satomi Saito

LIEUTENANT DAVID KLEIN

James Ellroy
(1948–)

James Ellroy's description of himself as "the greatest crime writer who ever lived" may be hyperbolic, but there is no doubt he is one of the major figures in contemporary crime fiction.[2] His novels offer a bleak yet powerful vision of

American history and human nature, and do so in a sharply stylized prose that shames the sometimes pedestrian writing of mainstream crime fiction. Yet his investigative figures sit uneasily alongside the luminaries of the genre. While many fictional detectives exhibit character flaws and weaknesses—think of Sherlock Holmes's cocaine habit, or the social isolation and alcoholism of many hard-boiled detectives—Ellroy's investigators shatter the central distinction between detective and criminal.

Lieutenant David Klein is a perfect example of this sort of transgressive Ellroyian figure. He appears in *White Jazz* (1992), the final novel in the LA Quartet, a series that charts the links between crime, politics, the entertainment industry, and the justice system in 1940s and 1950s Los Angeles. Klein's career has been shaped by the systematic corruption and endemic moral failure of his world. He joined the Los Angeles Police Department (LAPD) in 1938, fought against the Japanese during World War II, and returned to the force in 1945, joining an "ex-Marine goon squad" dedicated to strike-breaking and off-the-book law enforcement. Meanwhile, Klein put himself through law school by doing strong-arm work for the Mob, becoming known as "the Enforcer."[3] A brief flirtation with a Hollywood acting career led to more lucrative blackmail work targeting homosexual celebrities.

This background obviously compromises Klein as a representative of justice, but worse is to come. Having killed two hoods for mistreating his sister, Klein has exposed himself to Mob blackmail and become their hit man, the role in which readers first encounter him in *White Jazz*. Assigned to protect boxer Sanderline Johnson, he instead throws him out of a hotel window to stop him from testifying for a federal investigation into mob infiltration of the sport. This role inversion is essential to Klein's character: he does not just work on both sides of the law but is the antithesis of *everything* we believe—or at least hope—the police are.

Klein's transgressions are not limited to his professional life; he is also personally compromised. For example, his dual police/criminal career has obviously had financial rewards; this is one policeman—and as Ellroy represents the LAPD, he is not alone—who does not have to rely on his salary and pension. Instead, Klein has ploughed the profits of his illicit career into the slum properties he manages with his sister. When tenants are late with the rent, he sends gun-for-hire Jack Woods around to beat up the deadbeats. His relationship with his sister is similarly disturbing, as Klein has long harbored incestuous desires for this "woman [he] had no business loving."[4] Incest is one of our strongest and most persistent social taboos, and it is no accident that Klein's desires lead him toward breaking this rule too.

If this were all there were to Klein, he would be an example of a truly villainous character, too reprehensible perhaps to be considered even an antihero, and his position as a policeman would be little more than a final irony. But Klein is more complex than this. He is, first of all, an able detective, despite the fact that he is "a commanding officer, not a case man."[5] After being assigned to a burglary at the home of the Kafesjians, LAPD snitches and unofficially licensed drug dealers, Klein displays formidable investigative prowess despite the family's lack of cooperation and departmental pressure to go easy on the investigation. Through a combination of "shitwork"—grinding through old files and forgotten paperwork—and "rolling shitwork"—trailing suspects, cruising the streets, and conducting stakeouts—alongside an impressive ability to interpret data, a disturbing readiness to resort to extreme violence, and finally, a sort of instinctive ability to "SEE IT," Klein is able to follow the trail that started at the Kafesjians ever further into a web of complicity involving the Mob, politicians, individual officers, and whole departments within the LAPD, the feds, and an array of other players.[6]

Even more important, however, than Klein's investigative ability is the transformation in his character that motivates it, a change that is central to the power of both Klein and the novel as a whole. For years, Klein has only worked, both as a cop and a criminal, to take care of himself and his sister, but his encounter with starlet Glenda Bledsoe changes everything. Assigned by the depraved Howard Hughes to accumulate dirt on her, he instead falls deeply in love, "thinking crazy: *Don't snitch her*," and eventually ends up protecting her from multiple accusations of murder.[7] Alongside, or perhaps because of, this unexpected passion, Klein begins to develop a sense that the life he has lived is untenable. As he puts it, "*It's dues time. I can feel it.*"[8] Klein's experience of love and his desire to both pay off his moral debts and escape from the network of corruption and vice that constitutes his world drive the novel forward.

Klein is an important investigative figure, touched by enough evil to allow readers access to a truly evil world, yet just good enough, or at least striving to become good enough, to allow for the possibility of moral redemption. It is this duality that makes him so typical of Ellroy's fictional world, and so effective as a fictional detective.

Selected Bibliography

The Black Dahlia (1987)
The Big Nowhere (1988)
L.A. Confidential (1990)
White Jazz (1992)
American Tabloid (1995)
My Dark Places (1996)
The Cold Six Thousand (2001)
Blood's a Rover (2009)
Perfidia (2014)

—Eric Sandberg

L

AUNT LALLI

Kalpana Swaminathan
(1956–)

Crime writing in India is fast becoming a dominant form of cultural expression, and Aunt Lalli is one of the best-known detectives in the postmillennial literary scene. Lalli is a sixty-three-year-old former police officer based in Mumbai who is still called on by her former colleagues to solve baffling crimes. They keep a file bearing the initials L.R.—meaning "last resort"—containing the cases that they call on her to solve. To date, her creator, Kalpana Swaminathan, who is a practicing pediatric surgeon, has written five Lalli novels, all narrated by Sita, Lalli's niece.

The Lalli mysteries are set in Mumbai, always involve murders, often quite gruesome ones, and are invariably cleverly solved by Lalli—and before anyone else has got remotely close to the solution. Lalli is well dressed, highly observant, and a collector of oddities, ranging from a ball of fluff and an unknown passenger's used bus ticket to a pile of unidentified powder, which eventually lead her to some of society's more outlandish individuals. Not much is known about her private life, as even her niece does not appear to be familiar with her aunt's past. In fact, in *The Page 3 Murders* (2006), where we are first introduced to this indomitable woman, Sita reveals that Lalli is "not a generic aunt" and that her father "for reasons both private and worrying, reclaimed this extremely peripheral twig of the family tree."[1]

Lalli's debut in *The Page 3 Murders* serves to vindicate the social role of older women as she unmasks the mastermind behind a prostitution ring. On one occasion, for instance, her capacity to take charge of the situation is challenged by one of the suspects who demands to see the corpse: "I would like to see for myself. I don't take orders from old women."[2] Yet despite the social prejudice she faces, "Last Resort Lalli" is calm, astute, forthright, and as comfortable with gory murder scenes as she is with the latest fashion crazes. This is nowhere more clearly seen than in the latest Lalli offering, *The Secret Gardener* (2013), which centers on the discovery of a mummified finger. In attempting to solve this mystery, Lalli seeks advice from Arifa, the boss of a reputable beauty parlor. The exclusive nail polish on the finger leads to the discovery of the victim's identity and thus to the solution of the murder. The solution to the third Lalli mystery, *The Monochrome Madonna* (2010) revolves around a photoshopped version of Raphael's famous painting featuring a gold-colored Sitara Shah instead of the Virgin Mary. A stranger lies dead in Sitara's drawing room and Lalli's niece, Sita, racks her brains to figure out the significance of an empty teacup and a set of fake golden toenails until her aunt finally makes her appearance on page 50 and takes charge of the investigation.

Sita's first-person narrative encourages readers to empathize with her and become her accomplice in the quest to find the solution to the crime. She is inevitably typecast as a Hastings figure, never quite as clever as Lalli herself who, in true Poirot fashion, refuses to disclose any hints until the very last minute. Clues are bandied about, but Sita never manages to fully understand their implications for the crime at hand. The niece often despairs at her aunt's unscrupulous methods: "There are moments when my aunt appalls me."[3]

The Lalli novels combine narratives of bloodthirsty crimes committed for abominable reasons with cynical pokes at the hypocrisy of Indian society. Swaminathan allows a certain amount of comedy to creep into her novels; the unfolding of the plot of *The Gardener's Song* (2007), for instance, is a spoof of the Lewis Carroll poem "The Mad Gardener's Song." In this way, the unpredictability of modern Mumbai life is reflected in the Victorian poet's nonsense verse. However, the comic exterior cannot conceal the horrors of dowry deaths: "Her mother-in-law set up the stove and made her light it. Then she bolted her in the kitchen and walked away. A very common story."[4] Lalli puts her finger on one of the major problems of Indian society, domestic crime concealed by a conspiracy of silence.

The popularity of this mature crime-solving lady is indicated by the blurb on the front cover of *The Secret Gardener*, in which the *Hindustan Times* hails Lalli as the first credible Indian woman detective in the English language. However, other reviewers have not been so generous. For Partha Chatterjee there is a clear lack of "the sociopolitical pressures that contribute to the making of a human being."[5] Likewise, Maitreyee B. Chowdhury misses "a more persuasive language [and] better description of characters."[6] Even if we accept these criticisms, however, Aunt Lalli exemplifies the recent trend in Indian crime writing to focus on the ills of twenty-first-century society, from female infanticide to the sexual exploitation of naïve young women. Patriarchy, not men, is the enemy to beat, and perhaps the Lalli novels, in addition to being entertaining and page-turning crime novels, will help to increase women's awareness of their own part in the perpetuation of these attitudes and their potential role in combating them.

Select Bibliography

The Page 3 Murders (2006)
The Gardener's Song (2007)
The Monochrome Madonna (2010)
I Never Knew It Was You (2012)
The Secret Gardener (2013)

—Felicity Hand

DUCA LAMBERTI

Giorgio Scerbanenco
(1911–1969)

Duca Lamberti is undoubtedly the most famous private detective in the history of Italian crime fiction. After decades of pale imitations of Sherlock Holmes, in the 1960s Italian crime fiction readers finally got "the hero that they had been waiting for."[7] A former doctor, struck off the register and imprisoned for practicing euthanasia, turned private eye, Lamberti (with his girlfriend, the unforgettable Livia Ussaro) is the protagonist of four hard-boiled novels published between 1966 and 1969, before crime writer Giorgio Scerbanenco's untimely death put an end to the detective's adventures.

No other Italian crime writer has been as influential as Scerbanenco. His novels have earned an international reputation, and he was the first Italian crime writer to have his books translated into more than one foreign language. The series marked the beginning of a wave of successful Italian novels that had close ties with their urban settings and offered a sustained focus on Italy's political and social conflicts, and Duca Lamberti's adventures inspired many subsequent Italian crime writers, such as Carlo Lucarelli and Massimo Carlotto, who have acknowledged the importance of this fictional character for their own work. Scerbanenco's novels have also inspired film and television adaptations, some of which are considered precursors to Quentin Tarantino's postmodern noirs. As a testimony to his enduring appeal, a collection of short stories written by sixteen Italian crime writers featuring Duca Lamberti as the protagonist was published in 2007 to celebrate this iconic character.

One of the basic facts that makes Lamberti notable is that he is one of the few private detectives in the Italian crime fiction tradition in which the most common character is a police detective, such as Andrea Camilleri's Inspector Salvo Montalbano, who mostly investigates alone but still has to work within the constraints of the organization for which he works. Just as importantly, through the figure of the detective, this series tackles important issues in Italian society of the 1960s. Set in Milan during the so-called Italian Economic Miracle (1950–1963), the series depicts rapid industrialization and unprecedented economic growth, accompanied by urbanization and the birth of a consumer society. In particular, from being what was in effect a big village, which had been heavily bombed during the Second World War, Milan was turning into a modern metropolis with the concomitant issues of growing criminality and social marginalization.

Duca Lamberti is himself a marginalized person struggling to find his place in the new Italy after his time in prison. In *A Private Venus*, guilt-ridden (his father died of a heart attack while Lamberti was locked up) and in search of a purpose to his life, Lamberti is hired by a wealthy industrialist to investigate his son Davide's past, in order to help him stop drinking. Davide soon reveals that he feels responsible for the death of a woman, Alberta Radelli. Lamberti finds the circumstances surrounding Radelli's alleged suicide suspicious and helps the police uncover a complex circle of prostitution and pornography. Prostitution is also at the core of

I milanesi ammazzano al sabato (The Milanese kill on Saturdays; 1969), while arms-trafficking features in *Betrayal* (1966), and juvenile violence in *I ragazzi del massacro* (The boys of the massacre; 1968).

Lamberti is an inflexible cynic and a critic of the superficiality and hypocrisy that characterized Milanese society in the 1960s. His frequent outbursts of anger are a vehicle for ferocious commentaries on consumerism and an expanding urban environment increasingly characterized by unauthorized building, pollution, and gratuitous violence. Lamberti is neither the muscular detective performing physical heroics nor the cerebral sleuth of classic detective fiction. He follows leads as they are presented to him and commits serious errors of judgment (such as when in *A Private Venus* he unwittingly causes his future girlfriend, Livia Ussaro, to be disfigured by a gangster). Success is sometimes a result of intuition, but it is largely a result of chance. Lamberti is hounded by his sense of justice but feels only sadness when he triumphs over evil, because he knows that his victories are only temporary.

Like the typical hard-boiled private eye, he is prepared to use illegal methods to ensure that criminals will be punished, but his code of honor prevents him, for example, from hitting women. Unlike the American gumshoe of the 1940s and 1950s, Lamberti does not discriminate against people, migrants or otherwise, on the basis of race or ethnicity (though he is homophobic). He is also fond of the elderly and lower-middle-class people who have been left on the fringe of the new hedonistic Italian culture. In contrast, he hates the new business-like criminals who haunt Milan: "These days there are bandits with lawyers in attendance, they cheat, they rob, they kill, but they've already worked out a line of defence with their lawyers in case they're found out and put on trial, and they never get the punishment they deserve."[8] Above all, he despises the opportunistic villain who shows no loyalty to anyone: "Her sort were ready to betray anyone, a dying mother, a daughter in labour, husband, wife, friend, lover, brother or sister. Any one of them would commit murder for a thousand lire, and turn state's evidence for the price of an ice-cream."[9] A committed lover to Livia, a friend to the elderly and marginalized, and a merciless crime fighter, Duca Lamberti is an Italian-style hard-boiled hero who walks the mean streets of Milan.

Selected Bibliography

A Private Venus (1966 [2012])
Traitors to All (1966 [2014]; also translated as *Duca and the Milan Murders* [1970] and *Betrayal* [2012])
I ragazzi del massacro (The boys of the massacre; 1968)
I milanesi ammazzano al sabato (The Milanese kill on Saturdays; 1969)

—Barbara Pezzotti

JUDITH LEE

Richard Marsh
(1857–1915)

While Richard Marsh's detective August Champnell, who appeared in a number of short stories and the hugely successful 1897 novel *The Beetle*, may be more familiar to some readers, his lip-reading, jujitsu-practicing female detective Judith Lee, who first appeared in the *Strand Magazine* in August 1911, is arguably the more interesting character. A lively first-person narrator, Lee featured in twenty-two short stories until her career was cut short by Marsh's death. An amateur detective, Lee is a professional teacher of the deaf-mute who uses her skills as an expert lip-reader to spy on criminals and thwart their plans in ways that seem to them almost supernatural: she *sees* their words from a distance, sometimes through binoculars, and her curiosity and sense of justice lead her to pursue the case to its conclusion. While Lee frequently reminds us that she is primarily a teacher of lip-reading (of an international standing), and not a detective, she could nonetheless be seen as an extreme example of the ocular power displayed by many scientific detectives, including Sherlock Holmes (whose adventures also appeared in the *Strand*).

"The Man Who Cut Off My Hair" (1911), the first story in the series, situates the beginnings of Lee's detective career in her brutal treatment by two burglars into whose clutches she fell as a prepubescent girl. The men tie her up and cut off her "beautiful" hair; the "fury" she feels at being "robbed" of "the dearest thing in the world" leads her to pursue the perpetrators until she can "cry . . . quits" with them over this symbolic rape.[10] Thereafter, Lee's career is characterized by a mistrust of men and a commitment to personal and economic independence. She observes, for example, that "so many men—nearly all of them" are "so silly" that she intends "never, never, never" to marry, and her ambiguous sexuality is confirmed by her frequently rapturous descriptions of feminine beauty.[11] Like other groundbreaking literary female detectives such as Catherine Louisa Pirkis's Loveday Brooke, Lee helps women combat romantic deception and unhappiness in such stories as "The Miracle" (1911), "Isolda" (1912), and "Mandragora" (1912).

More often, however, she deals with cases of murder, international crime, identity fraud, and property crime. In "Conscience" (1911), she pursues a mass murderer (of women) until he commits suicide; "The Barnes Mystery" (1916) sees her track down two doctors who have disposed of a murder victim through medical dissection; and in "The Finchley Puzzle" (1916) she escapes being murdered herself by a bomb concealed in a chocolate and a poisonous snake hidden in a bouquet of flowers. In "Matched" (1911), she tries—and fails—to track down an identity-switching female polygamist, while "Uncle Jack" (1912) sees her save a foolish old man from being robbed, only to have to convince him that she did not act out of love. Like the adventures of Grant Allen's globetrotting Lois Cayley, many of Lee's cases have an international flavor: "Auld Lang Syne" (1912) fictionalizes the Sidney Street anarchist siege of 1911; "The Restaurant Napolitain" (1912) sees Lee defend herself against the Italian Mafia in London; "My Partner for a Waltz" (1916) deals with continental counterfeiting; and in "Two Words" (1916), she thwarts a German spy's mission to steal British military secrets.

An independent young woman, Lee leads a relatively comfortable life in affluent West London. Her cases come to her during outings to restaurants, balls, and the opera, or while on holiday at the seaside or on a cruise. The series emphasizes both Lee's confidence in these public spaces and the financial and cultural rewards of her professional success. Lee's travels give her the opportunity to acquire foreign languages, and she is fluent in at least French, German, and Italian, besides English and sign language. She is a confident user of public transport and modern technology, making frequent use of trains and trams, the telephone, and the telegram. Nor is she physically helpless, using her skills in "jiu-jitsu—the Japanese art of self-defence" to send her antagonists spinning: "I am a woman, but no weakling," she declares. "I have always felt it my duty to keep my body in proper condition, trying to learn all that physical culture can teach me."[12] While many critics see early female detectives as essentially disappointing figures, Lee's absolute independence and fearlessness make her a truly subversive New Woman character within the often conservative genre of detective fiction.

Like Fergus Hume's gipsy detective Hagar, Lee is also ethnically "other." Described by her enemies as a "half-bred gipsy-looking creature" and a "black-faced devil's spawn," the petite, dark Lee claims in "Curare" (1916) to belong to "the greatest family of gipsies in England, perhaps in the world."[13] Her alignment with this much-maligned community, often associated with rootlessness, fortune-telling, and deception, may account for her tendency toward adventurous travel, her ability to disguise herself convincingly, the suspicion with which those in polite society seem to eye her, and the perception of her lip-reading skills as bordering on the supernatural. Intriguingly, however, Lee's profession, the teaching of lip-reading, is itself a practice that threatens, in a way, a minority group within the nation based on a shared language, sign.

Like many other "great" detectives, then, Lee marries personal enigma and transgression with an attempt to eliminate deviance. Arguably a predecessor of such unconventional detective figures as Laurell K. Hamilton's Anita Blake and Stieg Larsson's Lisbeth Salander, Judith Lee, whose adventures have recently returned to print in editions by Black Coat Press (2012) and Valancourt (2016), deserves a larger audience as one of the most intriguing and entertaining of early female detectives.

Selected Bibliography

The Beetle: A Mystery (1897)
An Aristocratic Detective (1900)
The Goddess: A Demon (1900)
The Joss: A Reversion (1901)
Strand Magazine (1911–1916)
Judith Lee: Some Pages from Her Life (1912)
The Adventures of Judith Lee (1916)

—Minna Vuohelainen

LITUMA

Mario Vargas Llosa
(1936–)

Peruvian Mario Vargas Llosa's recurring police detective Lituma made his literary debut in 1958 in the collection *The Chiefs*. One play and five novels later, the unpretentious policeman appeared most recently in the 2013 novel *The Discreet*

Hero. Unlike the traditional detective of the crime fiction genre, Vargas Llosa's antihero lacks a cohesive set of character traits. He can be prejudiced and empathetic, self-righteous and humble, abusive and heartbroken. If there were to be a Lituma on the big screen, the writer had suggested casting "an ordinary dark-skinned mestizo with trimmed hair, vivid eyes, medium height, rather stout with a beer belly and perhaps a gold tooth."[14] The chameleonic depiction of Lituma in each of his appearances has puzzled critics and fans but kept both groups eager for his next incarnation. Lacking a first name, Lituma embodies the ordinary man; he is an invisible nobody who, despite his personal flaws, is consistently good at his job.

The most memorable time of Lituma's life was the wild years he spent as a young man in his beloved working-class neighborhood of La Mangachería in the city of Piura. He formed the group Los Inconquistables (The Unconquerables) with his two cousins and a friend. They led a wild life of booze, women, and partying. More troubling for the reader than the questionable activities of the Inconquistables, as revealed in the play *La Chunga* (1986 [1990]), is the characterization of Lituma's relationship with his future wife in two interlaced story lines of the novel *The Green House* (1966). In one story, Sergeant Lituma has been punitively transferred to a post in the Peruvian jungle. There he attempts to seduce, and eventually forces himself on, Bonifacia, the servant of a group of missionaries. Lituma then marries her and takes her home to his native Piura. A second story line in the novel finds a titleless Lituma returning to his hometown after serving a ten-year sentence in a Lima jail for killing a man in a duel. He finds his wife in a brothel (the titular Green House), and instead of taking revenge on the man who enslaved her, he begins living off of her earnings and enjoying a life of drinking and gambling with his old buddies. Detective Lituma will later selectively evoke these years in a nostalgic mode by focusing on his life with the Inconquistables and by remembering his first love, Lira, a woman who left him when he joined the civil guard.

While the various versions of detective Lituma frequently stay on the sidelines of the action, the Piuran sleuth comes to the forefront in the novel *Death in the Andes* (1993 [1996]). Sent to a remote and volatile area of the Andean mountains in the 1980s, Corporal Lituma needs to solve the disappearance of three villagers that the Maoist guerrilla group Shining Path has most likely killed. He sees the unpleasant assignment as penance for his Inconquistable years. His fears go beyond the Shining Path: "Lituma had never believed in witches or magic, but here in the sierra he was not sure."[15] Coming from the urban, Europeanized Peruvian coast, Lituma derides the indigenous culture of the *serruchos*, a pejorative variation of *serrano*, or people from the sierra. The corporal consistently casts the descendants of the Incas as barbarians and sees himself as a pillar of rationality and (Western) civilization in that "backward" environment. Ultimately, however, even Lituma can hardly believe the truth behind the crimes: it was not the guerrillas but the villagers themselves who killed the victims, sacrificing and cannibalizing members of their own community to appease the gods over the construction of a highway. Lituma's contempt toward his indigenous countrymen reinforces centuries-long racial and cultural prejudices in Peru, and Vargas Llosa was harshly criticized for the portrayal of this Lituma. The halt in the construction of the highway—a metaphor for progress—signals in the novel that the Andean region, just like the Amazonian jungle of *The Green House*, remains too backward to be connected to the modern Peruvian coast.

Unlike more traditional serial detectives, Lituma's appearances in Vargas Llosa's works lack a cohesive timeline, often requiring a suspension of disbelief, or the willingness to entertain multiple possibilities simultaneously. What seems more important to Llosa is placing his sleuth in the context of some of Peru's important twentieth-century historical moments, such as the dictatorship of General Odría in the 1950s or the government's war in the 1980s against the Shining Path. In *The Discreet Hero*, a middle-aged Lituma notices the modernization of his native Piura in the 1990s against the backdrop of neoliberal economic policies. Even his old neighborhood has gentrified and his Inconquistable buddies have become respectable affluent citizens. Ironically, only Lituma has not changed.

Selected Bibliography

The Chiefs (1959 [2001])
The Green House (1966 [1990])
Aunt Julia and the Scriptwriter (1977 [1982])
Who Killed Palomino Molero (1986 [1987])
Death in the Andes (1993 [1996])
The Discreet Hero (2013 [2015])

—Patricia Catoira

DI THOMAS LYNLEY AND DS BARBARA HAVERS

Elizabeth George
(1949–)

Although an American author, Elizabeth George deliberately sets her Inspector Lynley mysteries in the United Kingdom, aiming not only to create a contemporary—albeit somewhat atypical—police procedural but also to paint a vivid picture of contemporary Britain and the issues it faces. The first novel in the Inspector Lynley series, *A Great Deliverance* (1988), for example, exposes a multitude of oppositions and rifts in British society, including issues of class, religious strife, the presence of immigrants in English society, and the flourishing of racism. Here George sets the scene not only for a murder inquiry but also for an inquiry into the complex stratification of a modern society made richer but also more dangerous and infinitely more vulnerable through the changes it has undergone.

Detective Inspector Thomas Lynley and Detective Sergeant Barbara Havers of New Scotland Yard epitomize this stratification and provide the crux of the novels' internal dynamics. This is a partnership of not just different individuals but also antipodal personalities. Everything about Thomas Lynley, the eighth Earl of Asherton, with his Eton and Oxford education, patrician voice, Belgravia townhouse, and the Cornish family estate, clearly signals his association with the upper crust of English society. With the face of a Greek sculpture, an abundance of personal charm, and a wardrobe from Savile Row, he is "too tall, too handsome, too well-groomed, and too splendidly dressed" for a policeman.[16] He is in fact the sort of character who would be arguably more at home in a Golden Age detective novel than in a contemporary police procedural. Barbara Havers, on the other hand, with her grammar school background and working-class accent appropriate to Acton's worst neighborhood, contrasts with golden boy Lynley in her sartorial nonchalance and complete indifference to personal grooming. Always hungry—despite the fact that her clothes are always sequined with crumbs—she is short, plump, and frumpy, but also "prickly, argumentative, [and] easily given to anger"; she is, as George writes, "bitterly aware of the enormous gap" between Lynley and herself, "an impassable chasm created by birth, by class, by money, by experience."[17]

However, what at first appears to be a grotesque and forced alliance in which Havers sees herself as a pariah turns into a fully functioning though still a very awkward professional relationship, evoking other unlikely partnerships in detective fiction. One is reminded, for example, of Colin Dexter's Inspector Morse and Sergeant Lewis. If Lynley stands for the center, representing authority and power with all the accouterments of fortune, class, and birth, Havers is a marginal figure, ill dressed, ill positioned, and ill equipped to deal with the nuances of an increasingly complex British society.

The differences between the two protagonists go far beyond their background. Although he appears to be a man with the perfect, seemingly imperturbable stiff upper lip and a convenient repertoire of engaging personas, Lynley is a man all too familiar with depression, desperation, and desire, a man whose exhibitions of compassion and understanding frequently threaten the pace of the pair's investigations. In contrast to this, Havers's approach is marked by a sort of ruthlessness, a pronounced suspicion and distrust of a world that has dealt her such a rotten hand of cards. Whereas Lynley is perfectly placed to understand the subtleties of the upper-class social dance, in Havers it provokes nothing but the utmost contempt; where Lynley treads lightly, Havers feels the urge to rush in kicking and stomping.

Throughout the total of nineteen novels in the Inspector Lynley series, George develops not only the core character traits of her two detectives but also their private lives. Their personal tragedies frequently feature in the main plot of the novels. Both Lynley and Havers, although they are in so many ways so different, are haunted by the demons of their respective pasts—Havers by her deeply troubled parents who sink into illness and madness after the death of her brother, Lynley by a guilty conscience over a car accident that left his best friend crippled for life. These personal traumatic experiences enable them to approach murder inquiries from different but complementary vantage points, as they attempt to piece together not only the fragments of the puzzling murders they investigate but also the fragments of their own lives.

Rich with intertextual references to both seminal works of detective fiction and classic British literature, George's Inspector Lynley mysteries usher readers into a world that at first seems very specific to a British context. Yet against the backdrop of political battles and scandals, social struggles and prejudices, general ignorance, and the trivial pastimes of the common people, Lynley and Havers aim for what should be universal—the human heart and human follies. They engage with professional questions, such as those of authority, the chain of command, professional responsibility, and the position of women in the police force, but also with life questions concerning parenthood and child-rearing, love and marriage, personal responsibility and selfishness, environmental problems, educational standards, and the criteria of success and happiness. By opting for this universal approach, Elizabeth George offers her readers an allegorical depiction of the poignant issues present in almost all societies, though one "filtered through the light of a different culture" and thus potentially more palatable.[18]

Selected Bibliography

A Great Deliverance (1988)
Well-Schooled in Murder (1990)
Missing Joseph (1994)
Deception on His Mind (1997)
A Place of Hiding (2003)
What Came before He Shot Her (2006)
Just One Evil Act (2013)
A Banquet of Consequences (2015)

—Nina Muždeka

M

CHIEF INSPECTOR JULES MAIGRET

Georges Simenon
(1903–1989)

In Georges Simenon's *Friend of Madame Maigret* (1950 [1959]), Madame Steuvels asks Chief Inspector Jules Maigret if he honestly believes her husband is guilty of "having killed a man and burned the body in the furnace." Maigret's reply reveals his character with absolute clarity: "He hesitated. He could have given her any answer that came into his head, but he was determined to be honest. 'I have no idea.'"[1] Maigret has no investigative method. He knows he must sit and wait, and reflect on human nature, until such time as the truth is revealed.

Georges Simenon tended to dismiss his most famous creation, describing him as "an accident to whom I attached little importance," preferring instead to focus on the rest of his prolific output.[2] But whether he liked it or not, the names of Georges Simenon and Inspector Maigret have become completely intertwined. Maigret appeared in seventy-five novels and twenty-eight short stories between 1931 and 1972, is constantly in print in over fifty languages, and has featured in films and television series across Europe. Simenon will never be able to escape his creation.

Thickset, heavily built, with a taste for beer and calvados, Maigret was born fully formed into a specific era but with no distinct chronology. Indeed, his "first" case, featuring him as a young police officer trying to earn his stripes, wasn't written until 1948, when he had already appeared in some tens of novels as an older man. Although Burgundian by origin, he has made Paris his home. He lives quietly with his wife in their flat in the Boulevard Richard Lenoir. He turns up to work every day at police HQ on the Quai d'Orfevres. His cases may take him out to the provinces, or even abroad, but mostly he walks the Parisian streets he knows so well.

And he knows them as a copper. In Maigret's era, a fictional police detective was a rarity in a narrative realm of wealthy amateurs or people whose position as, for instance, a priest or a journalist led them to investigate and solve crimes. But Maigret knows the criminals, the petty burglars, the unfortunate gamblers, and the women who earn a living as best they can. Under Maigret's steady, nonjudgmental gaze, these marginal characters come to life. There is a pronounced sympathy in Simenon's work for the underdog: many of the murders in his novels are motivated by desperation and poverty. By exploring the social and psychological causes of crime, Simenon gives his stories a powerful moral backbone. More than that, he bestows on his central character a believable, everyday heroism.

Maigret's quiet integrity is also expressed through his relationship with his wife, Louise. Childless, they are devoted to each other. Maigret manages to be sensitive to the charms of women and yet never, ever, yield to them. In turn, Madame Maigret adores her husband. She is a traditional housewife, concerned with her home and her chores; she provides a proper lunch to which he returns each day, often one that she has started cooking first thing in the morning. It is perhaps ironic that Simenon, whose own marital life was famously complicated, succeeded in creating this faithful, uxorious central character who, every time he gazes upon his wife, can't quite believe his luck.

But within the deceptive simplicity of Simenon's writing, there is a playfulness: about storytelling, about the detective genre, and above all, about the fact that Maigret has no method:

> "Are you disappointed, Mr. Pyke?" asked the Chief Inspector.
> "Why?"
> "I don't know. You came to France to find out our methods, and you discover there are none."[3]

This playfulness reaches its most concentrated form in *Maigret's Memoirs* (1950 [1963]), a collection of writings in which Maigret attempts rather grumpily to set the record straight about his career, after having been portrayed so fancifully by the bouncy young journalist "Georges Sim." But Maigret is constantly wrong-footed by his creator:

> "Tell someone a story," [Sim said], "any story. If you don't dress it up, it'll seem incredible, artificial. Dress it up, and it'll seem more real than life."
> He trumpeted out those last words as if they implied some sensational discovery.
> "The whole problem is to make something more real than life. Well, I've done that! I've made you more real than life."
> I remained speechless. For a moment I could find nothing to say, poor unreal policeman that I was.[4]

Simenon's writing is spare and poetic. The light touch of his prose allows for a luminosity of characterization. Even bit-part characters have a world beyond the confines of the story: the murderous dentist returning to his everyday routines; the gangster's unfortunate girlfriend making sure her little boy finds a safe adoptive family; the down-at-heel circus clown who, burdened by guilt, hangs himself four years after the end of the story; and the cobbler in the rue de Turenne who never admitted, "not even when he was dead drunk, that he had sent the anonymous letter."[5] And at the heart of it all sits Chief Inspector Maigret, moral, heroic, and utterly believable, waiting for the mist of doubt to lift.

Selected Bibliography

Maigret and the Tavern by the Seine (1931 [1940])
Maigret and the Yellow Dog (1931 [1939])
Maigret's First Case (1948 [1958])
Maigret and the Burglar's Wife (1951 [1956])
Maigret's Little Joke (1957 [1957])

—Alison Joseph

PHILIP MARLOWE

Raymond Chandler
(1888–1959)

Philip Marlowe, along with characters like Race Williams and Sam Spade, is a defining example of the hard-boiled detective. The genre's dingy realism continues to appeal to readers, and Marlowe stands alone among these sleuths with his scintillating humor and studiously poetic worldview that develops throughout the series (1939–1958). Marlowe's apparent misogyny and preening self-righteousness have received much criticism, and Chandler's lack of interest in traditional detective plotting often makes conclusions complicated even by hard-boiled standards. Nevertheless, the charm of Marlowe's first-person narration, with its distinctive playfulness, sentiment, and jarring metaphors that amplify the inherent discord of modernity, dazzled audiences from the first.

Marlowe is best known for his piercing, hard-boiled wisecracks, but the insight of his wit far surpasses any prior examples of tough-guy language. Though well built and pugnacious, he is an intellectual detective, who works alone and avoids violence when possible. He has a keen eye for detail, and remorselessly documents the grim extravagances of midcentury California. These powers of observation are frequently turned inward, as Marlowe ruminates upon all the "tired, clichéd mannerisms" of his trade.[6] Fired from the DA's office for insubordination, Marlowe, a "shop-soiled Galahad," follows a strict professional code that is both knightly and working class.[7] In his Los Angeles, wealth is inevitably corrupt, as it betrays the great American promise of hope typified by Midwestern values in tragic characters like Merle Davis in *The High Window* (1942).

Despite Chandler's genre experimentation, several of the novels such as *The High Window* and *The Lady in the Lake* (1944) initially follow the whodunit form, and Marlowe is an able reader of traditional clues. However, his greatest strength is psychological analysis, and he unfailingly uncovers weakness, fear, and avarice in suspects. Marlowe likewise reads institutional failings and corruption, thus ensuring that his workaday detection involves a class-based social criticism. Chess recurs as a figure for his detective work, and when alone he replays games of the grandmasters; like these solitary matches, many larger conclusions he reaches are unnarrated and only subsequently explained to the reader. Solutions to cases are often incidental, and the greater interest lies in

Marlowe's reflections on human frailty in a world where injustice and moral compromise are inevitable.

The development of Marlowe as a character is a complicated issue. *The Long Goodbye* (1953), the final completed novel written for the series (the 1958 *Playback* was adapted from an earlier screenplay), offers a wiser and less hostile Marlowe; however, he repeatedly appears bitter and self-indulgent, particularly regarding Terry Lennox's betrayal of their friendship. The detective's musings on loss and the fundamental loneliness of experience are some of the most perceptive in the series, but Marlowe's usual note of self-parody, which pushes the limits of his character and the genre, is missing. Nevertheless, Marlowe's outlook and mode of expression are expanded and refined throughout the novels, even as he surrenders prior ideals.

His knightly refusals of femmes fatales are infamous and often savage, but he still sees "enough melodic line for a tone poem" in Vivian Regan's legs in *The Big Sleep* (1939), and his flirtatious banter with women is some of the best hard-boiled dialogue ever written.[8] Noteworthy among the lethal women he encounters are the corrupt Quest sisters from Manhattan, Kansas, in *The Little Sister* (1949), whose ruthlessness dismantles Marlowe's fantasy of a purity still existing outside the Gomorrah of Los Angeles. The most significant women in Marlowe's life are Anne Riordan from *Farewell, My Lovely* (1940) and Linda Loring from *The Long Goodbye* (1953), *Playback* (1958), and *Poodle Springs* (1989). Riordan is a policeman's daughter and a talented amateur sleuth who becomes Marlowe's unprecedented collaborator, earning his respect and attraction. Loring, equal to Marlowe in wit and insight, actually wins his love, and Chandler envisioned the series ending with Marlowe succumbing to domestic life in the unfinished *The Poodle Springs Story* begun in 1958. This is a remarkable and innovative character change for the habitually private Marlowe and, at the time, an unheard of narrative arc for the hard-boiled genre.

In stark contrast to the contrived refinement of Golden Age mysteries, Philip Marlowe's adventures offer a brashly realistic view of the underside of modern life, stretching from skid row to Bel Air. The piercing clarity of his narration furthered the hard-boiled genre's examination of masculinity, camaraderie, and isolation in American experience, with exceptional humanity and unsurpassed humor. After Marlowe, hard-boiled fiction becomes as much about language as character and plot. Scores of intellectual and reflective tough-guy detectives (e.g., Lew Archer, Travis McGee, Dave Robicheaux, and John Rebus) are cut from Marlowe's cloth.

Marlowe continues to excite cultural fascination, with adaptations of the novels appearing in various media. To date there have been eight big-budget Marlowe films, although the best-known remain *The Big Sleep* (Howard Hawks, 1946) and *The Long Goodbye* (Robert Altman, 1973). Numerous radio dramatizations appeared in the 1940s and 1950s, and several television movies and series have been produced in the United States, the UK, and Canada. In the late 1990s and early 2000s, three graphic novels appeared that drew on the Marlowe stories (*The Little Sister* [1997], *Raymond Chandler's Marlowe* [2003], and *Playback: A Graphic Novel* [2006]), in addition to a number of videogame and short online film adaptations.

Philip Marlowe's witty distaste for the status quo perfectly embodies current reservations about things as they are, based upon the fading promise of what was supposed to be. His hopeful cynicism reminds us that honor and beauty remain accessible through playful, common language, even amidst the inherent nastiness of contemporary experience.

Selected Bibliography

The Big Sleep (1939)
Farewell, My Lovely (1940)
The High Window (1942)
The Lady in the Lake (1944)
The Little Sister (1949)
The Long Goodbye (1953)
Playback (1958)
Poodle Springs (completed by Robert B. Parker in 1989)

—Alexander N. Howe

MISS JANE MARPLE

Agatha Christie
(1890–1976)

Miss Jane Marple is synonymous with a particular version of English national identity. Her genteel manners and stifled emotional range associate her with a privileged English class, and she lives in a village, St. Mary Mead, that is the epitome of the traditional rural idyll often associated with England. It is the kind of landscape with an inherent "harmony and rest about it," a bastion of tradition and constancy.[9] Through Miss Marple, Agatha Christie personifies a longstanding value system of decency, etiquette, moral uprightness, tact, and discretion. She does so through the person of a physically frail woman of advanced age so as to place the focus on the cerebral rather than the physical dimensions of the art of detection. Marple reflects on her life experience in order to decode the crimes that happen around her. And crimes there are—many. For despite its Edenic image, St. Mary Mead is not as benign as at first appears: "What kind of place is this for a man to come to lie in the sun and heal his wounds? It's full of festering poison, this place, and it looks as peaceful and as innocent as the Garden of Eden."[10]

Though *Murder at the Vicarage* (1930) was the first Miss Marple novel, the character initially appeared in Christie's 1927 short story "The Tuesday Night Club": "She had on black lace mittens, and a black lace cap surmounted the piled-up masses of her snowy hair. She was knitting—something white and soft and fleecy."[11] From the first she demonstrates her capacity to disarm those around her with her benign appearance, providing her with countless opportunities to overhear private conversations or observe the behavior of those who do not notice her. This inconspicuousness is a key weapon in her detective's armory in each of the twelve "Miss Marple" novels and twenty short stories. The first appeared between the two world wars, and the last was published in the late 1970s, not long after Christie's death. Yet they all have in common the shared themes of family, community, and marital dysfunction, as well as the criminal motivations of sexual infidelity, jealousy, revenge, and economic greed. By the time of *Sleeping Murder* (1976), the last Marple story, she had been part of an array of cases featuring a remarkable number of examples of human duplicity and immorality.

But there is more to the Marple novels than immoral acts occurring within an idealized England. In the later stories in particular, the depiction of a world that is firmly located in an idea of the past gradually starts to give way to an awareness of the various ways in which the world is beginning to shift, displaying incremental signs of the wider social change that took place during the twentieth century. In the postwar novels this social transformation is even fundamental to the plotlines, with *The Mirror Crack'd* (1962), for instance, relying on the interaction of traditional and emerging social classes as a facilitating element of the central crime. And it is Miss Marple herself, so often seen as the embodiment of tradition and conservatism, who displays the most enlightened perspective. While certain other characters might lament the fact that "fifteen years ago one knew who everybody was" whereas now "every village and small country place is full of people who've just come and settled there without any ties to bring them . . . nobody knows any more who anyone is," Miss Marple is more at ease with the shifting social landscape.[12] She is comfortable with the young mothers pushing their children in prams around the previously peaceful streets of St. Mary Mead; she even employs one of them as her housekeeper. So, paradoxically, the aged detective becomes part of a picture of growing diversity: "The houses were different, the streets were called Closes, the clothes were different, the voices were different but human beings were the same as they always had been."[13]

Despite the interesting social layering of the later Marple novels, their modernity has been largely overlooked in the various screen adaptations of the stories, which tend to reproduce the familiar stereotypes of Englishness, as the films starring Margaret Rutherford, Helen Hayes, and Angela Lansbury, and the highly successful BBC TV series running from 1984 to 1992 starring Joan Hickson, all illustrate. Hickson was the epitome of this sense of Englishness in every gentle, kind, intuitive, compassionate, decent, and well-mannered moment. And whilst some of the more recent television adaptations, starring Geraldine McEwan and Julia Mackenzie, detour from this image at times, for the most part they too implicitly acknowledge that for many viewers, and readers, Miss Marple will always symbolize a comfortable, familiar world that, although it has now passed, will forever remain seductive.

Selected Bibliography

Murder at the Vicarage (1930)
The Tuesday Club Murders (1932)
The Body in the Library (1942)
The Moving Finger (1943)
A Murder Is Announced (1950)

They Do It with Mirrors (1952)
A Pocket Full of Rye (1953)
4:50 from Paddington (1957)
The Mirror Crack'd from Side to Side (1962)
A Caribbean Mystery (1964)
At Bertram's Hotel (1965)
Nemesis (1971)
Sleeping Murder (1976)
Miss Marple's Final Cases (1979)

—Neil McCaw

SHARON McCONE

Marcia Muller
(1944–)

While Sharon McCone is not the first female professional private investigator, she is the most enduring and influential. *Someone Always Knows* was published in 2016, the thirty-first McCone novel in a series that began in 1977. Her position as an independent woman whose feminist sensibility has developed over the years, and as an investigator whose thoughtful and introspective nature gives her an unusually rich interior life, has been praised by authors such as Sue Grafton and Sara Paretsky. Instead of forcing her character into the hard-boiled mold, Marcia Muller set out to change the mold to better fit a female sleuth. McCone thus became the template for popular characters such as Grafton's Kinsey Millhone and Paretsky's V. I. Warshawski, who were part of the groundswell of interest in the 1970s and 1980s in strong, active female characters taking on roles traditionally defined as male. Over nearly four decades, McCone has maintained her core of independence, decency, and compassion, but she has also reflected the significant changes taking place around her. Indeed, the last few decades of social transformation in San Francisco, her home base, and in America in general, can be traced through the series.

McCone's nephew and employee, Mick Savage, describes his aunt in this way: "Serenity wasn't Shar's thing. Keen concentration, purposefulness, action, yes. Laughter, tears, anger, and the occasional white-hot rage, too."[14] Most of those qualities have characterized McCone since her first appearance in *Edwin of the Iron Shoes* (1977). McCone is also, as she learns in *Listen to the Silence* (2000), adopted, a discovery that disrupts her sense of who she, and what her family, is. The dark complexion and black hair that made her stand out in the McCone family are clues to her newly discovered birth parents and Shoshone ancestry. This heritage is part of a broader, gradual transformation in Muller's character.

As the "soul-less" 1980s gave way to the "I got mine, so fuck you" 1990s and the paranoid post-9/11 world, McCone has become a darker figure, and one more aware of the gray area between right and wrong.[15] She has killed in self-defense and in defense of others, and has the nightmares and regrets to prove it.

The earlier novels' emphasis on social justice is less prominent in the later ones, an absence that tinges them with an unsentimental nostalgia. Social ills, such as homelessness, drug abuse, the disenfranchisement of minorities, and the transformation of her city into a place where only the rich can afford to live become a dark ambiance, invoking what at times borders on despair. Social issues move into the background, because McCone has come to recognize that she cannot fix the world, as once seemed possible: "Not the world, but some of its people anyway. We thought too big back then. Thinking small is more realistic."[16] She is not a hardened cynic, nor is she acquiescent, but she has become more pragmatic about what she can accomplish in a world dedicated to perpetuating the status quo.

Back in the 1970s, McCone worked as a security guard while she completed a sociology degree. Finding that her degree did not exactly open doors to employment, she took a job as an investigator for a poverty law cooperative, All Souls, in San Francisco. She became a licensed private investigator who sometimes carries a gun and is sometimes forced to use it. Later, she earned a pilot's license. However, the combination of social sensitivity and emotional awareness with which Muller has imbued McCone from the outset mitigates the hard-boiled investigative skills and sharp-edged personal qualities that she displays. Rather than charging through doors with gun blazing, McCone "listens to the silence," which might be the space between words where something is left out, or the space of a room where a crime has occurred. While the truism holds that money is the root of all evil, McCone often finds that secrets are at the root of crime.

Many of the friends she made in that early job remain friends and associates as she starts her own very successful agency. As they all enter their forties, McCone, like the rest, has changed. She experiences several personal crises that keep her character dynamic, appealing, and realistic. Among these life-changing events are her discovery of her birth family, her near murder of a man in cold blood, her brother's death from drugs and alcohol, a brutal shooting that leaves her temporarily paralyzed and mute, and meeting Hy Ripinsky, who will finally become her husband and then her business partner. This last event is particularly important, as one of the problems she struggles with throughout the series is how to maintain her personal integrity and independence in a relationship. In *Where Echoes Live* (1991), she finally finds the perfect partner, one whom she can love and rely upon without constant struggle and who values her work and her passion as much as she does.

McCone was formed in the tumultuous 1960s and 1970s. Her experiences, her evolving character, and her immersion in changing American concerns and attitudes from that now distant era to the present constitute an extraordinary personal journey through each of these decades. As a woman in a man's world, and as an idealist who has had to confront her own naïveté and learn how to live with compromise and failure, McCone has pushed detective fiction beyond its boundaries and retained her appeal as both an investigator of, and a guide to, American consciousness through forty years of change.

Selected Bibliography

Edwin of the Iron Shoes (1977)
There's Something in a Sunday (1989)

Trophies and Dead Things (1990)
Where Echoes Live (1991)
A Wild and Lonely Place (1995)
Listen to the Silence (2000)
The Dangerous Hour (2004)
Someone Always Knows (2016)

—Rebecca Martin

TRAVIS McGEE

John D. MacDonald
(1916–1986)

John D. MacDonald's Travis McGee belongs to the jaded knight-errant tradition of detectives originated by Chandler's Marlowe and Dashiell Hammett's Spade. McGee emerges amid the social tumult of the post-Kennedy assassination years and appears in a series of twenty-one novels, starting with *The Deep Blue Good-By* in 1964 and ending with *The Lonely Silver Rain* in 1984. This two-decade span is integral to McGee's characterization and affords MacDonald the opportunity to assess various social changes and follies, beginning with the countercultural dissent of the 1960s and concluding with the onset of the go-go Reagan era. Yes, MacDonald designs mysteries and creates thrills that turn pages, but the postmodern condition itself is the actual case McGee investigates throughout his career.

The signature feature of McGee's first-person narrative perspective is digression. With noteworthy insight, he offers asides on a range of sociopolitical subjects and opines fulsomely on sexuality, finance, ethics, and more. Nor will McGee hesitate to throw in a word or two on more prosaic matters such as physical fitness. In *The Green Ripper* (1979), for instance, he admonishes that "until a man can walk seven miles in two hours without blowing like a porpoise, without sweating gallons, without bumping his heart past 120, it is asinine to start jogging."[17] This does little to advance the plot but is vital to the fun of reading the McGee novels: you are privy to the man's hard-won wisdom.

The sandy-haired, Irish American McGee is a rangy but thick-boned six foot four and weighs in at just over two hundred pounds. He is a Korean War army veteran and recipient of a Silver Star and a Purple Heart. A former tight end, he played college and professional football before a knee injury abruptly ended his career. Still spry and solid somewhere in his midthirties, he is a shrewd fighter and has a familiarity with the martial arts. A handsome bachelor, he is taking his retirement in installments between cases and lives on *The Busted Flush*, a fifty-two-foot houseboat docked in Fort Lauderdale, Florida, at the Bahia Mar Marina. Florida, the nation's sandy annex that amplifies appetites peculiarly American, provides a tawdry frontier ripe for an array of scams, larcenies, and eco-disasters—an apt realm for rendering McGee's vision of a civilization careening toward apocalypse. His land transportation is called Miss Agnes, a fusion of the front end of a 1936 Rolls

Royce and the bed of a pickup truck. While this extravagant cross is amusingly parodic, its hybridity fittingly suggests both McGee's mistrust of the newfangled and his reasonable practicality. His good friend Meyer, who becomes a Watson-like interlocutor by the series' tenth novel, *Pale Gray for Guilt* (1968), is a voluble economist who lives a few boats down in Bahia Mar.

McGee is not a conventional detective. A self-proclaimed salvage consultant, he recovers stolen property for a fee of 50 percent of its value, which he collects only if the retrieval is successful. He is typically hired by friends, or friends of friends, who use him as a last resort. He is especially motivated to pursue cases in which the naïve and well meaning (usually females of some allure) have been swindled by dodgy adventurers (usually males of much nastiness).

Though in *Free Fall in Crimson* (1981) he admits to having "cut a wide swath through a wall of female flesh," McGee represents a departure from the blatant misogyny found in much previous detective fiction.[18] He counsels, nurses, and defends females throughout the series. His desire to protect and comfort is genuine, but a paternalistic strain is palpable in the novels. Although McGee loathes sex that lacks genuine emotional connection, he stands ready to perform as a sexual therapist if necessary; moreover, the damsels in need of his practiced attentions seem inexhaustible. His attitudes toward women were probably regarded as progressive by many of MacDonald's generation, but today they can be distressingly (and sometimes comically) dated. When it comes to McGee and women, read with caution. But also read with an eye to exhuming curious, if often chauvinistic, portrayals of romantic mores typical of the period.

McGee maneuvers easily enough among the well-to-do of polite society, but he is not one of them at heart. Yet as much as he decries the fads of bohemians and hippie reformists, like them, he desires an escape from the hollow avarice of the mainstream. The rub for McGee is that his inner beach bum wants a divorce from the wreck of consumer culture, but he finds the progressive alternatives no more promising than the social structures they aim to replace; furthermore, his moral conscience will not allow him to cold-shoulder the lost souls caught up in the complications of contemporary society, or abandon those who fall prey to the evils of human nature. McGee is profoundly suspicious of the authorities directing socioeconomic "progress," specifically those involving the alleged benefits of technological advances, such as contractors who "develop" the environment, or the hyper-bureaucratization of governmental and corporate enterprises. In *The Deep Blue Good-By* (1964), he reflects, "I am wary of the whole dreary deadening structured mess we have built into such a glittering top-heavy structure that there is nothing left to see but the glitter, and the brute routines of maintaining it."[19] McGee laments the massification of anything that fosters regimentation, and thus represents a novel extension of the conventional solitary detective.

Selected Bibliography

Nightmare in Pink (1964)
Dress Her in Indigo (1969)
The Scarlet Ruse (1972)
The Turquoise Lament (1973)

The Dreadful Lemon Sky (1974)
Free Fall in Crimson (1981)
Cinnamon Skin (1982)

—Kenneth K. Brandt

KINSEY MILLHONE

Sue Grafton
(1940–2017)

A fascination with mysteries with related titles inspired Sue Grafton to write a series of crime novels based on the letters of the alphabet. The series started with *A Is for Alibi* in 1982 and ended one book short of completion with Grafton's untimely death in 2017. All of the novels focus on the central character of PI Kinsey Millhone.

While many series authors condense narrative time, often to avoid a too-rapidly aging PI or police detective, this is rarely as clearly marked, or as integral to the works, as in the Kinsey Millhone novels. *Q Is for Quarry*, for example, is set in 1987, even though it was written in 2002, while *W Is for Wasted* (2013) and *X* (2015) both feature a thirty-eight-year-old Millhone and are set in 1989. Grafton keeps Millhone in her thirties, old enough to be cynical, jaded, and emotionally reserved. The novels' 1980s setting is also important, as this was a time period of particular interest and importance to the rise, post-second-wave feminism, of the female private eyes who challenged the old "hard-boiled" masculine heroes. Indeed, the Millhone novels are a paradigm of the "girl with a gun" subgenre, and one of the reasons that Millhone stands out as a "great detective" is her status as a trailblazer of the early and, at that time, groundbreaking idea that a female character could be a richly developed protagonist in crime fiction, instead of falling into one of the binary pair of "good girl victim" or femme fatale. Instead, Grafton portrays Millhone as an independent, sexually active woman.

Each novel describes her situation and offers a slightly different perspective on her life and business status, but this self-description from *W Is for Wasted* (2013) is typical: "My name is Kinsey Millhone. I'm a private investigator, female, age thirty-eight. I rent office space in a two-room bungalow with a kitchenette and a bathroom on a narrow street in the heart of Santa Teresa."[23] Millhone's fictional Santa Teresa is similar to Monticeto, California, Grafton's own hometown, and is the setting for many of her investigations. Twice divorced before the series begins, Millhone is introduced to the reader in *A Is for Alibi* as a single woman living in a converted garage in her octogenarian landlord, ex-baker Henry Pitt's backyard. Her relationship with Pitt and his siblings is a constant in the series, as is her independence at work; small changes occur, but a reassuring domestic continuity is provided near the start of every novel. Millhone has a habit of eating at Pitt's cranky sister-in-law's restaurant, and her confined living space demands little housework. This freedom from traditional domestic work frees her to concentrate on her professional life.

Grafton uses Millhone's attachment to Pitt and his extended family as a contrast with her hard-won independence in her professional and personal life, but it also works as part of the repetition that is a necessary element of this series. Grafton's formula involves Millhone's description of her business and home situation at the beginning of each novel, the constant presence of the father figure Pitt, and her repeatedly professed reluctance to allow anyone to get close to her. Pitt's presence is thus exceptionally important to Millhone; she sometimes muses that she is at least half in love with him, and one of the reasons for the extreme time compression of the series may be the fact that he is eighty-one when the series starts.

Despite the importance of Pitt, and her reluctance to become emotionally attached, Millhone does have other relationships. In *A Is for Alibi*, Grafton sets the pattern that Millhone's romantic relationships follow, albeit not always in such a definitive and violent manner. She starts to fall for lawyer Charlie Scorsoni, who turns out to be the murderer in the case she is investigating. Once she realizes his guilt, she confronts him and, as he tries to emotionally manipulate her, spots the knife he has in his hand. Realizing his intention is to kill her as well, she shoots him dead—"I blew him away."[24] Afterward Millhone tries, as she acknowledges, to keep her distance.

The Kinsey Millhone novels are comforting books, even exhibiting a certain predictability. Their 1980s setting also encapsulates an increasingly distant world. However, their continued success indicates that some things, such as our need for a detective hero like Kinsey Millhone, may not have changed much at all.

Selected Bibliography

A Is for Alibi (1982)
B Is for Burglar (1985)
C Is for Corpse (1986)
W Is for Wasted (2013)
X (2015)
Y Is for Yesterday (2017)

—Fiona Peters

KIYOSHI MITARAI

Sōji Shimada
(1948–)

With Seicho Matsumoto's realistic and hugely successful crime mysteries, Japanese detective fiction entered the age of the humdrum police procedural. The brainwork of private detectives was replaced by the legwork of police detectives. Writers scorned unrealistic depictions of murder and investigations set in unlikely closed-circle situations. The new generation even avoided casting detectives in multiple cases and aimed at dealing with the social issues affecting an economically prosperous Japan. During this 1980s "winter" for detective fiction, Sōji Shimada boldly ventured into the forgotten realm of the whodunit with his maiden work *The Tokyo Zodiac Murders* (1981 [2004]) featuring a new incarnation of the classical detective, Kiyoshi Mitarai.

In *The Tokyo Zodiac Murders*, Mitarai tackles a murder mystery no one has been able to solve for more than forty years. He takes the role of an armchair detective and solves the mystery only through newspaper articles and published documents. The author makes the case as challenging as possible by incorporating many of the elements of classical detective fiction: a locked room, serial murders, a strange testament left by a victim, and the dismemberment of the victims' bodies. He even inserts a "message from the author" twice in which he challenges the reader to solve the mystery before the final chapter. *Naname yashiki no hanzai* (The murder in the slanted mansion; 1982) introduces a closed-circle setting where Mitarai reconstructs the impossible murder of the prime suspect, later revealing that he built the eponymous mansion only to carry out the perfect crime of killing his unwanted guests. This is the kind of crime that writers of realistic police fiction would consider mere fantasy. Mitarai repeatedly expresses his hatred of police detectives who believe legwork always brings success. Considering the fact that Mitarai's age is the same as Shimada's, it is not difficult to see here a criticism directed toward mainstream police fiction.

In order to cope with these impossible mysteries, Shimada gradually transforms Mitarai into a sort of superhero of brainwork. Mitarai is first introduced as an astrologer who occasionally works on criminal investigations to satisfy his curiosity. His Watsonian friend, assistant, and the narrator of his stories, Kazumi Ishioka, describes him as a misogynistic, cynical, eccentric genius who suffers from frequent mood swings. When Ishioka mocks Mitarai by comparing him to Sherlock Holmes, Mitarai curses this fictional detective, calling him a "liar, barbarian and cocaine addict who always confused the real with the unreal," although this is Mitarai's unusual way of showing respect.[25]

According to Ishioka's research, Mitarai was born in 1948 to a wealthy family. His father was a high-ranking government official during the war but later went to the United States to be a music teacher. His mother was a professor of mathematics and was too occupied with her own research to be an effective parent. After their separation, Mitarai lived in his grandmother's house in Yokohama, until leaving Japan for the United States at eight to live with his paternal aunt in San Francisco. He entered a private high school at ten, Harvard at fifteen, and at twenty-one was already working as a researcher at Columbia University. After moving back to Japan, and after a lost decade, he opened a school to teach astrology in Yokohama in 1978. This was where he met Kazumi Ishioka. Mitarai is also musically talented (he attended the Juilliard School and says he is better at music than criminal investigation). He can handle the majority of world languages (except for hieroglyphics), and his IQ is said to be more than three hundred!

The success of the Mitarai series cannot be separated from the attractiveness of the series' characters. The narrator Kazumi Ishioka is particularly important since his common sense complements Mitarai's cynical view of human beings. When Mitarai is absent, he even becomes the protagonist by taking college student Satomi Inubo as an assistant in *Ryūgatei jiken* (The Ryūgatei murders; 1996). After her first appearance in *Kurayamizaka no hitokui no ki* (The cannibal tree of Dark Hill; 1990), actress Reona Matsuzaki also frequents the series, bewildering Mitarai with her straightforward emotion for him. She also acts as the main detective in *Hariuddo sātifikeito* (Hollywood certificate; 2001), in which she investigates a mystery surrounding the torturing and killing of Hollywood actresses. When Mitarai leaves Japan in 1994, the role of the narrator is handed to the German journalist Heinrich von Lehndorff-Steinort to add an international perspective to the series.

In the Mitarai case files, the adversary is not necessarily the perpetrator of a crime, but our limited perceptions that make a simple case appear extremely enigmatic. Mitarai often faces fantastic problems, such as a flesh-eating tree in *Kurayamizaka no hitokui no ki,* a mermaid in *Suishō no piramiddo* (The crystal pyramid; 1991), and a vampire in *Atoposu* (Atopos; 1993). Unlike the early generation of classic detective writers, Mitarai is not an evangelist of modern civilization. His role is to reveal the logic (including astrology) that operates behind what we may see as "fantastic" in our naïve belief in scientific knowledge. Mitarai mocks our arrogance and emphasizes how small and insignificant our everyday lives are in relation to the vast universe.

The success of the Mitarai series prepared the way for the revival of orthodox detective fiction in the 1990s, acting as a model for the new generation of crime writers. Yukito Ayatsuji, who became the central figure of the movement, thus named his detective Kiyoshi Shimada out of respect for the author and his iconic detective.

Selected Bibliography

The Tokyo Zodiac Murders (1981 [2004])
Naname yashiki no hanzai (Murder in the slanted mansion; 1982)
Kurayamizaka no hitokui no ki (The cannibal tree of Dark Hill; 1990)
Suishō no piramiddo (The crystal pyramid; 1991)
Atoposu (Atopos; 1993)

—Satomi Saito

EBERHARD MOCK

Marek Krajewski
(1966–)

In Raymond Chandler's celebrated *Big Sleep* (1939), there is a scene in which Philip Marlowe, having returned to his apartment, finds Carmen Sternwood naked in his bed. The knightly Marlowe remains composed and does not hesitate to send her on her way. Despite his indebtedness to Chandler's detective, and the hard-boiled genre in general, Marek Krajewski's Eberhard Mock would never have missed out on such an opportunity. This stocky but good-looking "lover of Antiquity and a woman's body" features in a series of so-called retro-style crime novels that have both revolutionized the Polish market for crime fiction and garnered considerable international attention.[26] Krajewski's take on noir has left an imprint on his numerous followers digging into Poland's prewar history, but the memorable and eccentric Mock, who in the inaugural *Death in Breslau* (1999 [2008]) is introduced by his peculiar habit of playing chess with naked prostitutes in a brothel, has so far found no equal.[27]

Mock's pedantry and dandified style (he wears an immaculate suit and a perfectly matching bowler) are well suited to the background of decadent Breslau (now Wrocław) where most of his investigations take place. Krajewski's books cover the period from the 1920s to the early 1950s, tracing the city's German (until 1945) and then Polish history. To a large extent, however, the setting is reminiscent of Chandler's Los Angeles, characterized by sex, alcohol, violence, and nightlife, all of which are indispensable parts of Eberhard Mock's life. He is a frequent visitor to houses of pleasure, taverns, cafés, and bars—where his beloved food and drink choices are meticulously described—as well as cabarets, theaters, and operas. On the other hand, the investigator paradoxically reconciles his predilection for sensual pleasures with an unwavering love of classical studies. The ancient Roman playwright Plautus and others like him are to Mock (a graduate in classical studies at the University of Breslau) what the violin is to Sherlock Holmes—they help him concentrate, restrain his anger, and maintain a comforting distance from everyday life. His knowledge of antiquity is also a prism through which he perceives reality. This helps him with his investigations, as some of his cases reenact classical myths, such as *The Minotaur's Head* (2009 [2012]) in which he pursues a perverted rapist and cannibal.

If the decadent milieu is part of the hard-boiled tradition, so too is Mock's manner of detection. Like his notable predecessors, he does not refrain from violence, breaking the law, or crossing the boundary between good and evil. The ruthless Cornelius Wirth and Heinrich Zupitza, members of the criminal underworld, are always at his disposal whenever radical (beating up) or ultimate (murdering) measures are required. Mock labels his favorite method of investigation "catching in a vice"; he gathers information about the suspect, such as phobias or secrets, and then uses it during interrogation, with a certain dose of brutality at the hands (and more) of Wirth and Zupitza. Mock is obsessed with bringing his cases to an end and administering justice, though not necessarily in accordance with the law. He is not a knight who believes in reinstating social, moral, and legal order, but a hunting dog, as he likes to call himself, tracking down and punishing criminals.

On the personal level, Eberhard Mock remains largely unchanged despite the long period of time covered by the series. His identity is in a way reaffirmed when the detective is confronted with his Polish alter ego, Police Commissioner Edward Popielski from Lwów, as they jointly solve the case of the Minotaur. Popielski is a carbon copy of Mock, and the similarities between them highlight what constitutes Eberhard Mock as a literary character. On the other hand, Mock is socially and professionally dynamic, both climbing the career ladder and changing occupation when the circumstances demand it. In *Death in Breslau* the flash-forwards concluding the narrative present Mock as an Abwehr captain (in the 1940s) and a CIA agent (in the 1950s), while the other novels in the series, which sometimes precede and sometimes follow the events of the first book, show Mock's promotion from the position of criminal assistant in *Phantoms of Breslau* (2005 [2010]) to criminal commissioner in *The End of the World in Breslau* (2003 [2009]) and criminal counselor and finally criminal director in *Death in Breslau*. To ensure his position, Mock demonstrates capabilities usually associated with a detective's criminal antagonists, such as Arthur Conan Doyle's James Moriarty. He takes advantage of Freemasonry's backing, resorts to blackmail and "vice," joins the Abwehr to protect himself from the Gestapo and the CIA to protect himself from the Communists. The mask he puts on during the war and in its aftermath to cover his damaged face can be taken as metonymic of his ongoing masquerade, despite the stable essence beneath.

In his renowned description of the hard-boiled hero as "a man of honor . . . in search of a hidden truth" in an evil world, Raymond Chandler optimistically concludes that "if there were enough like him . . . the world would be a very safe place to live in, and yet not too dull to be worth living in."[28] No one will ever be bored in the company of Eberhard Mock, and even if making the world a safer place is not his real objective, we can rest assured that if there were enough like him, all of those who deserve it would be tracked down and duly punished.

Selected Bibliography

Death in Breslau (1999 [2008])
The End of the World in Breslau (2003 [2009])
Phantoms of Breslau (2005 [2010])
The Minotaur's Head (2009 [2012])

—Jakub Lipski

INSPECTOR SALVO MONTALBANO

Andrea Camilleri
(1925–)

Over the last two decades, Italian crime fiction has grown enormously, producing a number of detectives and policemen that are drawing the attention of a vast readership both in Italy and abroad. Inspector Salvo Montalbano, the creation of Sicilian crime writer Andrea Camilleri, is undeniably the most widely acclaimed of them all. Since his first outing in *The Shape of Water* in 1994, Montalbano has appeared in twenty-four novels (translated into more than thirty languages), and in a number of short stories, comics, and audiobooks. His success, fostered by the television adaptations first aired in Italy in 1999, was celebrated in 2009 with the official unveiling of his statue in Porto Empedocle, Camilleri's hometown.

Camilleri's achievement, however, has not always been received so positively. A number of Italian scholars have harshly criticized his writing and seen Montalbano as a product of lowbrow popular culture, a mere restyling of spent detective fiction clichés. Camilleri's admirers, on the other hand, see Montalbano as an original, inspiring creation and an appropriate fictional tool to explore and comment on the state of Italian society, politics, and law and order.

Camilleri has indeed reworked, often with irony, forms and features of the archetypical detective of both the Golden Age and the hard-boiled schools, but by blending tradition and innovation, seriousness and humor, he has developed an enhanced version of the ethical sleuth. According to many commentators, Montalbano is less one-dimensional than many of his literary predecessors; he is not an unrealistic, infallible superdetective but a convincing, multifaceted character.

Montalbano is an ordinary policeman with an extraordinary sense of justice who struggles against everyday difficulties. His political sympathies are left wing, and he is concerned about citizens' welfare and civil rights. This often brings him into conflict with his self-serving superiors and the institutions he should represent. Although he is assisted by a loyal team of (sometimes disorganized) police officers, such as Sergeant Fazio, he prefers to investigate alone, to follow his own intuition and instincts in his quest for truth. He explains this need to his ambitious deputy: "I've realized I'm sort of a solitary hunter. . . . I do like to go hunting with others, but I want to be the only one to organize the hunt."[29] Montalbano is a skillful investigator and an intelligent, cultivated man with a passion for literature, history, philosophy, and painting—interests that frequently facilitate his inquiries—but he can also be unwise and impatient.

He displays traits and quirks that make him a sympathetic figure with which readers (and television viewers) can easily identify. He is short-tempered and heavily influenced by the weather; he grows frustrated with the slow pace of bureaucracy and the lethargy of public officials, and gets furious with his men—but always remains compassionate with the victims of crime. He detests paperwork, meetings, and press conferences; he is hopeless with technology; he has a deep aversion to flying. He also betrays a fear of commitment, which is noticeable in his stormy long-distance relationship with his Genoese girlfriend Livia, an unchanging presence who often functions as Montalbano's advisor, confessor, and conscience. Montalbano is a rather conservative man, honest and faithful, and he does not let women other than Livia tempt him—until he begins to dread aging. His personal crisis and increasing worries are explored in a number of novels, for instance, *August Heat* (2006 [2008]) and the significantly titled *The Age of Doubt* (2008 [2012]).

Importantly, Montalbano is a gourmet with a predilection for traditional Sicilian cuisine and occasionally a heavy drinker, who prefers to savor his large meals in silence. The many descriptions of local dishes that underscore Montalbano's obsession with food are far from trivial. They reinforce Montalbano's Sicilian identity, a sense of place that is highlighted by frequent references to his expert knowledge of his native island's geography, history, and art, and his deep understanding of its impenetrable cultural codes.

Camilleri has emphasized that his character's cases originate in real events and are influenced by their historical and political moment. Therefore, Montalbano's investigations regularly echo topical issues: international terrorism in *The Snack Thief* (1996 [2003]), arms smuggling in *The Terracotta Dog* (1996 [2002]), organ trafficking in *Excursion to Tindari* (2000 [2004]), bank fraud in *The Smell of the Night*

(2001 [2005]), and the exploitation of migrants and police brutality in *Rounding the Mark* (2003 [2006]). Inquiries are normally set in the fictional town of Vigàta but are interspersed with allusions to recognizable true cases of corruption, abuse of power, and misgovernment in Sicily and mainland Italy. Unexpectedly for these Sicilian stories, the Mafia rarely appears at the center of Montalbano's investigations, although its presence, influence, and violence are skillfully braided into the social and political framework offered by the author. By contrast, crimes of a more private nature emerge as recurring plot lines: family feuds, betrayal, and deceit, for instance, are explored in *The Patience of the Spider* (2004 [2007]) and *The Potter's Field* (2008 [2010]).

After more than twenty years in the limelight, Montalbano is still dividing opinion, but he has become an international sensation, one of the greatest detectives in world literature. His admirers do not seem to tire of reading about his cases, or of watching them unfold on television against the vibrant Sicilian scenery.

Selected Bibliography

The Shape of Water (1994 [2003])
The Snack Thief (1996 [2003])
The Terracotta Dog (1996 [2002])
Excursion to Tindari (2000 [2004])
The Smell of the Night (2001 [2005])
Rounding the Mark (2003 [2006])
The Patience of the Spider (2004 [2007])
August Heat (2006 [2008])
The Age of Doubt (2008 [2012])
The Potter's Field (2008 [2010])

—Lucia Rinaldi

INSPECTOR MORSE

Colin Dexter
(1930–2017)

The fictional Detective Inspector Morse first appeared as the rather nondescript "lightly built, dark-haired" lead investigator of Colin Dexter's *Last Bus to Woodstock* (1975).[30] From that point, across the thirteen-novel "Morse" series that concluded with *The Remorseful Day* in 1999, readers followed the career and personal life of a hardworking, though often less than extraordinary, detective. Morse has his idiosyncrasies, true, such as his love of crosswords and alcohol, but perhaps the most notable personality trait in the earlier novels is his rampant lasciviousness—a trait, it is suggested, that is entirely in keeping with the world around him. The novels explore the ongoing tensions between the detective's own truculent irascibility and the nature of a modern world often characterized by "volleys of bricks and insults from gangs of yobbos clapping the skidding-skills of youths in stolen cars," but readers get little sense that either Morse's method or his acumen make him an equal of (say) an Inspector Bucket, a Sergeant Cuff, a Sherlock Holmes, or a Hercule Poirot.[31]

So, while many of the Morse novels are relatively successful in fashioning him as a distinct, contemporary manifestation of the literary detective, it was not until these texts were adapted for television that Morse joined the ranks of his more esteemed predecessors. What is clear is that, from the very first adaptation, *The Dead of Jericho* (1987), Morse was destined to become one of the most popular detectives in the history of fiction and broadcasting. The *Inspector Morse* television adaptations produced by Carlton television (1987–1997) offered thirty-three film-length snippets of "quality" television franchised across the globe to more than two hundred countries, bringing Morse to places as diverse as Mongolia, Malawi, El Salvador, and Papua New Guinea. By the time it concluded, the franchise was one of the most significant exports in the history of British television drama, with "a billion people, just under a sixth of the world's population" having watched at least one episode.[32]

Crucial to the success of this global Morse franchise was a fundamental rewriting of the detective himself. On television Morse is a much more layered, charismatic, engaging figure whose life, and particularly his continually disastrous love life, binds together the various strands of each film episode. His idiosyncrasies are ramped up, making him an Opera-obsessive, real-ale-drinking misanthrope, a man alienated from most elements of mainstream society, continually at odds with authority, but also (perhaps crucially) with much-enhanced investigative skills that allow him to decode the mysteries of life with a dexterity and mental acuity beyond that apparent in many of the Dexter novels. And to emphasize his greater capabilities and status, the character of Sergeant Lewis was also recast, as a younger, less experienced, and less knowledgeable man, to re-create the familiar dynamic of detective-partner established by earlier writers including Edgar Allan Poe, Arthur Conan Doyle, and Agatha Christie.

This rewritten version of Morse contributes toward a particular vision of Englishness. He is an erudite man of high culture, always with an apposite literary allusion to hand, someone who works among the towering spires of the University of Oxford, with its medieval architecture and quaint pastoral backwater locations that reinforce the stereotypical sense of an English nation rooted in nostalgia for an Edenic past. He is a detective who solves cases that themselves often accord with such an imagined national landscape, whether it be victims drifting Lady of Shallot–like down rivers in punts, or dead bodies found incongruously in picturesque, ancient buildings. His classic burgundy Jaguar (it was a less heritage-influenced Lancia in the books) winds its way through the streets of an Oxford that are curiously devoid of the litter, traffic, street violence, and the sense of urban threat that one might find in the real Oxford. Morse thus plays the role of a gentlemanly knight-errant whose quest is to ameliorate the grubby urbanity of the modern world. Everything about him is tinged with nostalgia, including his regular retreat into the mythical worlds of the past typified by the poetry of A. E. Housman and the operas of Wagner. He symbolizes a cultured disillusionment with the vulgarity of the present and a longing for an imagined national past.

The Janus-faced-ness of Morse—being one character in the earlier novels and another in the television adaptations and the later novels—does not detract from his legend. For while it is certainly the case that Dexter's novels were thoroughly sanitized for television in a way that echoed with the English tradition of detective fiction most explicitly articulated by Agatha Christie, many of the central elements of the TV series, such as the driven, selfish, eccentric detective at odds with the world around him, were there all along. What the Morse films do, however, is remove the sociopolitical specificity of the original stories, instead focusing on the apparently more timeless questions of love, hate, jealousy, revenge, and secrecy within an idealized English-heritage setting. This combination maximized their national and international appeal.

Inspector Morse has thus taken his place as one of the most charismatic and beloved detective figures in the history of English detective fiction. He is a comforting presence in a televisual Oxford that itself embodies many of the idealized qualities of English pastoral, a haven for a mythical national identity light years from the gritty, multicultural reality of the present. Morse soothes the audience's anxieties by reassuring them not just that crimes will be solved but also that no matter how frightening modernity might become, there will always be the sanctuary of culture: the books, music, architecture, and ideas that fend off the relentless push of the contemporary world.

Selected Bibliography

Last Bus to Woodstock (1975)
Last Seen Wearing (1976)
The Silent World of Nicholas Quinn (1977)
Service of All the Dead (1979)
The Dead of Jericho (1981)
The Riddle of the Third Mile (1983)
The Secret of Annexe 3 (1986)
The Wench Is Dead (1989)
The Jewel That Was Ours (1991)
The Way through the Woods (1992)
The Daughters of Cain (1994)
Death Is Now My Neighbour (1996)
The Remorseful Day (1999)

—Neil McCaw

N

INSPECTOR GRAZIA NEGRO

Carlo Lucarelli
(1960–)

Grazia Negro is arguably the most successful of the few fictional female detectives in Italian crime fiction. Female protagonists are rare in a genre that in Italy (and elsewhere) is still dominated by male characters—typically narcissistic, immature men prey to midlife crises. The first Italian female sleuth appeared as far back as 1909, the protagonist of mystery writer Carolina Invernizio's *Nina, la poliziotta dilettante* (Nina, the amateur detective). However, it was only in the late 1980s that a number of female crime writers emerged in Italy and the first successful fictional female detectives were born. Among the most important authors in this tradition are Laura Grimaldi (1928–2012); Fiorella Cagnoni (1947–), who created Alice Carta, an amateur lesbian detective; Nicoletta Vallorani (1959–); and Grazia Verasani (1964–), author of the successful and long-lived Giorgia Cantini hard-boiled series. These female writers have used crime narratives as a vehicle to investigate sensitive issues in contemporary Italian society, such as discrimination and violence against women, following a trend initiated by American feminist crime writers of the 1980s and 1990s. The protagonists of their books are private investigators or amateur detectives who often fight against authority, the police included, and a patriarchal society.

Within this group of female sleuths, Grazia Negro stands out for many reasons. First of all her creator is a male writer, Carlo Lucarelli, a successful crime novelist and creative journalist. Second, she is a police inspector, and therefore she works for the state and not against it. Third, her investigations are not confined to the private sphere but involve the hunt for psychopaths and serial killers, always men who pursue both male and female victims. Finally, while in Italy the crime genre is still dominated by stories of psychological investigation, Grazia Negro and her team rely on forensic science and technology to solve crimes.

Writer Carlo Lucarelli attributes his decision to choose a woman as the protagonist for his stories to his work as a police reporter: "I wanted to describe reality, and in real life there are now a lot of women in the police force."[1] Lucarelli also wanted to create an Italian version of Thomas Harris's *Silence of the Lambs* (1988). Based on a real woman, a friend of Lucarelli's brother and a trumpet player, with whom the fictional police detective shares her name, physical appearance, and personal history, Grazia Negro occupies more and more "space" throughout Lucarelli's series. For example, in *Lupo mannaro* (The werewolf; 1994) she is a secondary character, a twenty-two-year-old recruit who works as an assistant for Inspector Romeo. She is very efficient but insecure. She often has an "anxious look," and she is "careful and trustful."[2] She is in love with her boss, who is hospitalized for a degenerative disease at the end of the novel. In *Almost Blue* (turned in 2000 into a movie directed by Alex Infascelli), she is promoted to inspector and joins a task force for the analysis of violent crimes (UACS) under the leadership of psychiatrist Vittorio Poletti. She is now more assertive, and her new boss trusts her "fierce, animal instincts."[3] However, he also patronizes her, and her subordinates resent being managed by a woman. But by the end of the novel she has gained her colleagues' respect and is able to tell her boss, "Don't call me sweetheart anymore. It bugs the hell out of me."[4] The last two adventures also see Negro in charge of difficult and dangerous investigations, and she is invariably pivotal in solving these cases.

Negro comes from the south of Italy and, in a tradition made famous by crime writer Leonardo Sciascia (1921–1989), has difficulty in understanding the city where she works—Bologna, a sprawling modern metropolis. Sciascia used this feeling of estrangement in *The Day of the Owl* (1984), in which Captain Bellodi, coming from the northern region of Emilia-Romagna but fighting the Mafia in Sicily, finds it hard to understand local culture and the code of silence in particular. Since then the topic of the northern and southern culture clash has been used many times in Italian crime fiction. Negro, however, is not only a "foreigner" but also a woman pursuing a career dominated by men. In this sense the Negro police procedural series shares with other novels featuring female detectives an interest in the status of women in Italy.

If Negro at first fails to be the detective-flâneur who confidently navigates her urban space, she soon learns how to make sense of Bologna thanks to her rationality and the power of technology. Lucarelli's writing style, very visual and characterized by an almost manic attention to detail, focuses considerable attention on technology: the use of monitors, modems, and scanners, searches of chat lines, and psychological offender profiles. The continuous references to technological devices seem to deliver a message: the modern metropolis may be unknowable, urban sprawl may have made interpreting and controlling life difficult, but technological devices can help to make sense of this new environment. It is thus thanks to technology, and in spite of being a woman, petite, and young, that Negro manages to conquer a space in the male-centric tradition of Italian crime fiction.

Selected Bibliography

Lupo mannaro (The werewolf; 1994)
Almost Blue (1997 [2001])
Almost Blue (film, 2000)
Day after Day (2000 [2004])
Acqua in bocca (Take it for yourself; 2010) with Andrea Camilleri
Il sogno di volare (The dream of flying; 2013)

—Barbara Pezzotti

THURSDAY NEXT

Jasper Fforde
(1961–)

A relative newcomer to fictional law enforcement, with her first print appearance in 2001, Thursday Next is a literary detective in the most literal sense. In an alternate version of England, she is a leading light in SO-27, the special police force that fights literature-related crime. SO-27 not only undertakes detective work with which Scotland Yard might be familiar, such as identifying copyright violations and counterfeit books, but also combats felonies that arise from the extreme mania for the written word that grips almost everyone in this reality. Next's remit in SO-27 includes "overtly free thespian interpretations" of Shakespeare's plays (which are banned by law) and violent political factionalism based around the controversy over their authorship.[5] And these are only the Shakespeare-related crimes!

However, the greatest entertainment to be gleaned from Jasper Fforde's rollicking recounting of Next's career comes from her second detective job. Through her supernatural ability to enter the very fabric of fiction, Next has discovered that the worlds of literature are as real as our own is, and arguably more so. In *Lost in a Good Book* (2002) she joins Jurisfiction, the BookWorld's equivalent of SO-27. Jurisfiction is a police force with a difference. As Next relates, "Our mandate . . . was to keep fictional narrative as stable as possible. As long as it was how the author intended, murderers walked free and tyrants stayed in power."[6] Ably assisted by master detectives including Miss Havisham and the Cheshire Cat, Next deals with assaults upon fiction's integrity including the illegal trade in bootleg plot devices and attempts to assassinate Heathcliff for his treatment of Catherine in *Wuthering Heights*. Fforde even amusingly reveals that many of the characteristics of the literature we know and love are actually caused by criminal activity in BookWorld, such as thieves pilfering the punctuation from *Ulysses*' final chapter or the humor from Thomas Hardy's novels.

Despite the odd procedural mistake, a self-admitted inability to grasp the complexities of human emotion, and the painkiller addiction she has developed in recent years, Next has proved an incredibly capable detective. The fighting skills she gained in her military service (and in the ultraviolent World Croquet League) have saved her skin on many occasions. She is also intellectually brilliant. Next is so knowledgeable about literature that she knows every reference to hedgehogs in Shakespeare's plays, and her affinity with the workings of narrative means that she can identify patterns of evidence and motive that BookWorld citizens, confined to their individual character roles, and unable or unwilling to look beyond them, cannot.

These abilities have enabled Next to solve numerous crimes in RealWorld and BookWorld alike, some of which threatened their very existence. In the former, she has foiled master criminal Acheron Hades's attempts to hold the manuscripts of *Martin Chuzzlewit* and *Jane Eyre* to ransom, and stopped the sinister Goliath

Corporation from physically destroying future time to sell their goods to a compliant population interested only in the present (and thus unable to concentrate on the written word). In the latter, she has prevented a plot to establish totalitarian control of the BookWorld and undone the unauthorized merging of *Hamlet* and *The Merry Wives of Windsor* by locating a Shakespeare clone in the RealWorld and having him reproduce the original manuscripts of both. Most thrillingly, she has defeated nefarious attempts to use the BookWorld to control the RealWorld, and vice versa. She exposed Goliath's plans to win the still-ongoing Crimean War by spiriting deadly plasma rifle technology from fiction into reality, and their later project to destroy the planet, transport its population from reality into fiction, and establish a new society in which the corporation rules supreme. In arguably her greatest triumph, during *Lost in a Good Book* (2002) Next halted the attempts of the politician Yorrick Kaine, a crazed escapee from vanity publishing, to filch the lost Shakespeare play *Cardenio* from the BookWorld, release it into the public domain, and thus earn enough popularity to become dictator of England. Thinking ingeniously on her feet, Next coaxes Kaine into "revealing his fictional roots by his inability to follow undedicated dialogue."[7] This case provides a telling example of how her success as a detective relies not only on her knowledge of the BookWorld's literature and how the RealWorld receives it but also on her ability to navigate the similarities and differences between realms.

Next's fans are legion in the BookWorld and the RealWorld in which she works and also in our reality, what we might call the RealRealWorld. Every year, admirers of Fforde's books gather for the Fforde Fiesta convention, primarily to celebrate his most beloved character's exploits. And why would they not? After all, not only is Next a great literary detective, but also her tireless work in protecting the BookWorld from harm, tyranny, and even outright destruction makes her the most important literary detective of all. Although she appeared in print long after Sherlock Holmes, Miss Marple, and Hercule Poirot, these characters would not exist in their current form without her efforts. In fact, when we consider that the BookWorld she protects includes nonfiction as well as fiction, it becomes apparent that even the book you are reading now owes its existence to her. So, on behalf of myself and my fellow writers, many thanks, Thursday Next.

Selected Bibliography

The Eyre Affair (2001)
Lost in a Good Book (2002)
The Well of Lost Plots (2003)
Something Rotten (2004)
First among Sequels (2007)
One of Our Thursdays Is Missing (2011)
The Woman Who Died a Lot (2012)

—George Twigg

P

DON ISIDRO PARODI

Honorio Bustos Domecq
Jorge Luis Borges (1899–1986) and Adolfo Bioy Casares (1914–1999)

Honorio Bustos Domecq's investigator Isidro Parodi made his first appearance in 1942, in a story collection entitled *Seis problemas para don Isidro Parodi* (translated by Norman Thomas Di Giovanni as *Six Problems for Don Isidro Parodi*, 1981). Parodi's first adventures were followed by *Crónicas de Bustos Domecq*, which appeared in 1967 (*Chronicles of Bustos Domecq*, 1976, also translated by Di Giovanni). Although Borges and Bioy Casares frequently collaborated, Bustos Domecq was to become their most famous nom de plume, which they chose by combining the surnames of their highborn great-grandparents: Bustos and Domecq respectively.[1]

The law-abiding Don Isidro Parodi is a hairdresser by trade who is wrongly imprisoned. Cracking his cases while confined to the legendary cell 273, and thus without visiting the crime scene, he epitomizes the armchair detective. He first establishes himself as a sharp sleuth after helping a journalist clear his name; after this, he begins to take on referred clients, but only if he deems the challenge worthy of his prowess. While proving his own innocence would present no obstacle for a detective of his caliber, the conviction of the actual perpetrator would be against the system's interests. Holy Hoof, the thug who committed the crime, and the only witness, delivers his gang's votes to the establishment candidate: Parodi is a scapegoat, while Hoof walks free. Additionally, Parodi was incarcerated by a police clerk who owes him money. By abusing the system for his own benefit, this petty administrator embodies the unpalatable truth behind the official Peronist dogma.[2] Thus, Parodi's "armchairness" could be read as an ideological as well as physical condition.

The Bustos Domecq stories feature many covertly satirical references to contemporary Argentine culture. In "The Nights of Goliardki," for instance, Gervasio Montenegro, an actor accused of theft and murder, visits Parodi for help. Montenegro is described as a tall, distinguished man with a dyed moustache. His use of circumlocutions and affected language (overusing, and sometimes misusing, French and Latin phrases) is humorous, as the register is clearly inappropriate for the situation. Montenegro comments in passing that he shares Parodi's dislike for the radio; a theatre actor, he finds the microphone a cold instrument for communicating with his audience. This can be read as an allusion to Eva Duarte,

Perón's second wife. Her rise from humble origins to model and B-movie and radio actress in the capital, and soon to first lady and spiritual leader of the nation, was for her followers a fairy tale come true.[3] Like many of Parodi's clients, Montenegro represents the rising class of the nouveau riche, whose unfamiliarity with appropriate etiquette hints that their wealth is not hereditary. For example, to celebrate a stroke of luck at a card game Montenegro drinks a particular brand of "champagne," El Gaitero (The piper), which is actually an inexpensive local brand of cider. Furthermore, he orders only half a bottle, suggesting he is parsimonious, although keen to boast about his supposedly expensive tastes.

While crime fiction was at the heart of Argentine literary production throughout the 1900s, the 1940s constitute a particularly important decade for the development of the genre. Considered part of "a cultural operation" promoted by literati such as Borges and Bioy Casares, detective fiction, predominantly of the type associated with Golden Age crime writing, was one of the main genres cultivated by this generation of writers.[4] This is epitomized by the *Séptimo Círculo* crime fiction collection. Published by Emecé, and endorsed by Victoria Ocampo through her literary magazine *Sur*, the *Séptimo Círculo* transformed the genre in terms of both popularity and prestige. It released its first title in 1945 (Nicholas Blake's *Beast Must Die* [1938] translated by Juan R. Wilcock as *La bestia debe morir*) and issued 366 novels in total, the last in 1983. As editor-creators, Borges and Bioy Casares's stamp was most evident in the first 121 issues in which they vigorously supported and promoted foreign authors (Borges, in particular, was closely associated with Anglo-Saxon literary culture). Parodi's adventures reflect this internationalism; an educated reader could appreciate their homage to authors such as G. K. Chesterton. After the *Séptimo Círculo*, the detective novel was no longer seen as "news stand literature," and while not published in this collection, the figure of Parodi was also central to this transformation.

Arguably, the most enduring feature of the Parodi series was not only its contribution to the elevation of the genre but also its exploitation of detective narratives as a form of pastiche, allowing for humor and satire. As the name of Borges and Bioy Casares's most famous sleuth suggests, cultural references are parodied, mocked, and ridiculed in his stories. It is precisely here that the stories' complicity with their readership lies: while Parodi solves the mystery, the reader decodes and deciphers the cultural references.

Selected Bibliography

Seis problemas para don Isidro Parodi (1942); *Six Problems for Don Isidro Parodi* (1981)
Crónicas de Bustos Domecq (1967); *Chronicles of Bustos Domecq* (1976)

—Carolina Miranda

JOSEPH PETERS

Mary Elizabeth Braddon
(1835–1915)

The Trail of the Serpent was Mary Elizabeth Braddon's first novel, and with it she created what was arguably an entirely new genre: the detective novel. It first appeared in serial form in Beverley, East Yorkshire, as *Three Times Dead; or, The Secret of the Heath* in 1860, but it was republished in London with much greater success as *The Trail of the Serpent* in 1861 by Braddon's publisher and future husband, John Maxwell. This success lies firmly at the door of Joseph Peters, the police detective with a difference. In many ways, Peters is an extraordinary detective: he is mute; communicates using sign language; is adept at disguise; and has an adopted son whom he brings up in the detective line. Taken together, these traits make Peters one of the most intriguing, challenging, and unique detectives of the genre.

While the detective novel may have begun with Braddon, Peters draws upon literary and true-life forerunners, such as the fictionalized memoirs of the French police chief Eugène Vidocq, and the British Bow Street Runners. Both are referenced within the novel. The Bow Street Runners were established by Henry Fielding in 1749 and are considered the first British professional police force. In the 1840s, the detective branch of London's Metropolitan Police grew out of this service. Based in Scotland Yard, these police officers were plain-clothed, permanent detectives, who were called upon when local police could not solve a case.

Peters, while not a Scotland Yard officer, is a plain-clothed, working-class policeman who retires from the force halfway through *The Trail of the Serpent* in order to continue investigating the case of a wrongly accused murderer. In doing so, Peters transforms from an outsider into one of the novel's central characters, thus taking a more significant place within the narrative than his predecessor, Charles Dickens's Inspector Bucket in *Bleak House* (1853), or his successor, Wilkie Collins's Sergeant Cuff in *The Moonstone* (1868). The fact that *The Trail of the Serpent* is a "howdunit," rather than a "whodunit," makes it distinct from the Newgate Novel of the 1820–1840s, because, as the updated title indicates, it prioritizes both the villain as the central figure (serpent) and detection as a process (trail). In the end, Peters enlists the help of Liverpool's police force to capture the criminal and resolve the narrative—though he has his own unique skill set that leads him to decide "on a strange step, and arrest . . . the dead."[5]

Braddon's depiction of Peters and his muteness is one of the most positive portrayals of a disabled character in Victorian writing, especially as it is a vital aspect of his success: people misunderstand his disability and therefore underestimate him, a fact he uses to his advantage. For instance, people assume that as well as being mute, Peters is also deaf, so they talk freely amongst themselves in his presence, thereby unknowingly divulging their bloodiest secrets. Furthermore, Peters's use of sign language—the "dirty alphabet"—is a key skill.[6] Outside his colleagues and close friends, no one can understand him, and so he is free to communicate across public spaces without revealing his plans. In the novel's climax, for example, Peters and another policeman hide in a crowded dockyard to apprehend the villain; the policeman's communication is disguised as rearranging his cravat.

This is not the only detective technique Peters draws upon. Before Sherlock Holmes perfected the practice, Peters also adopted disguises to further his investigation. In the dockyard scene, Peters goes incognito as an Irish laborer, "keeping quite aloof from the rest of his kind," and thus hiding himself in plain sight.[7] Peters also preempts the detective convention of junior assistance through his adoption of a young boy whom he saves from drowning in the local river. Slosh (named after said river) is trained in the detective arts from infancy, giving Peters a highly skilled and loyal sidekick who acts as another pair of eyes and ears, as well as access to areas he cannot go himself—playing a similar role to Holmes's Baker Street Irregulars. Peters's final detective skill is his ability to analyze physical evidence in an almost forensic fashion; he "reads," for instance, a supposed suicide scene on a heath, deducing that it is in fact a murder because the bottle of poison is not clasped in the deceased's hands but is off to one side. These cunning tropes have been staples of the genre ever since, demonstrating not only Peters's effective detective skills but also Braddon's many contributions to the genre.

Overall, the crimes Peters solves in his only appearance are two murders, a house robbery, identity theft, forgery, and its associated embezzlement, and all within a wider narrative that contains another (attempted) murder, bigamy, fraud, and illegitimacy. He also helps the wrongfully condemned suspect break out of the mental asylum he was confined in. This multiple criminal narrative, with the detective Joseph Peters at its center, opened the door for other fictional literary detectives—and the detective novel as a genre. Both Agatha Christie and Dorothy L. Sayers reference Braddon in their own work, demonstrating her key influence on the Golden Age of detective fiction and beyond.[8] Braddon's novel is back in print after almost a century, in an edition with an introduction by Sarah Waters, bringing long-overdue attention to one of the earliest and most fascinatingly entertaining examples of the literary detective and shedding light on the roots of crime fiction as a genre.

Selected Bibliography

The Trail of the Serpent (1861)
Lady Audley's Secret (1862)
Rough Justice (1898)
His Darling Sin (1899)

—Janine Hatter

HERCULE POIROT

Agatha Christie
(1890–1976)

Hercule Poirot has been one of the most phenomenally successful creations in detective fiction, appearing in thirty-three novels and sixty-five short stories spanning fifty-five years. His appearance in Christie's "whodunits" first started during—and indeed largely helped to create—the Golden Age mystery form, with its closed circle of known suspects in an isolated setting, a country house party, a girl's school, or a stranded train such as the Orient Express. The narrative gives all the necessary clues, alongside a number of red herrings, and teases the reader to guess the murderer before Poirot reveals them at the close. Poirot's "death," in *Curtain*, brought an actual obituary on the front page of the *New York Times* in 1975, while the Belgian town of Ellezelles claims to hold his birth certificate. Perhaps after writing him for forty years, Christie was entitled to exclaim, "Why did I ever invent this detestable bombastic tiresome little creature? . . . Eternally straightening things, eternally boasting, eternally twirling his moustaches and tilting his egg-shaped head," but his publishing success and enormous fandom have helped to keep Christie on the "dead celebrity rich list" with an estimated £40 million amassed since her death in 1976.[9]

Poirot appeared in Christie's first novel, *The Mysterious Affair at Styles*, in 1920 alongside an ineffectual sidekick, Captain Hastings. Where Hastings is a tall, masculine English war hero, Poirot is small, round, fussily concerned about his attire and magnificently curled moustaches, outrageously conceited about his own prowess, and overtly foreign, at least when it serves his purpose: "Everyone tells everything to me sooner or later. I'm only a foreigner, you see, so it does not matter. It is easier because I am a foreigner."[10] These aberrations from traditional English masculinity hide the exceptional brain, the famous "little grey cells," which outperform every one. An ex-detective from Belgium, Poirot's concern for small, often domestic, clues baffles Hastings and the reader alike but proves crucial in indicating changes in normal routines that indicate stress points for the suspects. From paper spills to light a fire to the position of a dog's ball, the very things that have the reader wondering why Poirot has become so obsessed are exactly the subtle clues that will indicate how the murder was committed.

Increasingly, however, alongside the overlooked clues too unimportant to worry the plodding police, Poirot comes to rely on his conception of character, a form of psychological reading of the suspects, to arrive at his conclusions. When, in *Cards on the Table* (1936), Mrs. Lorrimer tries to shield the murderer by claiming she did it, he rejects her smoke screen with the statement, "Either the killing of Shaitana was planned beforehand—*or you did not kill him at all*," because he is convinced that an impulsive murder is not in her psychological makeup.[11] It is not that he does not believe that she is capable of murder, because Poirot, like his creator Agatha Christie, believes that every single person is capable of murder given the appropriate circumstances. Indeed, in *Curtain*, Poirot's last case (published in the seventies but written during the London Blitz, in case she was hit by a bomb), both Hastings and Poirot prove capable themselves. The impossibility of trusting even the nearest and dearest adds to the frisson of anxiety and duplicity surrounding those within the closed circle of Christie's "whodunits."

After Hastings marries a character from *Murder on the Links* (1923) and debunks to Argentina to raise cattle and a family, Poirot is accompanied by other supporting characters, often the fictional crime writer Ariadne Oliver in the later novels, but perhaps most notably in *The Murder of Roger Ackroyd* (1926) by the doctor who provides the narrative voice and subtly omits to mention his own culpability. This denouement created a critical furor for being too tricky and not "fair play," making Christie internationally famous in 1926. Even Poirot's peripatetic love interest, the Countess Rosstikoff, is not blameless; she is in fact a successful jewel thief. Christie has enormous fun allying the small fussy dandy to the flamboyant, glamorous, and large faux countess. Though not always trustworthy, she is never a murderer, because to kill is in Poirot's eyes always evil—he "disapproves" of murder. For the majority of the villains, Poirot knows that their apprehension will lead to the gallows, but a number of culprits are allowed to take their own lives to escape public opprobrium, and in one famous case, *Murder on the Orient Express,* Poirot deems all the murderers to have suffered sufficiently to allow them to go free. Within the fictional world, justice must always be served, but occasionally that does not include police detention.

Poirot's characteristics can span the stern to the twinkling eyed. He is often sympathetically avuncular toward innocent suspects but resolute in exposing the murderer. His grasp of the truth is portrayed through a "strange cat-like gleam in his eyes."[12] When this appears, toward the end of the novel, the detective has apprehended the truth and now has only to prove it—which of course he does, in all ninety-eight of the texts that he appears in. His overbearing pride in his own abilities is genuinely earned, for all its un-English boastfulness.

Selected Bibliography

The Mysterious Affair at Styles (1920)
The Murder of Roger Ackroyd (1926)
Murder on the Orient Express (1934)
Appointment with Death (1937)
Dumb Witness (1937)
The Hollow (1946)

—Merja Makinen

ELLERY QUEEN

Ellery Queen
Manfred Bennington Lee (1905–1971) and Frederic Dannay (1905–1982)

Ellery Queen, a New York mystery writer and amateur detective created by cousins Manfred Bennington Lee and Frederic Dannay under the pseudonym Ellery Queen, made his debut, along with his father Inspector Richard Queen, in 1929 in *The Roman Hat Mystery*. By 1971 Ellery had appeared in more than thirty novels, as well as a huge variety of novellas, short stories, and radio plays. From the early 1940s onward, his name, like that of Sherlock Holmes before him, has been in common parlance a virtual synonym for a fictional detective.

Apart from being one of the most famous literary sleuths of the twentieth century, Queen is undoubtedly one of the most complex and multifaceted characters of the so-called Golden Age of crime fiction. Unlike the many detectives who remained flat and stereotypical throughout their literary careers, his character profoundly evolved over the decades. Physically and psychologically modeled on S. S. Van Dine's Philo Vance, Queen was initially described as a tall, slender, snobbish Harvard graduate, dressed in tweeds and wearing pince-nez, and quick with a scholarly quotation. In the first nine novels, published between 1929 and 1936, Dannay and Lee presented Queen as a young bibliophile interested in abstract problems rather than people, who solves crimes exclusively because he finds them intellectually stimulating. In this period, Queen is a thinking machine capable of fairly and rationally explaining some of the most convoluted puzzles in the history of the genre, ranging from the supremely bizarre locked-room problem underlying *The Chinese Orange Mystery* (1934) to the disappearance of an entire house in the novella "The Lamp of God" (1935). While Philo Vance's solutions largely depend on intricate psychological analyses of the suspects, few detectives can match the early Ellery Queen's ability to make perfectly logical deductions from empirical evidence.

From the late 1930s, Dannay and Lee began to redefine the detective as a less all-knowing and more human character. His criminal cases are blended with human-interest elements and gradually lose their intrinsic bizarreness. The locations also change, with New York progressively giving way to Hollywood (*The Four of Hearts*, 1938); Wrightsville, a fictional but powerful and fairly realistic microcosm of the United States (*Calamity Town*, 1942); and the isolated fascist domain in which *The*

King Is Dead (1952) was set. Throughout the 1940s, at the peak of his celebrity, Queen progressively gave up his show-off habits, becoming more practical and more emotionally involved in his cases. Indeed, he is often torn by them. As a consequence, his methods of investigation significantly change. He becomes less concerned with physical clues, conversely paying more attention to psychological ones, and begins to apply his broad knowledge of psychology and religion. His detection comes to rely on intuition rather than deduction, as can be seen in novels such as *The Door Between* (1937) and *The Scarlet Letters* (1953).

Interestingly, from the late 1940s Queen began to become a much more fallible character, less confident in his capacity to solve mysteries. In *Ten Days' Wonder* (1948), except for a purely intellectual victory that comes too late, he was bested and outsmarted by his adversary, and holds himself responsible for causing at least two deaths. At the beginning of his next novel, *Cat of Many Tails* (1949), Queen's recent failure causes him to renounce his habit of intervening in the lives of others: "I don't want to hear about the case . . . just let me be . . . I've given all that up. I'm not interested any longer." As the narrator remarks, in the previous case "he had found himself betrayed by his own logic."[1] Nonetheless, he decides to take the case, only to be once again shattered by its solution and the fact that his failure to comprehend it has cost lives. This fallibility was reiterated and even reinforced in 1960s novels such as *And on the Eighth Day* (1964), in which Ellery solves the crime but, once again, fails to avert its dreadful consequences: "It's too much . . . too much, too much, too much; it's more than reason can bear. . . . Too much, an infinite complexity beyond the grasp of a man. Acknowledge. Acknowledge and depart."[2] The later novels feature a detective increasingly disillusioned with his life and his career, as we can note in *The Fourth Side of the Triangle* (1965), where Queen, incapacitated and offstage for most of the book due to a skiing accident, is humiliated and surprised by the solution of the case.

In conclusion, like the novels in which he appeared, the character of Ellery Queen, both in terms of his methods and his personality, evolved dramatically over time. He thus embodies some of the changes that both the crime novel and American society underwent over a span of forty years, moving from a stable, even arrogant, self-confidence to a less secure and more vulnerable identity. We cannot but agree with the critic Anthony Boucher when he affirms that "Ellery Queen *is* the American detective story."[3]

Selected Bibliography

The Roman Hat Mystery (1929)
The Chinese Orange Mystery (1934)
"The Lamp of God" (1935)
The Door Between (1937)
The Four of Hearts (1938)
Calamity Town (1942)
Ten Days' Wonder (1948)
Cat of Many Tails (1949)
And on the Eighth Day (1964)
The Fourth Side of the Triangle (1965)

—Stefano Serafini

DANIEL QUINN

Paul Auster
(1947–)

Daniel Quinn is a writer of crime fiction who publishes stories about his detective hero, Max Work, under the Poesque pseudonym of William Wilson. At the beginning of Paul Auster's *City of Glass* (1985), the first installment of *The New York Trilogy* (1987), Quinn is mistaken for a detective named Paul Auster and employed by a mysterious, dyslexic youth, Peter Stillman, to keep a watchful eye on his father, also named Peter Stillman, who has recently been released from jail and ostensibly plans to kill his son. From this tangled but ultimately conventional situation, the story develops into a postmodern puzzle, where Quinn's detection becomes a quest for identity, if not for the meaning of reality itself. Soon he gets lost in a maze of clues and hypotheses that multiply exponentially, and in the end he is forced to acknowledge that "nothing was real, except chance."[4]

City of Glass is an "anti-detective story," a literary subgenre that William Spanos considers "the paradigmatic archetype of the postmodern literary imagination," whose purpose is "to evoke the impulse to 'detect' . . . in order to violently frustrate this impulse by refusing to solve the crime."[5] Talking about Italo Calvino's *If on a Winter's Night a Traveler* (1979)—a probable inspiration for Auster's story, along with works by Samuel Beckett, Edgar Allan Poe, Nathaniel Hawthorne, and Miguel de Cervantes—Stefano Tani described it as a "metafictional anti-detective novel" where "the writer is no longer an 'absent' third-person narrator but part of his text, which he enters and leaves continuously."[6] The same is true of *City of Glass*: when Quinn is stuck in his detection and cannot possibly find a solution to the case, he goes to Auster (his author?), assuming he is a real detective, and asks for clues, only to find out that Auster is a writer too and cannot help him. The postmodernist author can no longer play the role of the detective—a surrogate reader who interprets ambiguous or misleading signs and "solves" the reality of a text by composing the events and clarifying them for the reader; on the contrary, the author is as lost as his own characters.

While following Stillman through the streets of New York, Quinn records the man's seemingly random itinerary in a red notebook. In order to draw a map of Stillman's movements, the writer-become-detective must become writer again; since "walking and writing were not easily compatible activities," Quinn must develop a technique that allows him to simultaneously write and walk.[7] However, when he later studies his detailed notes and maps, they do not make any apparent sense. He shapes the maps in the form of words, but conventional language, the writer's tool, is no longer able to represent the hieroglyphic reality of the streets. The metropolis, which is the true protagonist of Auster's story, communicates through signs that the writer/detective cannot interpret.

Having taken upon himself the role of detective, Quinn is forced to find a solution, to provide a *telos*, or goal, for his narration in order to solve the case, even though he lacks enough proof to formulate a sensible hypothesis, and the evidence he does have points to inconsistent hypotheses. Reality is not structured as in crime fiction, where every word is significant as a clue to a solution; on the contrary, the city is made of fragile and reflective glass, more akin to the ontologically hesitant text of a postmodernist fiction, where each fragment reflects multiple, contradictory meanings: "Was he scribbling nonsense?" Quinn asks himself, "or was he trying to find something? Either response, he realized, was unacceptable" because "he continued to disbelieve the arbitrariness of Stillman's actions. He wanted there to be a sense to them, no matter how obscure. This, in itself, was unacceptable."[8]

Quinn's inability to accept the nonsense and embrace the doubt and the inherent mystery of reality—his resolve to find a univocal and final meaning, however arbitrary—will condemn him to failure; Stillman will prove unreadable as well as unreachable, his movements and motives, transparent yet inaccessible. In the end, Quinn himself literally disappears from the story, until Auster ultimately finds him in the pages of the red notebook; he gives the notebook to a friend, who abruptly appears in the last page of *City of Glass*, revealing himself as the narrator of the whole story. Quinn is briefly mentioned again in *The Locked Room*, the third part of the trilogy, as a detective who wanted to help but who mysteriously disappeared; at the end of the book, the narrator states, "These three stories are finally the same story, but each one represents a different stage in my awareness of what it is about."[9]

In 1994, Paul Karasik and David Mazzucchelli adapted *City of Glass* into a critically acclaimed, experimental graphic novel, published in a discontinued series called *Neon Lit*, which in the idea of the coeditor Art Spiegelman (who also illustrated the pulp-magazine-style cover of a 2006 reissue of *The New York Trilogy*) would present comic adaptations of urban noir-inflected literature. By linking words with images, as well as by pushing narrative strategies typical of comic books to their limits (varied word balloons, innovative paneling, different drawing and lettering styles, a particular distribution of gutter spaces, and a creative arrangement of page layout), Karasik and Mazzucchelli remediated not only Auster's story but also its reflections on the limits of language and detection, the unreliability of the author and the investigator, the fundamental instability of meaning, and the linguistic ambiguities of contemporary life.

Selected Bibliography

Squeeze Play (1982; as Paul Benjamin)
The New York Trilogy (1987)
Leviathan (1992)
Invisible (2009)

—Paolo Simonetti

QUIRKE

Benjamin Black (John Banville)
(1945–)

Quirke, the protagonist of seven crime fiction novels published by Irish novelist John Banville under the pen name Benjamin Black, is a middle-aged Irish pathologist. He is a surly yet charismatic man who lives in 1950s Dublin, where he is in charge of the morgue at the Holy Family Hospital. Quirke, whose first name we never learn, is a well dressed but shambolic figure, a big man with improbably tiny feet and a mane of silver hair. He experiences life with the passionate intensity of a child, having failed to acquire an adult's thicker skin. He smokes too much and drinks to excess, both to remember and to forget. The Dublin he inhabits is a boozy, dank, shabby city dominated by a duplicitous Catholic hierarchy and a few powerful but secretive cliques. In fact, Black's novels are as much a portrait of Dublin in the 1950s, ruled over by what he has described as the "iron ideology" of Irish Catholicism, as they are murder mysteries with a crime to be solved and a culprit to be caught.[10]

Quirke's career as a reluctant amateur detective commences in *Christine Falls* (2006) when a young woman's corpse mysteriously disappears from his morgue. In the course of his quest to learn the fate of the woman, finally identified as Christine Falls, Quirke discovers an elaborate network of intrigue and deceit springing from the Catholic Church's stranglehold on Irish society. Christine died in childbirth; the father of her child was Judge Griffin, Quirke's revered adoptive father, and her death was covered up while the baby was smuggled to America. Quirke eventually links the crime to the Knights of Saint Patrick, an exclusive Catholic group consisting of the highest echelons of Dublin society, which runs a profitable trade in illegitimate babies with the collusion of priests, politicians, and businessmen. As abortion was illegal in Ireland in the 1950s (and still is unless the life of the woman is in danger), young pregnant girls were ostracized and isolated, and often forced to spend their confinement in places like the Mother of Mercy Laundry. This institution, run by hard-hearted nuns, features in several Quirke mysteries. Despite its misleading name, the girls housed in the laundry are treated like slaves: overworked, unpaid, and despised. Once the babies are born, they are forcibly taken from their mothers and shipped to Boston for adoption by wealthy Americans.

If the criminal plots of Quirke's novels shed light on hidden involutions of Irish society, so too do Black's characters, who struggle to find meaning in an atmosphere poisoned by secrets and lies. The Quirke of *Christine Falls* is a widower racked by guilt because, instead of mourning his dead wife, he continues to obsess over the loss of Sarah, his first love, who married Quirke's adoptive brother Malachy twenty years ago, a union that apparently produced one child: Phoebe. By the novel's end Quirke learns that Phoebe is actually his daughter, that Judge Griffin is his own biological father, and that Malachy was aware of the knights' questionable activities and the judge implicated in them. *The Silver Swan* (2008) takes up Quirke's story two years on. Sarah has died and Judge Griffin, paralyzed by a stroke, is speechless and immobile. Quirke continues to smoke but has accepted that he has become an alcoholic and that he must give up whisky, his preferred tipple, or die prematurely. The easy intimacy he once enjoyed with Phoebe has gone, their relations irreversibly tarnished by his guilt and her recriminations. In *Elegy for April* (2010), Phoebe and Quirke achieve an uneasy reconciliation when she contacts the father she has angrily shunned to ask for his assistance in finding one of her best friends, April Latimer, a junior doctor at a local hospital who has suddenly disappeared. While unraveling the mystery, Quirke discovers yet more about the Irish Church and its abuses of power and privilege. He also finds that Latimer had had a black lover and uncovers a startling vein of racial hatred in the city.

Quirke is an introspective and endlessly curious man who feels a greater affinity for the dead than for the living. The dead lie passively on his examining table, yielding up their secrets without resistance, but the living prove more intractable, obstinately thwarting his attempts to understand them. Perhaps because of this Quirke dwells in the shadowy world of memory and reflection. His default mode is fruitless regret, but the forensic skills he has honed during his long years as a pathologist allow him to morph effortlessly into a sleuth dedicated to solving mysteries. Quirke's professional mission—to discover how people died, the physical causes that hastened their end—transforms into a quest to discover why they died and who might have wished them dead. He is assisted by an amicable working relationship with Inspector Hackett, an uncouth but astute policeman who steps in when Quirke needs to enlist the authority and resources of the police.

Quirke was portrayed by Gabriel Byrne in a three-part miniseries in 2014 based on the first three Quirke novels. The four subsequent novels represent variations on the themes that dominate the trilogy: Quirke remains a lonely man with a conflicted sense of identity; he broods over his position as the illegitimate son of Judge Griffin, whom he had adored as an adoptive father; he regrets his failed marriage but, even more, his failed romance with Sarah; and the crimes he investigates inevitably arise from the tight and iniquitous grip of the Catholic Church on Irish society.

Selected Bibliography

Christine Falls (2006)
The Silver Swan (2008)
Elegy for April (2010)
A Death in Summer (2011)
Vengeance (2012)
Holy Orders (2013)
Even the Dead (2016)

—Wendy Jones Nakanishi

R

MMA PRECIOUS RAMOTSWE

Alexander McCall Smith
(1948–)

Precious Ramotswe, the irrepressible proprietor of the No. 1 Ladies' Detective Agency, solves the crimes and personal dilemmas of her customers while drinking bush tea, advocating for "traditionally built ladies," and sharing wistful reminiscences about bygone Botswana, a time of cattle, close community, and manners. Mma Ramotswe defies the conventions of the male detective, instead manifesting a type of investigative skill rooted in social rituals and observation:

> Mma Ramotswe had a detective agency in Africa, at the foot of Kgale Hill. These were its assets: a tiny white van, two desks, two chairs, a telephone, and an old typewriter. Then there was a teapot, in which Mma Ramotswe—the only lady private detective in Botswana—brewed redbush tea. And three mugs—one for herself, one for her secretary, and one for the client. What else does a detective agency really need?[1]

Mma Ramotswe was able to start the agency after selling the cattle left to her by her father, Obed Ramotswe, whose life lessons form the foundation of Mma Ramotswe's investigative technique, which relies heavily on respecting others, having patience, and working hard. She credits Agatha Christie and Clovis Andersen, the fictitious author of Ramotswe's detective reference manual, *The Principles of Private Investigation*, as her sleuthing mentors. She is joined by her assistant, Mma Makutsi, whose 97 percent score on her final exams at the Botswana Secretarial College serves as her epithet, and the earnest Mr. J. L. B. Matekoni, who becomes Mma Ramotswe's fiancé at the end of the first book in the series. Mma Ramotswe's lengthy engagement with Mr. J. L. B. Matekoni is a feature in the subsequent books, and he finally becomes her husband in *The Full Cupboard of Life* (2003). Both Mma Makutsi and Mr. J. L. B. Matekoni participate in Mma Ramotswe's investigative endeavors, occasionally taking the lead themselves.

Ramotswe's form of detection focuses on unpacking the complex cultural and personal narratives of the people who seek her help. In each book, Mma Ramotswe solves several crimes and resolves multiple incidents rather than solving one major case. She is called upon to uncover embezzlement schemes, to identify fraudsters, and to find lost dogs (beneath her position but a necessary evil when money is needed) and missing children. Suspicion of spousal infidelity brings many clients to Mma Ramotswe's office in Gabarone. All of these mysteries focus on conflicts that disrupt society. While sometimes these disruptions are crimes, they might also be social issues or personal problems. For instance, the plot of *Morality for Beautiful Girls* (2001) revolves around Mr. J. L. B. Matekoni's depression. In *Tea Time for the Traditionally Built* (2009), Mma Ramotswe helps Mma Makutsi outsmart the predatory Violet Sephotho, who is intent upon stealing her love interest.

In Mma Ramotswe's investigations there is always time for thought, and it is during these periods of reflection that we see Mma Ramotswe as a character embodying the conflict of tradition and modernity. A modern, progressive woman, Mma Ramotswe wrestles to reconcile the new Africa with the past. She laments what she sees as the loss of manners and traditions that build a strong community, even as she celebrates her economic independence and the new opportunities afforded to women and girls.

Despite the fact that the historical and cultural background of the novels has led to a popular sense of their authenticity, Alexander McCall Smith has been accused of cultural appropriation. However, Smith's depiction of Mma Ramotswe, the country of Botswana, and the residents of the African continent has led many to appreciate his novels as love letters to the small African nation. The use of extensive description and historical detail, particularly concerning Botswana's search for a postindependence national identity, depicts the nation and its people as a postcolonization success story. However, the echoes of Miss Marple in Mma Ramotswe's character could be seen as an example of contemporary cultural colonialism.

Despite this controversy, the novels have achieved enormous popularity worldwide—including in Botswana. Besides the fifteen books in the series, there has been a critically acclaimed joint production by BBC and HBO filmed on location in Botswana, with Jill Scott playing the role of Mma Ramotswe. In addition to television success, McCall Smith has dramatized the series for a radio production that aired on BBC Radio 4 (2004–2015). In a relatively short time, Mma Ramotswe has become an internationally celebrated character as millions of readers, television viewers, and radio listeners have followed her progress from amateur sleuth to professional detective. Along the way, they have been treated to warm, humorous stories that capture the universal foibles and passions of human nature.

Selected Bibliography

The No. 1 Ladies' Detective Agency (1998)
Tears of the Giraffe (2000)
Morality for Beautiful Girls (2001)
The Kalahari Typing School for Men (2002)
The Full Cupboard of Life (2003)
In the Company of Cheerful Ladies (2004)
Blue Shoes and Happiness (2006)
The Good Husband of Zebra Drive (2007)
The Miracle at Speedy Motors (2008)

Tea Time for the Traditionally Built (2009)
The Double Comfort Safari Club (2010)
The Saturday Big Tent Wedding Party (2011)
The Limpopo Academy of Private Detection (2012)
The Minor Adjustment Beauty Salon (2013)
The Handsome Man's De Luxe Café (2014)
The Woman Who Walked in Sunshine (2015)

—Corinna McLeod

EZEKIEL "EASY" RAWLINS

Walter Mosley
(1952–)

The hard-boiled detective is a familiar figure. He (and classically it is almost always a he) is a lone wolf. He is drawn to women who are usually better described as femmes fatales than maidens in distress. An exemplar of street smarts, the private eye knows both who to speak to in urban underbellies and how to speak to them, employing a tough vernacular when necessary. The crimes he investigates reflect their mid-twentieth-century settings: police corruption, bootlegging, and gangsters abound.

However, hard-boiled detective fiction is historically skewed toward white protagonists, with few characters of color appearing in the genre, despite the fact that they are often set in ethnically and racially diverse areas such as Southern California. Walter Mosley's Ezekiel "Easy" Rawlins novels take on many of the traditional hard-boiled elements while simultaneously pressing at their constraints, primarily in terms of race. Easy Rawlins is a black, amateur detective turned private eye who works among the diverse communities of Los Angeles. He typically works for favors, rather than money, and influences the sociopolitical landscape in which he is embroiled as he solves his cases, thus aligning the personal with the political.

Unlike the majority of hard-boiled detectives, who tend toward flatness, Easy Rawlins is a fully rounded character; he is tough with his enemies but gentle with his children, steeped in the history of his times, and constantly evolving. Emphasizing his multifarious influences and range of reference, the self-taught detective explains, "André Malraux, Langston Hughes, Zora Neale Hurston and T. S. Eliot lived in me just as surely as backcountry lynchings and the scent of a lover's sex."[2] Indeed, the Easy Rawlins novels are as much about his development from a streetwise US veteran to a complicated man deeply embroiled in his historical purview as they are about his detective work.

Easy Rawlins's adventures span from the late 1930s in the retrospective novella *Gone Fishin'* (1997) to the late 1960s in *Charcoal Joe* (2016). Despite his numerous liaisons, from *A Little Yellow Dog* (1996) onward Rawlins finds himself increasingly bound to his on-again, off-again French Guianese–American lover Bonnie Shay. Rawlins and Shay's conflicts are as political as their contexts, which emphasize the impact of larger historical events, such as the 1965 Watts riots in *Little Scarlet* (2004) and the Vietnam War in *Blonde Faith* (2007), on individuals' lives. In addition to the usual jealousies and arguments, the lovers are torn between African and US nationalism and struggle with the boundaries of identity.

Further complicating his status as a hard-boiled detective, a type known for independence, Easy Rawlins works with and for his community and family, the two ever more entwined as the novels progress. Like most private eyes, Rawlins tends to do his detective work alone; however, he occasionally collaborates with others, including Saul Lynx, a white investigator, and his best friend, the notorious killer Raymond "Mouse" Alexander. He relies on the members of his social network for success and survival as much as they rely on him. He also literally invests in his community, owning a substantial amount of property, another trait atypical of the private-eye archetype. Moreover, Rawlins finds, saves, and adopts Jesus and Feather, orphans caught up in the crimes he solves in *Devil in a Blue Dress* (1990) and *White Butterfly* (1992). Similarly, he serves as surrogate father figure to local schoolchildren in his role as head custodian at Sojourner Truth Junior High School in several of the novels, a job that acts as another bridge between his familial and social bonds.

The lines between white and nonwhite Los Angeles are a constant topic for Rawlins, who is able to traverse the policed borders of his world more fluidly than most for the same reason that he is able to solve crimes that others cannot: he understands what people see and what they don't. Helping him to move from one world to the next is his facility for what might be described as slippage, as he moves between the large spheres of black and white Los Angeles, and within their respective microcosms, with a few deft costume changes and code switches. In addition, Rawlins's powers of observation are so legendary that the police department frequently, if reluctantly, calls upon him for aid. Mouse tells him, "You read a man's face like a little kid readin' Dick and Jane," while the sage Mama Jo puts it even more directly: "You look at the world and see what's there."[3]

Rawlins's insight also applies to himself. Although protean when necessary for his cases, he refuses to change to fit others' expectations, even sticking to the speech patterns of his Texas youth: "I never did like it when a man stopped using the language of his upbringing. If you were to talk like a white man you might forget who you were."[4] Just as he tries to see people and situations as more than their base components, he asks his audience to see *him*—contradictions, flaws, and all—rather than their projections of what they think he should be.

Although many believed *Blonde Faith* (2007) would be the end of the series, three more Easy Rawlins novels have appeared since its publication, bringing the total at the time of writing to fourteen. While the Easy Rawlins novels are set in the past, the social justice issues with which he contends, from the geopolitics of power to police brutality, rage on in the present, making Rawlins's role as a mediator more necessary than ever.

Selected Bibliography

Devil in a Blue Dress (1990)
Red Death (1991)

White Butterfly (1992)
Black Betty (1994)
A Little Yellow Dog (1996)
Gone Fishin' (1997)
Bad Boy Brawly Brown (2002)
Six Easy Pieces (2003)
Little Scarlet (2004)
Cinnamon Kiss (2005)
Blonde Faith (2007)
Little Green (2013)
Rose Gold (2014)
Charcoal Joe (2016)

—Katherine E. Bishop

DI JOHN REBUS

Ian Rankin
(1960–)

Ian Rankin's Edinburgh-based police detective John Rebus first appeared, with the rank of detective sergeant, in *Knots and Crosses* (1987). According to Rankin, this was supposed to be a stand-alone novel, a modern rewriting of R. L. Stevenson's *Dr. Jekyll and Mr. Hyde*. In the novel, Rebus is not only the detective hero but also a suspected serial child killer. Of course readers today will not see Rebus as the potential culprit, as *Knots and Crosses* is just the first in a hugely successful series of novels featuring the detective. Nineteen books later, the detective is a permanent feature of the Scottish crime fiction landscape and a reference point for new crime writers and their characters. Even though Rankin decided to part with his protagonist and sent him into retirement in *Exit Music* (2007), the detective proved to be so popular with readers that Rankin decided to bring him back in *Standing in Another Man's Grave* (2012), in which the retired policeman continues to work as part of a team that investigates cold cases.

At first glance, the character of Rebus owes a lot to the tradition of the American hard-boiled detective. He is a lonely and obsessive individual who drinks and smokes too much, has trouble sustaining relationships, and often faces violence. Rebus is also characterized by his cynicism and by a wisecracking abrasiveness that clearly echoes Raymond Chandler's Philip Marlowe. From the beginning of the series the detective is shown as alienated both in his private life (he has difficult relationships with his brother, his ex-wife, and his daughter) and at work where he is seen as an outsider. Rebus is an antiauthoritarian figure, whose tendency for insubordination leaves him in a permanent state of job insecurity. In *Fleshmarket Close* (2004) he does not even have his own desk—a clear message from his superiors that they would like to see him go. Unlike many of his colleagues, Rebus becomes emotionally involved in the cases he investigates and tends to follow his instincts rather than rational analysis or police procedures. He often talks about having "a gut feeling" and follows his own "hunches." These unconventional procedures naturally help him to solve his cases.

In contrast to many other crime series characters, Rebus ages between the books and is affected by every case he works on. He is both metaphorically and literally haunted by past cases, dead colleagues, and murder victims. Consequently, in all of the Rebus novels the feelings, emotions, and memories of the detective are as important as the crime plot. Throughout the series, we learn about Rebus's childhood and teenage years in his hometown of Cardenden, his army days, his failed marriage and unsuccessful relationships with various women, and his drinking problem. His deep love of music is a constant feature of his life: "Women, relationships and colleagues had come and gone, but the Stones had always been there. He put the album on and poured himself a last drink. . . . I don't have much, Rebus thought, but I have this."[5] Except for music the only real relationship that Rebus has is with his job. His obsession with casework is a way of escaping his own problems, but it also has a particularly Scottish resonance: "He lived to work, and in a very real sense he worked to live too: the much maligned Protestant work-ethic."[6]

What is most interesting about Rebus is that from the very beginning he is presented as a dubious hero, with all too much in common with the criminals he is opposed to. Sometimes his crimes are petty, such as when he steals rolls and milk from his local shop, or when he locks out his former girlfriend's cat (although the cat ends up dead), but sometimes they are far more serious. For example, in *The Black Book* (1993) he uses a rehabilitated pedophile, Andrew McPhail, to catch Cafferty (a dangerous gangster and Rebus's nemesis). As a result, McPhail ends up in the hospital, badly beaten. Rebus, however, feels no remorse; on the contrary, he thinks that McPhail got what he deserved. In *Black and Blue* (1997), he sticks up for his colleague and protégé, Brian Holmes, although he has beaten up a suspect during questioning.

Rebus is aware of his dark side. For example, in *Black and Blue* he acknowledges his own conflicting thoughts about rape: "Rape was all about power; killing, too, in its way. And wasn't power the ultimate male fantasy? And didn't he sometimes dream of it, too?"[7] This dual representation of the protagonist is one of the key underlying features of the whole series. Despite the fact that Rebus owes a lot to the clichés of the alienated private investigator, he is a complex and original character who represents an invaluable contribution to the development of the crime novel.

Selected Bibliography

Knots and Crosses (1987)
Hide and Seek (1990)
Let It Bleed (1995)
Black and Blue (1997)
Set in Darkness (2000)
Fleshmarket Close (2004)
Exit Music (2007)
Standing in Another Man's Grave (2012)

—Agnieszka Sienkiewicz-Charlish

BERNARD GRIMES RHODENBARR

Lawrence Block
(1938–)

Arthur Conan Doyle once warned against making a criminal the hero of a story.[8] Fortunately, Lawrence Block flouted this advice, or we would have been deprived of one of crime fiction's most charming detectives, Bernard Grimes Rhodenbarr. Bernie is a burglar by trade, a detective only by necessity; he has an unfortunate tendency to stumble over corpses during break-ins, and only by solving these murders is he able to stay out of jail. In the eleven-book Rhodenbarr series, Block boldly realizes the pure entertainment value of the crime genre, presenting murder and larceny stripped of social critique and criminal psychopathology. The series proves that crime fiction can be genuinely and unashamedly funny.[9]

Unsurprisingly, Bernie's approach to detective work disregards generic norms. Rather than going door to door interviewing witnesses, pinning evidence to murder boards, scouring the crime scene for clues, or tabulating lists of suspects and drawing maps of crime scenes, most of his sleuthing is done over the telephone or by breaking and entering. As Bernie narrates his own adventures, he is also able to keep much of the evidence he uncovers, as well as key stages of his investigations, from the reader, who thus remains puzzled until the denouement. This is certainly not Golden Age fair play.

Perhaps the most unconventional feature of Bernie's investigative technique, however, is his complete disregard for due process. Undeterred by police regulations or ethical qualms, he routinely withholds information to protect people when it suits him, while planting incriminating evidence to ensure the arrests of others. This type of unorthodox and legally, not to mention morally, questionable behavior is not what we have come to expect of our detectives, and readers anticipating a "problem of logic and deduction" will certainly be disappointed. In fact, the Rhodenbarr books are not really about crime at all; it is merely "dropped in like the olive in a martini" to provide a suitable framework for Bernie to be himself.[10]

Apart from being a criminally inclined and reluctant detective, there is at first glance nothing very remarkable about Rhodenbarr. He first appears in *Burglars Can't Be Choosers* (1977) as a pleasant and surprisingly erudite ex-con in his midthirties, living on New York's Upper West Side. Apart from Ray Kirschmann, "the best cop money can buy," Bernie has few acquaintances, and his only real friend is Carolyn Kaiser, a lesbian dog groomer introduced in *The Burglar Who Liked to Quote Kipling* (1979) who becomes Bernie's "soulmate" and "occasional henchperson."[11] Bernie is one of those fortunate fictional characters who does not age; in fact, he does not change much at all after his unexpected acquisition of Barnagut Books, a used bookstore in Greenwich Village. Bernie remains the same cheerfully polygamous and unrepentantly larcenous bookseller throughout the rest of the series.

Nor do the novels' plots vary much: there's a burglary (or two), there's a murder (or two), and there's a girl (or two). Bernie sells a few books and then he solves the mystery. Surprisingly, it is precisely this predictable routine that constitutes the true allure of the novels, or perhaps allows it to flourish. The twists and turns of the plot are incidental. It is the entertaining discussions and digressions on topics ranging from handy burglar's tips (plastic wallet calendars for jimmying locks) via the merits of rhubarb jam (best with tea) and the symptoms of Morton's foot (an ailment peculiar to joggers) to the question of Kinsey Millhone's sexual orientation (opinions differ) that matter most. As Bernie's routines become increasingly familiar—reading (and theorizing about) crime fiction, training Raffles the working cat with scrunched-up balls of paper, eating ethnic lunches and having after-work drinks with Carolyn at their local, the Bum Rap—a kind of creative stasis familiar to readers of P. G. Wodehouse occurs. Nothing terribly exciting goes on, but the reader hopes it will never stop. And so do Bernie and Carolyn:

> "You'll keep on washing dogs, and Raffles will keep on playing shortstop, and I'll keep on doing what I was born to do, selling books and breaking into people's houses."
>
> "And we'll live happily ever after, huh, Bern?"
>
> "Happily ever now," I said, and reached to pet my cat.[12]

As long as Bernie and Carolyn keep talking, readers will gladly suspend disbelief and share their eternal present. And if a dead body appears along the way, who is going to complain?

Selected Bibliography

Burglars Can't Be Choosers (1977)
The Burglar in the Closet (1978)
The Burglar Who Liked to Quote Kipling (1979)
The Burglar Who Studied Spinoza (1980)
The Burglar Who Painted Like Mondrian (1983)
The Burglar Who Traded Ted Williams (1994)
The Burglar Who Thought He Was Bogart (1995)
The Burglar in the Library (1997)
The Burglar in the Rye (1999)
The Burglar on the Prowl (2004)
The Burglar Who Counted the Spoons (2013)

—Johanna Sandberg

COMMISSARIO LUIGI ALFREDO RICCIARDI

Maurizio De Giovanni
(1958–)

Commissario Luigi Alfredo Ricciardi is an Italian police investigator who solves homicide cases in the vibrant yet secretive city of Naples in a series of noirish novels by the Neapolitan writer Maurizio De Giovanni. Two things set him apart from other popular Italian literary sleuths such as Guido Brunetti, Aurelio Zen, Nic Costa, and Salvo Montalbano. First, Ricciardi operates in the historic setting of the 1930s, under the shadow of Il Duce's fascism. Second, this commissario has a special power: he is able to see and hear the final moments of the lives of people who have died violently.

Ricciardi first discovered this frightening ability as a young child on his wealthy family's Salerno estate, when a man with a large pruning knife in his chest looked at him with half-closed eyes and said, "By God, I didn't touch your wife."[13] Young Luigi Alfredo ran away screaming but learned later that the man had been murdered on that spot five months earlier. Since then, he has lived alone with his terrible secret. At the time of "The Incident" (as he calls it), Ricciardi was already a lonely and unhappy child. His father had died young and his mother was mentally ill. The young Ricciardi's only comfort came from his beloved nanny, Tata Rosa, who is still caring for the thirty-one-year-old man as a housekeeper in his Naples apartment as the series begins.

From a life steeped in sorrow, Ricciardi has developed an emotion-driven theory of crime: all homicides are motivated by either hunger or love, a perception he uses to solve the murders of a succession of victims. Armchair detectives would do well to remember this theory as they attempt to solve the whodunit at the heart of each book. The first victim is a renowned tenor who is murdered in his dressing room in Naples' famed San Carlo Theater. His final words—"I will have vengeance"—are from an aria in Leoncavallo's *Pagliacci* and are softly sung to Ricciardi by his corpse; they give the book its English title.[14] In *By My Hand* (2011 [2014]) a wealthy couple is found in their home in a sea of blood; the man's dying words are "I don't owe you a thing!"; the woman's are a puzzling question: "Hat and gloves?"[15] In a haunting scene from *The Day of the Dead* (2010 [2014]), the body of a young boy is discovered sitting motionless on the Capodimonte steps. Mysteriously, here Ricciardi sees and hears nothing, which tells him—but no one else—that the body has been moved from the murder scene.

Commissario Ricciardi is a complex loner. He is a rich baron but ignores the family fortune and never uses his title. He is darkly handsome, with piercing green eyes. He is also highly intelligent and adept at solving crimes quickly. Leery colleagues steer clear of him, and to Ricciardi's disgust his superiors follow the official fascist line: "There are no suicides, no homicides, no robberies or assaults. . . . Not a word to the people, especially not to the press; a fascist city is clean and wholesome, there are no eyesores."[16]

Ricciardi has two loyal allies in his investigations: Dr. Bruno Modo, an antifascist medical examiner who trades friendly insults with Ricciardi, and his stalwart second-in-command Brigadier Raffaele Maione. Maione is a bear of a man, gruff and impatient with reluctant witnesses who observe the code of silence known as *omertà*. Maione is grieving over the murder of his policeman son, a crime that threads its way into a number of succeeding plots. In investigations, Brigadier Maione has his own secret weapon: a transgender prostitute named Bambinella who seems to know all there is to know about the city's extensive demimonde. Bambinella imparts information freely to Maione, along with a good amount of unwelcome flirtatious repartee.

Although unmarried and without a girlfriend, Ricciardi still has two women in his life. Enrica Colombo is a young woman who lives in the building opposite Ricciardi's. Watching this beauty at her needlepoint, Ricciardi has fallen in love but cannot act on his feelings because of his cursed power, thinking it would be unfair to impose this burden on her and their potential children. Unknown to Ricciardi, Colombo returns his love but is paralyzed by shyness and old-fashioned rules of behavior. The second woman is the beautiful soprano Livia Lucani Vezzi, widow of the famous tenor whose murder opens the series. Vezzi falls in love with Ricciardi and returns in succeeding books as a devoted would-be lover. De Giovanni skillfully adds to the suspense of his narratives with a running subplot dealing with the unspoken rivalry between Colombo and Vezzi that is fully observed only by the reader.

But it is Naples that makes the greatest claim on our attention: beautiful yet threatening, this city of narrow streets and blind, unwelcoming neighborhoods, with its extremes of heat and cold and a thousand varied assaults on the senses, together with its people, whose superstition and distrust are balanced by their strong family values and great capacity to feel and to love, is brilliantly brought to life in the series' best passages. The scarred soul of Commissario Ricciardi could not ask for a more pungently appropriate milieu in which to nurse his wounds and bring murderers to justice.

Selected Bibliography

I Will Have Vengeance: The Winter of Commissario Ricciardi (2006 [2012])
Blood Curse: The Springtime of Commissario Ricciardi (2008 [2013])
Everyone in Their Place: The Summer of Commissario Ricciardi (2009 [2013])
The Day of the Dead: The Autumn of Commissario Ricciardi (2010 [2014])
By My Hand: The Christmas of Commissario Ricciardi (2011 [2014])
Viper: No Resurrection for Commissario Ricciardi (2012 [2015])

—Joseph Sgammato

S

KAY SCARPETTA

Patricia Cornwell
(1956–)

Kay Scarpetta: first among forensic detectives. As the *Mail on Sunday* claims, "Cornwell almost single-handed popularized forensic crime fiction, and can lay claim to being the literary godmother of hit TV shows like CSI, Dexter and Silent Witness."[1] The forensic detail in the series is crucial, but Scarpetta is also a recognizable and distinctive detective on the side of truth and justice, perhaps the more important factor in making her one of the most popular and influential detecting figures of all time.

Scarpetta's character and circumstances have evolved over the twenty-five years of the series, and readers have had the opportunity to see her life change and develop. Kay Scarpetta is an attractive figure: small (five foot three), blonde, slim, and good-looking. Although forty when we meet her in the first book, *Postmortem* (1990), Patricia Cornwell has said recently "she will stay around fiftyish, with good bones and good genetics, while the rest of us struggle."[2] She is strong and assertive, and although coming from a poor Italian immigrant family, she has risen to a position of power. Scarpetta herself says, "I went to Cornell, to Georgetown Law and Johns Hopkins medical school. I'm a special reservist colonel in the Air Force. I've testified before Senate subcommittees and have been a guest at the White House. I'm the chief medical examiner of Massachusetts and director of the crime labs."[3] Scarpetta does not take kindly to any type of disrespect, particularly in relation to her gender.

Above all Scarpetta is a scientist. She is the first forensic investigator to appear in mainstream crime fiction, and her meticulous investigative procedures have remained the focus throughout the series. Scarpetta delves into bodies with her hands, scalpels, saws, and measuring instruments. She observes dead bodies as carefully as she can and has even honed her sense of smell to help her detect clues. She makes a point of not flinching and says that "isolating potentially significant smells from the awful stench of dirty bodies and rotting flesh is rather much like archaeology."[4] Scarpetta "listens" to the dead and pays respect to them by not turning away. She is deeply sensitive and empathetic, and one of the unique features of the series is the way it invites the reader to feel with her through every step of the investigation. This is perhaps what has kept the series consistently on the best-selling lists.

Perhaps to help alleviate the horrors of her job, Scarpetta is a sensual woman who enjoys good sex, quality clothes, fine architecture, art, and wine, and takes a keen interest in interior design. Hers is a material world, and she is sensitive to physical nuance in her life. In contrast to her high profile and very public professional life, Scarpetta is actually a domestic person; she gardens and pays attention to furnishing and domestic details. This is manifested most consistently in her love of cooking healthy and rustic Italian food: homemade pasta flavored with garlic, olive oil, herbs, quality cheese, and Italian tomatoes. She is perhaps most happy when she is cooking, and her food invariably sounds delicious. Indeed, two cookbooks of "her" recipes have been published, *Scarpetta's Winter Table* (1998) and *Food to Die For: Secrets from Kay Scarpetta's Kitchen* (2004).

Scarpetta frequently cooks for her family: her niece Lucy, her (sometime) husband Benton Wesley, and her closest friend and sidekick Pete Marino. This family is the most important thing in her life. Lucy was neglected by her mother, Scarpetta's sister, and has come to take the place of a daughter. Pete Marino, a police investigator and close friend, acts as family too. He is a gifted detective, big, crass, and macho but also unfailingly loyal to Scarpetta. Despite the fact that both Lucy and Marino can be almost impossibly difficult at times, Scarpetta will always stick by them both. Benton Wesley was an FBI agent with whom Scarpetta had an affair until it appeared he had been murdered in *Point of Origin* (1998). However he returns years later in *Blow Fly* (2003), apparently having spent the interval in a witness protection program. We find out they have finally married in *Scarpetta* (2008). They enjoy an intense, highly physical relationship that has never really had the chance to run smoothly.

Cornwell's portrayal of Scarpetta has changed over the years. In the fourteenth book of the series, *Predator* (2005), the narrative shifted from the first to the third person. This continued for the next three books, *Book of the Dead* (2007), *Scarpetta* (2008), and *The Scarpetta Factor* (2009). These books provided another type of insight into Scarpetta's character. However, when Scarpetta's own voice returned in *Port Mortuary* (2010), it was a relief to many fans. It is Scarpetta whom we want to hear and whom we trust. In the most recent books Scarpetta has become increasingly suspicious of government agencies, and Lucy has moved into an almost survivalist mode of living (on a heavily armed and surveilled fifty-acre estate). However, Scarpetta has not withdrawn, and she is still meticulously investigating crimes. The original forensic detective, she will never lose her hard-won place at the top of her field.

Selected Bibliography

Postmortem (1990)
Cruel and Unusual (1993)
Black Notice (1999)
Blow Fly (2003)
Predator (2005)
Red Mist (2011)
Dust (2013)
Depraved Heart (2015)

—Ruth Heholt

SAM SPADE

Dashiell Hammett
(1894–1961)

One way of thinking about the success of crime fiction from the nineteenth century to today is to view it as a response to the increasing anonymity, uncertainty, and unreliability of the modern world. The fictional detective's job is to help us navigate the complexities of modernity, making sense of the senseless and explaining the inexplicable. Few detectives have accomplished this more successfully than Dashiell Hammett's Sam Spade, perhaps the single most influential hard-boiled private eye, and a model of the radical distrust that is central to the role.

Sam Spade's fame rests largely on a single novel, *The Maltese Falcon* (1930), set in an interwar San Francisco in which nothing is what it seems, and in which to trust anyone would be impossibly naïve, if not suicidal.[6] The narrative revolves around a group of criminals, led by the deceptively named Gutman (he is anything but good), and the fabled Maltese falcon, a priceless relic of the crusading order of the Hospitalers, which the gang has stolen and are now struggling over in an intricate pattern of betrayal and counterbetrayal. Spade is recruited by Brigid O'Shaughnessy to help her get her share of the money to be made from the "black bird" without getting killed in the process.[7] But everything about O'Shaughnessy is false: she appears under a false name, tells endless false stories, and tries to lure Spade into closer involvement through scenes of false vulnerability. Spade and O'Shaughnessy's "quest"—and this is a quest, if an ironically inverted one—winds through a tangled thicket of lies, tricks, disguises, intrigues, and evasions.

Even beyond the confines of this criminal plot, the world Hammett presents in *The Maltese Falcon* is utterly unreliable. Perhaps the best indication of this is the otherwise puzzling embedded narrative in which Spade relates the story of Flitcraft, a normal family man who, after a near accident, suddenly abandons his wife and children to start over. American life is seen here as an illusion, a mirage of stability and order overlying a barely contained chaos. The Maltese falcon is itself also a sign of the untrustworthiness and essential falsity of this world; ostensibly a priceless artifact, worth fighting over and even killing for, it is ultimately revealed to be no more "real" than anything else.

Sam Spade is peculiarly well adapted to navigate this unreliable world. His intense physicality, emphasized through the novel by Hammett's detailed, meticulous narration of his actions, from rolling cigarettes to slugging villains, is important, as is his tough resilience. So too is his extraordinary impassivity. His ability to remain calm, despite his fierce temper, is essential to his investigations. It allows him to suspend judgment and to wait for events to develop around him, rather than rushing to tendentious conclusions like the police, who suspect him of involvement in murder, or the district attorney, who erroneously links the investigation to gang wars. But most important of all is Spade's refusal to take anyone or anything at face value. This extreme skepticism insulates him from the duplicity of the world he lives in. When O'Shaughnessy arrives in his office with a story about an abducted sister, he does not believe her but does not let this interfere with the business of the investigation. Her dishonesty is a given, one more fact to be taken into consideration. Even after they have fallen in love—or at least started sleeping together—Spade is able to maintain his doubt. When presented with a choice between trusting her or Gutman, he quite ruthlessly forces her to literally bare herself to learn the truth: "I had to find out, Angel."[8] In Spade's world, trust is an impossibility, and only physical evidence can reveal the truth.

Indeed, Spade operates so effectively in the dishonest world of *The Maltese Falcon* that for much of the novel it seems he is actually part of this duplicitousness. His appearance is against him—he is repeatedly described as looking Satanic—as is the fact that he has been having an affair with his partner's wife. He is careful to always get as much money out of the various participants in the conspiracy as he can, and as he enters into the plotting over possession of the falcon, he aligns himself at times with one member of the gang, at times with another, as expedience dictates. As Joe Cairo points out, this is something the gang has counted on, for Spade has a reputation as a man who would not let anything interfere "with profitable business relations."[9]

Yet despite this apparent lack of probity, Spade is, in a way, an honorable man who uses his reputation for dishonesty to achieve honest ends. As he tells O'Shaughnessy, "Don't be too sure I'm as crooked as I'm supposed to be."[10] Spade has no great fondness for his murdered partner Archer, but his primary motivation throughout the novel is to discover and punish his killer. This impersonal loyalty represents a code of sorts and provides a moral compass, albeit a rudimentary one, in an immoral world: "When a man's partner is killed, he's supposed to do something about it."[11] When O'Shaughnessy is ultimately revealed as his killer, he does not let emotion stand in the way of justice. It is this ruthless dedication to the truth, however hard it is to obtain, however expensive to purchase in an untruthful world, that has made Spade such an extraordinarily resonant figure. His fame may well have much to do with the success of John Huston's 1941 film adaptation of *The Maltese Falcon*, in which Humphrey Bogart plays an unlikely yet utterly convincing Spade, but Hammett's novel stands alone as a landmark of crime fiction.

Selected Bibliography

The Dain Curse (1929)
Red Harvest (1929)
The Glass Key (1931)
The Thin Man (1934)
Nightmare Town (short stories; 1999)

—Eric Sandberg

SPENSER

Robert B. Parker
(1932–2010)

The hard-boiled genre, featuring tough private investigators searching for justice in a corrupt world, underwent a resurgence in the 1970s. Acknowledged by many as the key exponent of the neo-hard-boiled genre was Robert B. Parker, whose Boston-based private eye, Spenser (his forename is never mentioned), appeared in forty-one novels from 1973 to 2010.[12] While conforming to a template that was set in the mid-1920s, the avowedly "post-Vietnam figure" of Spenser faced new social imperatives in his contemporary adventures.[13] This tension between social forces and a seemingly outdated code of conduct is played out in the distinctiveness of Spenser's character within the somewhat formulaic novels in which he appears.

As is customary in the hard-boiled tradition, the novels often begin with a client calling on Spenser at his office with a case. Unlike a policeman, ex-cop Spenser is not caught in a potentially stifling hierarchic bureaucracy, keeping that sixth ball in the air, which might restrict his character. Spenser's private life, therefore, merges imperceptibly with his business, hence the foregrounding of his humor (especially self-deprecating humor) and pomposity-pricking wit, his clothes (which show minimal development over the forty-one novels), and his relatively innocuous pastimes (which are significant markers of character), namely, cooking, eating (doughnuts in particular), dog-loving (the later novels feature the pointer, Pearl), and reading.

Various indicators throughout the series also assemble Spenser's macho credentials, especially in the early stories, which appeared at a time when traditional gender roles were under scrutiny. His past as a heavyweight boxer and his war experience in Korea are characterized as trips through an existential proving ground that give him the right—and power—of judgment in his contemporary battles. His weightlifting and jogging connote a carefully maintained masculinity. There are also hints throughout the novels regarding Spenser's upbringing: he was raised by his father and two maternal uncles after his mother died during childbirth. Some of the details of how Spenser's male mentors taught him reading, cooking, boxing, and the difference between "right" and "legal" are not fleshed out until quite late in the novel cycle.[14] What is clear throughout, however, is that Spenser's self-aware masculinity, purveyed through numerous knowing references to sexism and contemporary perspectives on gender, always wins the day. Typical in this respect is *Looking for Rachel Wallace* (1980) in which Spenser is hired as a bodyguard for feminist writer Rachel Wallace. At a protest meeting of female insurance workers, Wallace is manhandled by a security guard who wants to eject her from the building, and Spenser reacts by punching the guard and his superior. Wallace is furious, sacks Spenser, and for lack of a bodyguard, is later kidnapped by an extreme right-wing group. Spenser is aware that his macho act, far from protecting Wallace, has put her in peril. However, now that there is a situation of recognizably acute danger, violence is needed to resolve it, and Spenser comes to the rescue.

The other connected key social change against which Spenser pits himself is the contemporary challenge to family roles. In consonance with the hard-boiled PI genre as a whole, throughout the cycle Spenser repeatedly rescues runaway children and uses his investigations to repair "broken homes." Indeed, the cycle's longevity allows Spenser to confront the infant offspring of a teenage pregnancy—Ty-bop—on more than one occasion, latterly when he has grown into a petty criminal. Spenser's constant concern with the state of the family is established in the first novel, *The Godwulf Manuscript* (1973), in which Terry Orchard's inadequate family background leads her to seek harmful surrogate families in radical student groups and mystical cults.

Because the Spenser novels are narrated in the first person, his interactions with characters close to him are crucial for delineating his character in relation to the changing social world. Significant in this respect is Hawk, a black ex-boxer who makes a living as a hired killer, and who becomes an independent sidekick for Spenser. Their interracial masculine bonding (part of an American literary tradition of which Parker was certainly aware) suggests that Hawk and Spenser, if not "two different sides of the same coin," are at least conjoined by the former's existence outside society and his occasional forays inside it and the latter's existence inside society and his occasional forays outside it.[15]

Susan Silverman, who has featured in the Spenser novels since *God Save the Child* (1974), serves a slightly different role. An educational psychologist and later a psychotherapist with a Harvard PhD, she is situated as both working with families and deciphering or elaborating Spenser's worldview. She enables Spenser to represent a balance of chivalry, commitment, and respect for the need for independence of others, establishing a dialogue between feminism and Spenser's macho code. As with Hawk, she is also Spenser's partner in the humorous banter that has enabled the Spenser novels to circumvent stagnation and to avoid becoming an anachronism.

Selected Bibliography

The Godwulf Manuscript (1973)
Crimson Joy (1988)
Paper Doll (1993)
Hugger Mugger (2000)
Sixkill (2011)

—Paul Cobley

DOC SPORTELLO

Thomas Pynchon
(1937–)

The dust-jacket blurb of Thomas Pynchon's *Inherent Vice* (2009), which he probably wrote himself, makes two claims: that the author is working in an unaccustomed genre and that those who remember the sixties weren't really there. The unaccustomed genre, we assume, is hard-boiled detective fiction, and the classic quip seems to refer both to the 1970 setting of the novel (the cusp between having lived in the sixties and having forgotten what it was really like afterward) and to the faulty "doper's memory" of joint-smoking protagonist Larry "Doc" Sportello.

At some level, all Pynchon's novels have been about detection, in the sense of looking for clues and attempting to piece them together: in *The Crying of Lot 49* (1965), Mrs. Oedipa Maas was appointed executor (or executrix) to search out the assets of an estate, and in *Vineland* (1990), Prairie Wheeler completed a personal quest to track down her long-lost mother. His attraction to, and reworking of, noir and hard-boiled detective fiction is clearest in his latest novels however. In *Bleed-*

ing Edge (2013), Pynchon presents readers with an actual professional investigator, if a slightly tarnished one, Maxine Tarnow. But Doc Sportello is his first licensed private-eye character and, since Paul Thomas Anderson rendered *Inherent Vice* into film in 2014, also his first mainstream—but not streamlined—detective. Doc operates "Location, Surveillance, Detection"—or LSD—Investigations from an office by the Los Angeles airport and meanders from one strange scenario to another in a narcotic haze.

Pynchon's colorful "surf-noir" reconditions genre conventions; the visit that kicks off the hard-boiled plot of *Inherent Vice* is not from a femme fatale like Rita Hayworth or from an occasional noir heroine like Katharine Hepburn but from Doc's ex-girlfriend, Shasta Fay Hepworth. To cops she may be "some hippie chick with boyfriend trouble, brains all discombobulated with dope sex rock 'n' roll," but she has actually fallen from her "old dirty-blond ways" and the beach look of casual "sandals, bottom half of a flower-print bikini, faded Country Joe & the Fish T-shirt" she favored while dating Doc. She has moved "inland" in every sense of the word to become the platinum blonde plaything of a real estate mogul, but even in "straight-chick uniform," she can still seduce Doc into taking on her case, which predictably, sets a more complex plot in motion.[16]

Habitual readers of Pynchon might expect a postmodern antidetective novel with an inconclusive end. On the one hand, a host of strange characters and potential plot lines are continually introduced to a detective so apparently ill-equipped to gather, select, and coordinate information that notes are taken on a match cover or, occasionally, in a logbook, which is "a sign not so much of professionalism as of Doper's Memory."[17] Doc's office furnishings and equipment, moreover, are repurposed domestic items salvaged from renovations or found at swap meets. Finally, his hippie lifestyle leaves him so out of touch with the classical genre that, though he argues based on Sherlock Holmes's use of cocaine that drugs and detecting are a good match, in spite of "all 'em alternate universes" complicating the job, he does not realize Sherlock (like himself, ironically) is a fictional character: "Wh—Naw. No, he's real. He lives at this real address in London. Well, maybe not anymore, it was years ago, he has to be dead by now."[18]

Inherent Vice may add psychedelic touches to the detective genre, but it has more direction than some Pynchon novels. Doc Sportello smokes joints while investigating and relies on extrasensory skills gained from years of dropping acid, but the way in which this "flatfoot" pursues one trail after another in the hope of eventual success, rather than "overthinking" himself, moves his MO from the deductive tradition toward the strategies of a police-procedural gumshoe with the stubborn streak and strong legs of an Ed McBain character. Doc is a more laid-back "gumsandal" though, and a romantic who laments the fact that the extraordinary PIs of old, Philip Marlowe, Sam Spade, and "the shamus of all shamuses Johnny Staccato," are losing out to cop shows like *Hawaii Five-O* on TV. His fear is that they make viewers "so cop-happy they're beggin to be run in. Good-bye Johnny Staccato, welcome and while you're at it please kick my door down, Steve McGarrett."[19]

A hard-boiled hippie detective will be in double conflict with the police, whose perceived inefficiency and corruption are staples both of the literary genre and of opinions formed in the sixties amongst members of the counterculture and the New Left. Their respective contempt for the buffoonery of individual "pigs" and suspicions toward a corrupt institution are reflected in three ways: in Detective

Lieutenant "Bigfoot" Bjornsen, a ridiculous character who nonetheless frames Doc as part of a bigger plot; in the bungled handling of the Manson murders that haunt the historical frame surrounding *Inherent Vice*; and in the mindset and political conviction detectable in Pynchon's novels from the sixties and seventies.

Looking back to that period Pynchon's current solution is not revolution but perhaps recycling. Doc is a "pure" hippie, the only one Hepworth had known not to shoot up, though he shoots in self-defense. He is powerless to address the corruption, conspiracy, and unjust world order he finds but relies on these for local closure by securing the family reunion of formerly heroin-addicted Coy, Hope, and Baby Amethyst Harlingen. In a world where apparently wholesome nuclear families are heroin-handling agents of criminal cartels, the moneyed elite, and corruptible government institutions, and at a time when the Manson Family perverted the hippie commune ideal, Doc Sportello's conscience, his selfless acts of kindness, and his reliance on local community helps salvage the real-life, fallible domesticity of individuals not central to the original plot but with lives blighted by it. Pynchon pays homage here to the honorable private eye of Raymond Chandler and Dashiell Hammett, and to the good intentions and benign collectivity born in the summer of love.

Selected Bibliography

V. (1963)
The Crying of Lot 49 (1965)
Against the Day (2006)
Bleeding Edge (2013)

—Inger H. Dalsgaard

NIGEL STRANGEWAYS

Nicholas Blake (Cecil Day-Lewis)
(1904–1972)

The Collins Crime Club published many of the great detective narratives of the Golden Age, including, in 1935, *A Question of Proof*, which introduced readers to the private detective Nigel Strangeways. Building on a well-established style, Nicholas Blake, the pseudonym of the poet laureate Cecil Day-Lewis, created an able and well-connected detective who was comfortably well off, a poet, and a philosopher. What make Strangeways so fascinating are the ways in which he responds to conventional justice systems, and the manner in which poetry and philosophy, above forensics and science, play a pivotal role in his detection.

Strangeways is the well-bred nephew of Scotland Yard's assistant commissioner, and this connection, along with his belief that "it is the only career left which offered scope to good manners and scientific curiosity," lead Strangeways to channel his talents into amateur detection. Apparently named after the famous Manchester prison, Strangeways originally resembled Cecil Day-Lewis's close friend and collaborator W. H. Auden: he is blond, disheveled, and short-sighted; makes angular movements; drinks too much tea; and sleeps under a suffocating collection of blankets and carpets. And of course Strangeways resembles Auden in another vital way: he is a poet.

It is therefore not unexpected that the Strangeways mysteries should be scattered with literary references and allusions, although they feel less heavily burdened with quotations than many detective novels written by Blake's contemporaries. Blake, for example, focuses his literary pedigree in *Thou Shell of Death* (1936) by reimagining the Elizabethan play *The Revenger's Tragedy*. In addition to literary allusions, however, it is Strangeways's knowledge and emotional understanding of literature that assists him as a detective. In *The Beast Must Die* (1938), for example, he unravels the seemingly impossible mystery of George's death when he understands that Frank Cairns's constructed confessional diary, which imagines a connection between his own plight and that of Hamlet, is too contrived: Strangeways understands that the diary hides Frank's "too sensitive conscience," and therefore his guilt.[20]

This leads to another important element of Strangeways's character: his understanding of human psychology. This relates to Strangeways himself, who is humanized by his flaws and recurrent psychological issues. For example, when we first encounter him in *The Beast Must Die* he is suffering from some sort of ennui, left "exhausted and depressed" by lack of mental stimulation. However, Strangeways's psychological understanding means he can view his situation objectively, and even attempt to have a "tete-a-tete with [his] unconscious."[21] Although he may not be able to cure himself, he is most certainly able to use this knowledge of the human mind in solving crime. Indeed, the Strangeways mysteries often concentrate on the psychological aspects of the crime rather than the physical, and Strangeways's personable approach and psychological understanding mean that he gets close to all involved, from witnesses to suspects, and understands what can turn someone to crime.

This understanding, and at times empathy, for the perpetrator as well as the victim leads to a fascinating relationship between Strangeways and the traditional judicial system as represented by the straight-talking Inspector Blount, a hard-headed Scotsman in charge of investigations for Scotland Yard with whom Strangeways has a respectful but playful relationship. What Blake was creating could be described as left-leaning detective fiction, something much rarer in the 1930s than it is today. And this can be seen in the many instances where the killers are punished outside of the judicial system, not only to offer a satisfactory denouement within the confines of the narrative, but also as a comment about what justice really is. There are several occasions, for example, where Strangeways offers suicide as a form of justice. This is related to his psychological understanding of the killers, murderers who are three-dimensional, and often tragic, characters.

In keeping with many traditional whodunits, the Strangeways mysteries often deal with the upper classes. However, there is a clear understanding in these novels of the complexities of class. Strangeways, like his author, understands the inequalities created by class division, and conflicts are often dramatized by reference to such imbalances, as seen in relationships between masters and servants, the role of the working-class author, or geographical divisions between Scotland, Ireland,

and England. That which is conventionally seen as undesirable or uncomfortable, such as crossing class boundaries, often acts as a positive place for friendship to develop, whereas traditional images of nostalgic Englishness are seen as dangerous: the beautiful Somerset landscape conceals murderers, and corpses are hidden within scarecrows and snowmen.

Although Strangeways does belong to the Golden Age of detective fiction, these novels spanned four decades, and Strangeways later found himself in a combination of classic whodunits and thrillers. Although the lone gentleman detective certainly is in keeping with classic traditions, Strangeways offers readers much more. Day-Lewis may have written popular fiction for financial gain, and the puzzle mysteries written under the pen name Blake certainly helped, but what he created was far more than a generic whodunit. Strangeways's adventures are better classed as psychological thrillers, and there is a real interest in them in the human conditions that lead to crime. We are not presented with two-dimensional villains or victims, and certainly not with a flat detective.

Selected Bibliography

A Question of Proof (1935)
Thou Shell of Death (1936)
There's Trouble Brewing (1937)
The Beast Must Die (1938)
The Smiler with the Knife (1939)
Malice in Wonderland (1940)
The Case of the Abominable Snowman (1941)
Minute for Murder (1947)
Head of a Traveler (1949)
The Dreadful Hollow (1953)
The Whisper in the Gloom (1954)
End of Chapter (1957)
The Widow's Cruise (1959)
The Worm of Death (1961)
The Sad Variety (1964)
The Morning after Death (1966)

—Rebecca Gordon Stewart

FAHNDERWACHTMEISTER JAKOB STUDER

Friedrich Charles Glauser
(1896–1938)

In early 1935, Friedrich Glauser described to girlfriend Berthe Bendel a new project he had started with Fahnderwachtmeister (Detective Sergeant) Jakob Studer: a crime novel that would take place in a Swiss village and capture the Swiss milieu. Though Glauser had already included a policeman named Studer in a handful of short stories, the character came into sharper focus in the 1936 novel *Wachtmeister*

Studer (literally Sergeant Studer, later translated as *The Thumbprint*). A 1939 film version starring the beloved Swiss actor Heinrich Gretler introduced a broader audience to this unassuming homegrown detective, and periodic television rebroadcasts of the movie secured Studer's status as an enduring cultural icon for the German-speaking Swiss.

To understand the popularity of Detective Sergeant Jakob Studer, one has to appreciate the cultural and political context in which he appeared. When the inspector from the Bern cantonal police arrived on the scene, detective fiction in the German-speaking world was dominated by translations of Arthur Conan Doyle and Edgar Wallace. Glauser was familiar with these authors and their works, but he preferred Georges Simenon's Jules Maigret crime novels. Emulating Simenon's attention to atmosphere, character, and detail, Glauser took what had been seen in Switzerland as a foreign genre and made it seem homespun. His success in merging international and domestic popular culture was confirmed by contemporary critics who dubbed Studer the "Swiss Sherlock Holmes."

The political climate of Switzerland in the mid- and late 1930s was conducive to the success of this local investigator. As Adolf Hitler's expansionist rhetoric intensified, the Swiss government emphasized a cultural and political legacy distinct from Germany's, preempting any claims that Switzerland should be annexed to the Reich. In time, Studer's rustic Swiss identity was appropriated by the state-sponsored *geistige Landesverteidigung*, or "spiritual defense of the homeland," as one of many examples of how the values of the two nations diverged.

Studer's Swissness is a blend of understated professional competence, ethics, and personability. He studied with the well-known criminologists Hans Groß in Graz and Edmond Locard in Lyon and, in a personification of Swiss multilingualism, speaks German, French, and Italian along with his native Bernese dialect. But lest he seem a hidebound agent of the law, Studer is an outsider in the police system. His involvement in some "business with [a] bank" before the Great War caused him to fall out of favor and to suffer a demotion.[22] Forced to start over from the bottom and now nearing retirement, Studer remains driven by his strong moral compass. On more than one occasion, the sergeant resists the temptations of power or money to persist with a thankless investigation.

Though he often avails himself of his criminological training, Studer also relies on his interpersonal skills to solve cases. The detective knows what language to use in order to build trust with his interlocutors, or to remind them of his authority. He listens to the way people talk to judge the veracity of their statements, he examines their social networks, and he takes in their milieus as carefully as other investigators might secure more tangible evidence. As Studer observes, "It's not so much facts I need as the air these people breathe, so to speak."[23]

The sergeant's career spans five novels written between 1936 and Glauser's death in 1938. *The Spoke* (1941 [2008]) and *The Chinaman* (1939 [2007]), like *The Thumbprint*, take place in fictive Swiss villages. Here, Studer's investigations frequently reveal the putative Swiss idyll as irrevocably compromised: corrupt community leaders and oppressive social ties are only the most obvious expressions of a deteriorating social fabric. At times, Studer himself comes across as a crusty traditionalist annoyed by social pretensions, women who wear too much powder, tepid coffee, and pulp fiction. Yet the sergeant is also critical of outdated, inhumane social institutions and is capable of profound empathy. When he witnesses a moment of tenderness between a murderer and his wife, the detective reflects, "Things in life were always different from the way you imagined. A man might be brutal, but not all the time, at others, apparently, he could be quite different."[24]

In *Fever* (1938 [2006]) and *In Matto's Realm* (1937 [2005]), Studer is sent to other locales the author knew from experience: in the former, an outpost of the French Foreign Legion; in the latter, a psychiatric clinic. *In Matto's Realm* has drawn critical acclaim for its multilayered exploration of the human psyche. Here, even Studer's investigative powers fall short. After his solution to the crime is exposed as faulty, Studer must concede: "Suddenly everything was clear. He felt ashamed. He had understood nothing."[25] It is Dr. Laduner, acting director of the clinic, who accurately reads the forensic and psychiatric clues of the case and solves the mystery; Studer fails both on both counts.

If Studer's initial popularity stemmed from his Swissness, later generations of readers—for whom the patriotism of the 1930s seemed unpalatable if not downright embarrassing—appreciated Glauser's subtle social criticism and accorded him a place in Swiss literary history. The Bernese police commissioner Hans Barlach, a postwar creation of fellow countryman Friedrich Dürrenmatt, is unthinkable without Sergeant Studer. New editions of Glauser's novels along with graphic novel and radio play adaptations have enshrined Studer as the personification of the 1930s Swiss zeitgeist, and assured him of better name recognition than even his author.

Selected Bibliography

The Thumbprint (1936 [2004])
In Matto's Realm (1937 [2005])
Fever (1938 [2006])
The Chinaman (1939 [2007])
The Spoke (1941 [2008])

—Julia Karolle-Berg

INSPECTOR ERLENDUR SVEINSSON

Arnaldur Indridason
(1961–)

When Reykjavík police inspector Erlendur Sveinsson was ten years old, his father brought him and his younger brother Bergur to round up some sheep that had left the herd. In a typically sudden and brutal Icelandic snowstorm, the father lost track of both his sons. Erlendur was later rescued, severely frostbitten, but Bergur was never seen again. This childhood experience affected Erlendur so profoundly that he has never been able to leave it behind. The traumatized child became the troubled man.

When we are first introduced to Erlendur Sveinsson in *Jar City* (2000 [2004]) he is around fifty years old and divorced. He has troubled relationships with both his ex-wife and his two grown children. However fraught it may be, however, his relationship with his children, and especially with his daughter Eva Lind, rarely leaves him in peace. Like his memories of his dead brother, his children are constantly on his mind. In fact, trying to help Eva Lind with her serious drug problems—and generally tumultuous life—and to find evidence of what happened to his brother so many years ago are the two principal "cases" of his life, in part because he cannot solve them, unlike the many criminal cases he encounters during his police career.

Sveinsson's background can be detected in the "peculiarly mournful expression on his face."[26] He is quite conservative, and though not unkind to people, he remains reserved in most social situations. He has difficulties comprehending new phenomena and trends, he does not understand computers, and he dislikes the fact that English words occasionally find their way into the Icelandic language. He falls asleep at the theater, which he calls "artificial drama," presumably in comparison to his work and personal history.[27]

Sveinsson has lived alone since his divorce, the even tenor of his life sometimes interrupted by a more or less aggressive and confrontational Eva Lind, who resents him for leaving her mother, or later in the series, by a woman, Valgerdur, with whom he gradually develops a warm romantic relationship. When he is not working a case Sveinsson reads books about mysterious disappearances; one of them even contains an account of his brother's disappearance. He reads this story to his daughter, hoping it will help her understand him better. The child Erlendur is described in the book as "inconsolable" and "barely capable of human interaction," descriptions that illuminate the adult Erlendur for both Eva Lind and the reader. We also learn that he "continued searching for his brother's remains for as long as the family lived at Bakkasel."[28] Eva Lind wishes Sveinsson would let his brother go, and he admits that he too wishes it were possible, yet the reader knows that this will never happen unless something very radical occurs in his forty-year-old investigation.

In later novels in the series, such as *Reykjavik Nights* (2012 [2014]), the reader is introduced to a younger Erlendur Sveinsson who has just started working as a police officer, and these novels make it clear he has never changed and might not even be capable of it. Sveinsson might strike an unfamiliar reader as a rather dull and flat character who does not develop during the series. This is not true, however. His relationship to his children changes, and he starts to open up, especially to Eva Lind, and later to Valgerdur. His criminal cases lead him to meet new people and gain new perspectives on life. It is only his sadness that is perpetual and unchanging.

In comparison to Sveinsson's past experiences, and the many books about disappearances he devours in his spare time, the crimes that he solves in the novels are more ordinary, even pathetic and clumsy, and are never the result of a brilliant criminal scheme. However, he is not oblivious to the tragedy of each case, and Sveinsson's past does not affect his work. He is on the contrary a balanced and thorough investigator: "Erlendur walked around the flat and pondered the simplest questions. That was his job: investigating the obvious."[29] He treats the victims, witnesses, and suspects with the utmost respect, even though he maintains a personal distance. He is, however, especially moved by the death of a young immigrant boy in the novel *Arctic Chill* (2005 [2005]), whose body he covers with his own coat as if to protect him from further harm, a response that can naturally be traced back to the disappearance of his brother.

In *Strange Shores* (2010 [2013]), Sveinsson leaves Reykjavík to go back to the root of his trauma, the small village where he grew up. He sleeps outdoors, he talks to the people he encounters, and while he is officially investigating another old disappearance, he is also searching for clues to what happened to Bergur. This is the most intense and dramatic portrait of Sveinsson's psyche in the whole series, and the ending of the novel is left intriguingly open. Compared to many other Scandinavian urban detectives, it is ultimately due to Sveinsson's extremely intimate relationship to the landscape, with its lonely beauty and ever-present danger, that he is one of the most iconic detectives in contemporary Nordic noir.

Selected Bibliography

Jar City (2000 [2004])
Silence of the Grave (2002 [2005])
The Draining Lake (2004 [2007])
Arctic Chill (2005 [2005])
Strange Shores (2010 [2013])

—Katarina Gregersdotter

TEODOR SZACKI

Zygmunt Miłoszewski
(1976–)

The rapidly developing tradition of crime writing in Poland is dominated by two major tendencies. On the one hand, there is the so-called retro style, best exemplified by Marek Krajewski and his Eberhard Mock series, which feeds on the past, especially the interwar period. On the other hand, there are socially inclined writers who follow in the footsteps of Scandinavian authors, most notably Stieg Larsson, contextualizing crime within a faithful representation of contemporary society. Zygmunt Miłoszewski's Teodor Szacki trilogy is the most successful product of the latter tendency, even if while illustrating the social dynamics of twenty-first-century Poland the author demonstrates the imprint of the past on the present. Miłoszewski's protagonist Teodor Szacki, a state prosecutor originally based in Warsaw, is given the role of a misfit, so that he can combine his investigations with distanced observation, thus complementing the narrator's commentaries on the everyday life of the city and country that start each chapter of the novels.

Prosecutor Teodor Szacki reveals most of the symptoms of a midlife crisis. He is world weary, rather cynical, irritably sexist, and largely burnt out both at home and at work. In *Entanglement* (2007 [2010]), the first internal monologue, of which there are many throughout the trilogy, defines him in this way: "A coalface miner feels more rested than I do."[30] He finds consolation in a pedantic attentiveness to his looks—sharing with the reader his satisfaction with an impeccable haircut and a quality suit—and more or less serious affairs with young and attractive women. He survives professionally by strict adherence to rules and procedures, an approach that at times verges on a stultifying routine. Not unlike others of his kind, Szacki is truly moved and excited by one thing only—the case.

What adds to his—and our—excitement is the fact that none of the cases in the trilogy are what they first appear to be. They are characterized instead by a peculiar series of mistaken identities and false clues. In *Entanglement*, a locked-room scenario reveals far-reaching and politically charged implications, and in *A Grain of Truth* (2011 [2012]), a staged ritual murder covers up a surprisingly straightforward story of jealousy and revenge, whereas in *Rage* (2014 [2016]), an unearthed skeleton that is about to be classified as an archeological find turns out to be only several days old. One gets the impression, as Szacki does, that these mysteries are meant for him to solve, that only a detective of his intelligence and perceptiveness is able to tackle them; in fact, in *Rage* the case is addressed to Szacki and initiates a game between the prosecutor and the criminal. Partly because of his devotion to social order, and partly because of the sheer pleasure he derives from being involved in such games, Szacki is only truly alive when on a case.

Szacki's investigations depend both on his professionalism and intuition. In the Polish legal system, the role of the prosecutor resembles that of the American detective—he is responsible for gathering evidence strong enough to be used in court and for orchestrating the investigation with a group of experts and police. Prosecutor Szacki enjoys his leadership role, displaying both management skills and the ability to concentrate on many things at once. His cases are demandingly interdisciplinary, with Szacki combining archival, historical, chemical, medical, and psychological investigation. On the other hand, when confronted with a dead end, Miłoszewski's investigator puts aside empirically verifiable evidence and relies on intuition. He can enjoy moments of unexplainable illumination, as in *A Grain of Truth*, when a series of "clicks" helps him rearrange the clues to come up with a solution.

A typical representative of the Polish legal system, Szacki believes that the law is the only guarantee of society's continued functioning. As a rule, he refrains from moral judgments and emotional responses, and chooses to follow the law to the letter. This is how he understands justice. His weak point is the safety of his daughter—one cannot help thinking of other fictional tough guys here, such as Henning Mankell's Kurt Wallander or Luc Besson's Bryan Mills—and this makes him compromise his beliefs. In *Entanglement*, concern for his family's security makes him choose pragmatic withdrawal when a seemingly closed case appears to have serious political implications, with loose ends concerning the still powerful Communist secret service. In *Rage*, having been led to believe that his daughter was murdered, he loses control and administers vigilante justice himself. He gradually comes to understand that justice and the law do not necessarily go hand in hand, and that his role as a civil servant should at times go beyond the written rules. This is where the Szacki series comes to an end.

Miłoszewski's success proves that there is considerable potential in the character of Prosecutor Teodor Szacki and that he may well become an internationally recognized figure. It is perhaps unlikely that he will equal the popularity of his models—Larsson's Mikael Blomkvist and Mankell's Wallander—but he can definitely compete with them as a charismatic and memorable investigator of considerable psychological depth. To become part of the popular collective consciousness, he will need a more extensive presence in other media. So far, Szacki has appeared in a moderately successful film adaptation of *A Grain of Truth* (2015), featuring Robert Więckiewicz and directed by Boris Lankosz, and in a BBC radio adaptation of *Entanglement* (2015), dramatized by Mark Lawson as part of the Reading Europe series, but only time will tell what the future holds for Szacki.

Selected Bibliography

Entanglement (2007 [2010])
A Grain of Truth (2011 [2012])
Rage (2014 [2016])

—Jakub Lipski

T

PHILIP TRENT

Edmund Clerihew Bentley
(1875–1956)

The charismatic artist and amateur crime solver Philip Trent holds a fascinating position in the history of the Golden Age detective novel. Prefiguring and profoundly influencing the emergence of many later dilettante detectives such as Lord Peter Wimsey and Miss Marple, the amenable and genteel Philip Trent is often overlooked as one of the great literary sleuths. While for some Trent represents a more complex and nuanced realization of the often one-dimensional and mechanical ratiocinative detective (as embodied by characters such as C. Auguste Dupin and Sherlock Holmes), for others he was little more than a pale imitation and comic lampooning of these arguably more iconic and enduring figures.

Such polarization is due in part to Trent's origins. Exasperated by the infallibility and cold, analytical detachment of the detectives that had come to populate the genre, E. C. Bentley set out to create a sleuth who was not only more compassionate and sympathetic but also ultimately more flawed and inconsistent in his judgments—both romantically and professionally. Although Bentley does this by presenting Trent as a comedic imitation of previous beloved detectives, this does not detract from his individuality or impact as a literary figure. Such playfulness and irreverence had an enduring effect on the development of the Golden Age novel and is undoubtedly what makes Trent one of the most unique and endearing characters in the history of the genre.

Introduced to us in Bentley's masterpiece *Trent's Last Case* (1913), Trent is initially characterized by a combination of both investigative brilliance and bohemian insouciance. Having recently solved a murder "much like Poe had done in the murder of Mary Rogers," using nothing but "the newspapers to guide him," Trent is hired by a prominent London tabloid to solve the mysterious murder of misanthropic entrepreneur and millionaire financier Sigsbee Manderson.[1] Although initially noncommittal and seemingly disinterested when given the details of the case, Trent eventually, and somewhat begrudgingly, agrees to assist in the investigation. Described as a young and "loosely built" artist with a "high boned, quixotic face," "rough tweed clothes," and an "untidy" moustache, the eccentricities and oddities of Trent's appearance are mirrored in his equally unconventional and eclectic approach to criminal investigation.[2] His emphasis on introspection and observation, combined with his bizarre expertise in obscure fields of knowledge, such as the qualities of shoe leather, continue to baffle his investigative rival Police Inspector Murch. Trent complements these idiosyncratic techniques and practices with more objective, scientific analysis, utilizing everything from photography to fingerprint analysis.

Despite some early successes with his deductions, *Trent's Last Case* is more notable for Trent's *failures* as a detective than for any display of analytical prowess. Trent stumbles incompetently through the case, misinterpreting clues, drawing false deductions, and ultimately identifying the wrong culprit—twice. Even though Trent is correct about certain facts related to the case, he is wrong in the surmises that he bases upon those facts, misreading and misinterpreting the clues and causal links that led to Manderson's death. Not only is this a failure of logic and deduction, but also it is a failure of the analytical detective's visual paradigm of interpretation, one that emphasizes sight as the primary sense-making organ. Such prioritization of vision as a conduit to truth is fundamental to the history of detective fiction. As such, it becomes clear that the nature of Manderson's death—he is shot through the eye—operates as a symbolic manifestation of a wider denigration of vision within the text, foreshadowing the eventual failure of the "all seeing, all knowing" ratiocinative detective. Frustrated by his own failures and by the ultimately arbitrary solution to the murder, at the end of the text Trent decries the "impotence of human reason," vowing to "never touch a crime mystery again."[3]

Yet, there is more to *Trent's Last Case* than a simple deconstruction of the detective format. It is also a romance. Not only does Trent bumble incompetently through the case, but also he falls in love with one of the chief suspects, Manderson's widow Mabel. It is through this relationship that Bentley increasingly transforms Trent into a tangible, complex, and seemingly "real" character who is more than just a scientific reasoning machine. Trent's relationship with Mabel is the beating heart of the story, and their eventual union at the climax of the text more than compensates for Trent's failings as a detective.

In spite of Trent's vow to never return to crime, fortunately Bentley did bring him back for both the collection of short stories *Trent Intervenes* (1938) and another full-length novel, *Trent's Own Case* (1936). Featuring a number of satisfying mysteries that provide a welcome venue for the charismatic and urbane artist/amateur sleuth, these later stories nonetheless fail to replicate the ingenuity and originality of Bentley's first Trent mystery. Once described by Agatha Christie as "one of the three best detective stories ever written," the popularity of *Trent's Last Case* has certainly not abated.[4] All of the Trent mysteries remain in print, and *Trent's Last Case* has also been dramatized for radio and adapted three times for the big screen, the most notable version being Herbert Wilcox's 1952 adaptation featuring Michael Wilding as Philip Trent and the great Orson Welles as the misanthropic millionaire Sigsbee Manderson. Over a century after its initial publication, *Trent's Last Case* remains a humorous, sophisticated, and gripping masterpiece of detective fiction, and Trent himself is still one of our most compelling, charming, and multifaceted detectives.

Selected Bibliography

Trent's Last Case (1913)
Trent's Own Case (1936)
Trent Intervenes (1938)

—Nathan Ashman

V

CAMILLE VERHŒVEN

Pierre Lemaitre
(1951–)

Commandant Camille Verhœven, the main detective in Pierre Lemaitre's incredibly successful crime novels, is one of a kind. He is a bald man in his fifties and is as sharp as a razor, but his most obvious feature is his size, which without exception influences every other character's first impression of him and the way they interact with him from there on. Measuring 140 centimeters (approximately four feet seven inches) as a result of his mother's incessant smoking during pregnancy, Camille, as he is usually referred to in the books, is constantly confronted with shocked, bemused, or bewildered reactions to his appearance.

People respond to Camille's height with openly hostile or condescending remarks, uneasy political correctness, or motherly solicitousness, none of which is to his liking. Camille is in fact angry at the world. In addition to the conflicting emotions of love and hate that he entertains toward his dead mother, he dislikes the authorities and defies his superiors by repeatedly breaking rules during police investigations. Camille doesn't even like himself very much.

Camille's other main notable characteristic also stems from his mother, a famous painter. He is a skillful draftsman who processes his relations with and assessment of other people by sketching them. During a mental collapse following his wife's death at the end of the first novel, *Irène* (2006 [2014]), and the four difficult years that elapse before he returns reluctantly to detective work in the second novel, *Alex* (2011 [2013]), sketching becomes an obsession, his only way of coping with a relentlessly hard world.

Camille's personal relations are in fact crushingly difficult: first his wife Irène is abducted and savagely tortured to death (their unborn child is ripped from her belly and crucified), and then, when he finally meets another woman it turns out that this "Anne" is not who she claims to be; their relationship was set up by a criminal intent on manipulating the commandant into doing his bidding. Camille's junior colleague Maleval, who is like an adopted son to Camille, inadvertently betrays him (thereby causing Irène's death), and ultimately turns bad. Camille's life is characterized by numerous other personal losses: his mother is dead at the outset of the series whereas his father's death is an important element in the initial parts of the second novel. The third and last novel *Camille* (2012 [2015]) begins with a funeral: Camille's longstanding colleague and friend Armand has just died from cancer.

Classified as noir thrillers, the Verhœven trilogy blends features from thrillers and police procedurals. Each story displays its own singular mix of thriller elements like rapid point of view shifts, a sense of urgency, and the presence of serial killers, combined with aspects of classic police investigative novels centered on crime solving.[1] Gruesome violence and intricate murder abound. In *Alex* (2011 [2013]), for example, a woman is left naked in a wooden cage too small for her to move at the mercy of starving giant rats brought there by her abductor. There is always a twist in the narrative that takes the reader by surprise, as when it is revealed that Camille's badly beaten girlfriend Anne had willingly participated in the attack that almost killed her.

Camille is described as a legend in the police force because of his wife's tragic fate and, more importantly, his exceptional professional track record. It is therefore striking that most investigations end with at least a partial failure on the part of the police. As mentioned, *Irène* ends with the serial killer capturing and murdering the commandant's wife and unborn child. While the perpetrator is ultimately put in prison by Camille, this happens only after he has carried out his plan and committed all the murders he wanted to, which means that he goes to prison in triumph. In *Alex*, Camille and his team are incapable of catching up with the eponymous serial killer, who also manages to murder all of her intended victims before escaping justice through suicide; in *Rosy and John*, the police are blackmailed by a bomber into releasing his mother from prison, but Camille cannot foresee that his true intention is to kill her, and himself, in the violent explosion with which the story ends. *Camille* is somewhat different, as it ends with the commandant actually resolving the case and catching the main villain, but only after being severely manipulated, bending all rules—which entails destroying his relationships with colleagues and superiors, and exposing petty criminals to harm or death—and also losing his current girlfriend.

These partial failures by the police can be seen as a form of social commentary. The lack of the narrative closure that would reestablish order is common in sociocritical or political French crime fiction. Social critique, the failure of authorities, and the inability to protect subordinate groups like children and women are common themes in the stories about Camille, which denounce sexual violence and abuse. In *Alex*, Camille goes as far as putting a man in prison for a crime he hasn't committed in retaliation for crimes of which he is guilty but cannot be accused, namely, the rape and abuse of his half sister. Andrew Pepper is correct in counting Lemaitre among current radical crime writers with leftist sympathies, and also in detecting a poignant critique of neoliberal capitalism in his work.[2]

Camille closes with Verhœven's voluntary resignation from the police force, a gesture that is presented more as a reconciliation with life and a new start than as an imposed misfortune. Given that Lemaitre has since preferred to write stand-alone novels, it unfortunately seems unlikely that we will see more of this investigator in the future. But the Camille saga stands as one of the fiercest, most powerful, and most fascinating contributions to twenty-first-century crime writing.

Selected Bibliography

Irène (2006 [2014])
Blood Wedding (2009 [2017])
Alex (2011 [2013])
Camille (2012 [2015])
The Great Swindle (2013 [2015])
Rosy and John (2013 [2017])

—Andrea Hynynen

INSPECTOR KURT WALLANDER

Henning Mankell
(1948–2015)

Few detective characters are more representative of the Scandinavian crime fiction wave that has swept the world over the past decades than Henning Mankell's Inspector Kurt Wallander. Wallander started his career as a police officer in Malmö, Sweden, in 1969. In 1976, he transferred to the Ystad police where he remained until retirement, and Ystad and the surrounding, rural area of southern Skåne is where most of the stories take place. Occasionally, however, Wallander's investigations also take him further afield, to places like Copenhagen, Oslo, Riga, Berlin, and even South Africa.

As an investigator, Wallander relies heavily on his gut feelings, while simultaneously being a logical and effective—although somewhat forgetful—detective, who methodically sorts through the leads. He often makes mistakes but has strong morals and truly believes that police work is important to society—something that makes him prioritize his job over his family and personal life. He is a loner, but he receives a great deal of support from his team, including characters like Rydberg, Martinsson, Svedberg, Höglund, Hansson, and Nyberg, some of his most important colleagues over the many years of his career.

While in one sense the Wallander stories are resolutely local, they all, in one way or another, describe the effects of globalization and a concomitant increase in racism in Swedish society. Wallander is portrayed as a man shaped by the past who is having a difficult time understanding the changes in society. Already in *Faceless Killers* (1991 [1997]), he states that "as a policeman, he still lived in another, older world."[1] Wallander's difficulty in adjusting to his changing world runs throughout the series. Despite his uncertainties, however, he always tries to fight his own prejudices and to remain open minded.

Like many detectives before him, Wallander loves music—particularly opera—and whisky, and does much of his thinking while listening to opera in his car, or under the influence of whisky late at night, alone in his apartment. Some of his favorite composers are Puccini, Verdi, and Rossini, and he particularly admires singers Jussi Björling, Maria Callas, and Barbara Hendricks. Wallander sometimes drinks a little too much, and he is overweight and a bit of a slob. He loves junk food (which he inevitably spills on his shirts) but tries—unsuccessfully—to give it up in order to improve his health.

Wallander's poor health mirrors the society he lives in, a society that, like the one portrayed by Swedish crime writers Maj Sjöwall and Per Wahlöö in the 1960s and 1970s, is "sick." While the earlier writers depicted their Inspector Martin Beck progressing from severe colds and flus in their first novel to depression in their last, Mankell has Wallander diagnosed with diabetes—a result of his unhealthy lifestyle—in *One Step Behind* (1997 [2002]), and in the final novel in the series, *The Troubled Man* (2009 [2011]), he is slowly developing Alzheimer's. Mankell also dedicates extensive space to describing the weather and the seasonal changes of the Skåne landscape, which are also used to illustrate Wallander's moods and how his investigations are progressing.

Wallander's personal life constitutes an important part of the novels. When the series begins, Wallander's wife, Mona, has left him, and until the final novel he struggles to get over their divorce. In *Dogs of Riga* (1992 [2001]), Wallander falls in love with a Latvian woman, Baiba Liepa, whom he regards as the love of his life. They never become an official couple but stay in contact for the rest of the series. Wallander has a complicated relationship with his daughter, Linda, but they grow progressively closer during the series. Linda eventually follows in her father's footsteps and becomes a police officer, and in the last two novels they are colleagues in Ystad. The birth of Linda's daughter gives Wallander's life new meaning. He has a sister, Kristina, but they are not close, and his only living parent, his father, is an artist who detests Wallander's profession. Until his death, the old man is a constant source of frustration and guilt. Wallander has few friends. Most important are his colleague and mentor Evert Rydberg and Sten Widén, Wallander's oldest friend, but both of these men die during the series.

The popularity of the Wallander novels—and the many films and television series based on the novels—has contributed greatly to putting Swedish crime fiction and the melancholic Swedish police detective as represented by Wallander on the international crime fiction map. Nevertheless, in *The Troubled Man*, Wallander realizes that he has become obsolete and that a new generation has to take over, a generation that regards itself as European rather than Swedish and that is better equipped to deal with a new, transnational criminality. The fading of Wallander thus marks a turning point in Swedish crime fiction, as the traditional police detective is revealed as an outdated figure ripe for replacement. Kurt Wallander, the flawed, lonely, male detective with a limited, national perspective is no longer the best representative of Swedish crime fiction, instead marking an important stage in its historical development.

Selected Bibliography

Faceless Killers (1991 [1997])
The Dogs of Riga (1992 [2001])
The White Lioness (1993 [1998])
The Man Who Smiled (1994 [2005])
Sidetracked (1995 [1999])
The Fifth Woman (1996 [2000])
One Step Behind (1997 [2002])
Firewall (1998 [2002])
The Pyramid (1999; short stories [2008])
Before the Frost (2002 [2005])
An Event in Autumn (2004; novella [2014])
The Troubled Man (2009 [2011])

—Kerstin Bergman

MEI WANG

Diane Wei Liang
(1966–)

Like the "old China hands," mostly Caucasian, who have shaped Sino-US relationships throughout the twentieth century, a crop of "new China hands," mostly of Chinese descent, has emerged in the post-Mao, post–Tiananmen Square era, interpreting for Western audiences the culture, society, and politics of an increasingly prominent China. In the cultural sphere, Diane Wei Liang's Mei Wang mystery series plays just such a role, setting crimes and detective narratives behind what used to the bamboo curtain.

New China hands who stake their careers on ancestry or "Chineseness" face an inescapable paradox. Their success is due to the West's magnetic attraction to twenty-first-century China, yet these writers arrive in the West in the first place because of the century-long Chinese idolization of the metropolitan West. Situated in the West, writing in the global lingua franca of English, and adopting a perspective that will endear them to a Western readership, they share to some extent the fascinated yet apprehensive white gaze at the Eastern dragon stirring from its slumber. The beauty of China, and these writers' pride in it, is always adulterated yet, antithetically, heightened by its ugliness, most frightening in the nadirs of contemporary China—the Cultural Revolution and the Tiananmen crackdown—that these writers often select as the settings of their highbrow fiction, popular romances, and detective mysteries. Faced with these upheavals and the general malaise, "backdoorism," and corruption of modern China, one can easily distinguish the persevering, comely protagonist—Liang's detective Mei Wang—from the ugly Chinese collective.

Liang launched her English writing career with a memoir, *Lake with No Name* (2003), which explores her identity as a refugee from the Tiananmen incident. Liang followed this with the first of her Mei Wang mysteries, *The Eye of Jade*

(2008), featuring a female detective operating in the wild west of Beijing. Having abruptly resigned from the Bureau of Public Security after refusing assignations with dignitaries, Mei runs her own private-eye business, albeit illegally under Chinese law. She has a male secretary from the notoriously poor and backward Henan Province, a gender reversal that appeals to Western readers. When Mei is tapped by her family's old friend Uncle Chen to search for a lost piece of ancient imperial jade, she uncovers a family saga of shame from the Cultural Revolution in which China's national stone, jade, comes to be clouded by modern insanity. Maoist national frenzy disrupts the narrative as characters remember family betrayals and forced relocations to the countryside for reeducation.

Yet this shameful behavior is not limited to Chinese history. Uncle Chen, for example, uses Mei for his own purposes, while her beautiful celebrity sister, Lu, turns out to be so egotistic and materialistic that she is entirely unconscious of her unbecoming conduct. Mei not only seeks to right the wrongs of the past—the lost jade and repressed family suffering—but also symbolizes the persistence of traditional values and abiding conscience. In contrast, Lu stands for the modernizing China, future oriented and self-engrossed, too busy furnishing her new upscale apartment to visit her hospitalized mother. The glamour of Lu and her millennial China that Western readers gravitate to is, in a dialectical reversal, born of China's gravitation toward the West: Lu's husband owns businesses with close ties to Western capital and markets, and his family lives in Vancouver, Canada.

Liang strews unidiomatic English across the ruined landscape of China to create a problematic experience of foreignness. Characters complain "What a heat!"; a museum "had went up in the flames"; Mei is urged to "keep your heart open wide."[20] As a cultural broker, Liang is also at liberty to reinvent China as she sees fit. The famous liquor *wuliang ye*, for instance, is translated as "five virtuous liquid" rather than the more accurate "five-grain liquid."[21] This is perhaps due to the fact that the People's Republic of China's Simplified Chinese turns the traditional word for "grain" from 糧 to 粮. Both share the left radical, or element of the character, for "rice," but the traditional script has "to weigh/measure/ponder" for the right radical, which the simplified script replaces with "virtue." The traditional connotation of "weighing grains" becomes, supposedly, "grains are good." By corollary, the new China hand Liang simply simplifies Simplified Chinese by getting rid of "rice" altogether: five virtuous liquid—voilà! To those who do not speak Chinese, this exegesis amounts to nonsense upon nonsense, an evolution from one shade of blackness to another. Even the more than one billion native speakers educated in Simplified Chinese since the 1950s would be hard pressed to trace the etymology outlined here. But Liang's (mis)translation offers a telling example of the way, through the revolutionary logic of *new* in *new China*, new China hands discard what is obsolete and ugly, along with complexities of historical memory and the mysteries of the human mind.

A similar problem occurs with the Zen-like denouement that from Sherlock Holmes to Hercule Poirot so frequently ends mystery narratives. In *The Eye of Jade* this moment revolves around the Henan secretary's unwitting revelation that the eponymous "eye of jade" from the ancient capital of Luoyang, Henan, refers in the local dialect to "a spy from the royal palace" rather than to an object.[22] Mei is bowled over by the sudden revelation of who was behind her parents' separation during the Cultural Revolution and who instigated the present hunt for the jade—namely, the eye, or spy, for the "emperor" Chairman Mao. Very pat and neat, but *yuyan* (jade eye) means no such thing anywhere except perhaps in Diane Wei Liang's personal Henanese dictionary.

The Mei Wang mystery series seems to have petered out after the sequel *Paper Butterfly* (2008), which revisits the Tiananmen Square Massacre. Fear not, though; new China hands will not be short handed, for the long arm of English education, starting as early as preschool (if not antenatally) among the urban elite, reaches across global China. So long as a powerful reciprocal Sino-US mutual desire exists, the supply of English-speaking Chinese blood to the Beautiful Country (*meiguo*, or the United States) will never run dry.

Selected Bibliography

Lake with No Name (2003)
The Eye of Jade (2008)
Paper Butterfly (2008)

—Sheng-mei Ma

V. I. WARSHAWSKI

Sara Paretsky
(1947–)

At the end of *Bitter Medicine* (1987), the fourth book in Sara Paretsky's series, V. I. Warshawski contemplates retirement: "Maybe I should get out of the detective business—sell my co-op, retire to Pentwater. I tried picturing myself in this tiny town, with twelve hundred people who all knew each other's business. A quart of Black Label a day might make it tolerable."[2] This typifies both the sardonic attitude and commitment to her work that the politically engaged and highly driven private investigator has demonstrated throughout the many years of her fictional career. V. I. Warshawski (Victoria Iphigenia or Vic to her friends) is a Chicago private eye who specializes in investigating corporate skullduggery. She is politically committed and always ready to fight for the underdog, even when she is driven to despair by the lengths both individuals and corporations will go to line their own pockets at the expense of those who are unable to fight back.

In *Bitter Medicine*, for example, Warshawski takes on the medical profession, antiabortionists, and the inequalities of health-care provision in 1980s America. Paretsky clearly displays her liberal beliefs in this novel, as she does throughout the series. *Killing Orders* (1985), for instance, confronts corruption within the Catholic Church, *Blood Shot* (1988) embraces environmentalism and calls chemical companies to account, while *Blacklist* (2003) investigates the secrets and lies of two prominent Chicago families. *Blacklist* also exemplifies the ways in which the Warshawski novels explore the dark shadows cast by the past on the present—Paretsky's novels are richly interwoven with past and present narrative strands.

The ex-lawyer Warshawski (a background that comes in handy throughout the series) first appeared in *Indemnity Only* (1982). Her exact age is difficult to calculate: it is implied that she was born in about 1950, but while Paretsky has always argued that her heroine ages in real time, *Hardball* (2010) shifts her birthdate to 1957 in order to allow her to plausibly carry out the novel's physically demanding action. Paretsky then had to rework Warshawski's past in order to fit this new chronology. But regardless of her age, Warshawski is always an avowedly feminist private eye, who packs a Smith and Wesson semiautomatic pistol and drinks Johnnie Walker Black Label, thus emulating masculine figures from the American hard-boiled era such as Philip Marlowe and Sam Spade. Paretsky has stated many times that she wants to disrupt the stereotypical representation of women in the crime novel, an intention that is also a key element of the political inflection of the Warshawski series.[3]

Paretsky created Warshawski at virtually the same time that Sue Grafton created Kinsey Millhone, and a comparison between the two is illuminating. Both remain identified with a particular place, Millhone with Santa Theresa, California, and Warshawski with Chicago. The fact that Santa Theresa is a fictional construct while Warshawski's Chicago is very much a real place is emblematic of the difference between the two. Paretsky's work is politically and socially engaged in ways that her readership can identify with wherever they live. Warshawski's fight for those disenfranchised by systems of government and private corporate interests resonates strongly with the real world, and although Millhone engages with similar issues, her smaller, less overwhelmingly urban, and timelessly fictional town allows for a coziness and distance that has little place in Paretsky's writing.

There are, however, many similarities. Both heroines live alone and have an older man as a significant, nonsexual "other" in their lives. In Warshawski's case, this role is played by her downstairs neighbor Salvatore Contreras. As well as providing a father figure for the parentless Warshawski, Contreras allows Paretsky to demonstrate her independence, since Contreras, whose paternal and protective instincts remain resolutely prefeminist, often jumps needlessly to her aid. While Warshawski accepts Contreras's sometimes hapless attempts to protect her, this tolerance does not extend to the other men in her life. Paretsky, like Grafton, has constructed here an independent female character who, unlike many later female detective characters, is not distracted by a desire for the domesticity of coupledom or children.

Warshawski and Contreras share two dogs, Peppy and Mitch, and Contreras, despite (or probably because of) his flaws, provides stability and continuity for Warshawski, while Dr. Lotty Herschel is a clear maternal figure. As consistent throughout the series as Contreras, the Viennese Herschel brings "old Europe" to contemporary America, especially in *Total Recall* (2001) in which her own story as a Holocaust survivor runs throughout the narrative, interwoven with more contemporary themes. Herschel also provides an important space for Warshawski to admit her fallibilities and share her anxieties.

These two figures prevent Warshawski from being cast adrift in the flawed and dangerous world she engages with and help her make sense of the fragmented nature of modern urban society, in both social and personal terms. While readers may identify with Warshawski on a personal level, the intricacy of the plots, the effectiveness of the storytelling, and Paretsky's ability to make her political points without preaching means that she has constructed not merely a strong and sassy female protagonist but one who surreptitiously encourages readers to consider the most contentious social issues with new eyes.

Selected Bibliography

Indemnity Only (1982)
Deadlock (1984)
Killing Orders (1985)
Guardian Angel (1992)
Tunnel Vision (1994)
Hard Time (1999)
Blacklist (2003)
Fire Sale (2005)
Breakdown (2012)
Brush Back (2015)
Fallout (2017)

—Fiona Peters

CHIEF INSPECTOR REGINALD WEXFORD

Ruth Rendell
(1930–2015)

Chief Inspector Reginald Wexford's explanation of the nature of evil at the close of *End in Tears* (2015) encapsulates many of the themes that Ruth Rendell explored over the course of his career. "Love," Wexford tells DC Coleman, "doesn't excuse everything. It doesn't excuse anything. This was the worst and the wickedest motive . . . for murder I have ever known. This was what evil is. Look no further."[4] Wexford is concerned with love, with evil, with hate, and with the interplay between the three, primarily in relation to the ways in which they lead to murder, and to crime more generally. Wexford's definition also reflects his increasing ambivalence about a changing world, a recurring theme that Rendell explores throughout her work.

The first novel that Rendell published, *From Doon with Death* (1964) introduced Chief Inspector Wexford, and the last novel to feature him as a serving police office was *The Monster in the Box* (2010). Although the character had by then been in existence for forty-six years, this was not to be Wexford's final case. *The Vault* (2011) finds him retired and spending part of his time with his wife Dora in a coach house owned by his daughter Sheila, now a successful actress, located in a desirable part of London. Retirement offers him a sense of freedom, both due to the absence of the rules and protocol that bound him as a policeman, and because his new life offers an alternative environment to the fictional market town of Kingsmarkham, the setting of the majority of the Wexford novels. However, the chief inspector also misses the power and sense of identity that his previous role provided, and *The Vault* and the further very recent Wexford novel *No Man's Nightingale* (2014) allowed Rendell to develop the character into not only the uncertainties but also the liberating potential of old age.

The Wexford novels offer a persistent, long-term stability in ways that Rendell's other work does not, insofar as there are recurring characters and their main focus is always on the police investigation. This is not to say, though, that many difficult and challenging themes are not explored in them, reflecting the social and legal preoccupations of their time. For example, *Harm Done* (1999) foregrounds the controversial topic of pedophilia, while *Not in the Flesh* (2007) features a subplot on female genital mutilation amongst Somali immigrants, an important issue for Rendell not only as an author but also in her political life. Every Wexford text grapples with contemporary cultural, political, and gender issues, both through the cases he investigates and through his constant reexamination of his own, and his closest colleagues', family situations. This allows Rendell to reflect on the profound societal and familial changes that have occurred over the many years of Wexford's career.

While he is closely associated with Kingsmarkham, he does occasionally leave. For example, in *Murder Bring Once Done* (1972), the chief inspector convalesces in London, staying with his nephew Howard, himself a detective inspector. Here he becomes involved in a murder that exposes him to religious cults, dysfunctional family dynamics, and deceit. This allows Rendell to develop her character, even at this early stage, by placing him in new territory and forcing him to step out of his familiar setting. In London, he has no official "police" status and authority, and Rendell uses this device to deepen Wexford's understanding of both the foibles and the underlying dysfunctionality he encounters in criminal and noncriminal alike.

Wexford spanned Rendell's writing life; she returned to him as a stable presence, interspersing the Wexford novels amongst her other work. Although the novels do not always offer happy endings, a sense of stability, however fragile, is maintained throughout, something very much lacking in most of her non-Wexford texts, especially those written under her pseudonym of Barbara Vine. Additionally, the long-running television series *The Inspector Wexford Mysteries* (1987–2000) worked to popularize Rendell's work generally, but especially cemented Wexford in the popular cultural imagination. She herself commented that actor George Baker's portrayal of Wexford made him a far better character than she intended and that this influenced subsequent Wexford texts.

Wexford is no John Rebus or Harry Hole; his family life is relatively untroubled, yet it reflects in a subtle and gentle fashion on the dysfunctions of human relationships that lie at the heart of the crimes he investigates. His two daughters Sheila and Sylvia represent the changing place of women in contemporary society, and through them Rendell foregrounds the vicissitudes of family life that have to be negotiated, more or less successfully, by everyone, criminal and policeman alike. The "family man" Chief Inspector Wexford thus stands as a low-key but seminally important twentieth-century detective.

Selected Bibliography

From Doon with Death (1964)
A New Lease of Death (1967)
Woolf to the Slaughter (1967)
The Best Man to Die (1969)
A Guilty Thing Surprised (1969)
No More Dying Then (1970)
Murder Being Once Done (1972)
Some Lie and Some Die (1973)
Shake Hands Forever (1974)
A Sleeping Life (1979)
Put On by Cunning (1981)
The Speaker of Mandarin (1983)
An Unkindness of Ravens (1984)
The Veiled One (1988)
Going Wrong (1990)
Kissing the Gunner's Daughter (1991)
Simisola (1994)
Road Rage (1997)
Harm Done (1999)
The Babes in the Wood (2002)
End in Tears (2005)
Not in the Flesh (2007)
The Monster in the Box (2009)
The Vault (2011)
No Man's Nightingale (2013)

—Fiona Peters

LORD PETER WIMSEY

Dorothy L. Sayers
(1893–1957)

Golden Age crime writing produced many enduringly popular detectives, but few have aroused the passions of readers as thoroughly as the foppish, aristocratic detective Lord Peter Wimsey. Criticized as both tediously conventional and as fundamentally unbelievable, he can be seen as embodying everything politically regressive and aesthetically dubious about detective fiction. On the other hand, for his many admirers he is not just an ingenious and entertaining detective but also one the most fascinating characters of early twentieth-century popular fiction, a literary creation who approximates a real human being, with all the depth, complexity, and ambiguity this implies. The explanation for this disagreement may lie in Wimsey's history, for few literary detectives have changed so much over the course of their careers. From his first appearance in 1923 to his last in 1942, Lord Peter developed from a two-dimensional figure of fun into a believable, nuanced, and sympathetic character whose main attraction is not how he solves murders but how he solves the problems of life and love.

Lord Peter began his career as a derivative figure combining the analytical abilities of Arthur Conan Doyle's Sherlock Holmes, the cultured urbanity of E. C. Bentley's Philip Trent, and the amiable fatuousness of P. G. Wodehouse's Bertie Wooster. He is an aristocratic lightweight, whose "long amiable face" looks as if "it had generated spontaneously from his top hat, as white maggots breed from Gorgonzola."[5] He combines an ostentatiously cultured persona—he collects incunabula, drinks vintage port, quotes incessantly from the classics, and plays Bach in his tastefully decorated bachelor's suite—with a stream of slangy banter. A good idea, for instance, "wangs the nail over the crumpet."[6]

He is also an able detective. Assisted by his manservant Bunter and his associate and eventual brother-in-law Detective Inspector Parker, he solves murders through physical analysis (in *Whose Body?* [1923] he "reads" a corpse to prove that it was disguised after death) combined with a psycho-sociological method based not infrequently on the interpretation of cultural markers such as literary and artistic taste. These skills, alongside an unexpected physical prowess, enable him to solve murders in *Unnatural Death* (1927) and *The Unpleasantness at the Bellona Club* (1928), and to save his brother from a false murder charge in *Clouds of Witness* (1926). In *Strong Poison* (1930), Wimsey must again challenge a seemingly open-and-shut police case in order to save detective writer Harriet Vane from hanging, and it is at this point that he begins his metamorphosis from caricature into character.

Wimsey's love for Vane, and the carefully staged romance that gradually develops between them in *Strong Poison*, *Have His Carcase* (1932), *Gaudy Night* (1935), and *Busman's Honeymoon* (1937), is central to this transformation. While Dorothy L. Sayers had already begun to develop his character through his experience of shell shock and his ambivalence over the sometimes-deadly results of his investigations, it is primarily through this relationship that Wimsey comes alive. As he says of Vane's writing, in one of Sayers's deft metafictional touches, a real book can only be written by abandoning the "jig-saw" detective puzzle format and dealing with "human beings" with all of their "violent and life-like feelings."[7] In the case of Lord Peter and Harriet, these feelings concern the importance—and difficulty—of maintaining individual integrity in personal relationships. Sayers's triumph is not the resolution of this problem but her protracted exploration of its existence.

Over the course of his remarkable literary career, Lord Peter did not just solve crimes and win the heart of his beloved; he also became a vital model of what the fictional detective could be. His aristocratic garrulousness, charm, and wit, and arguably excessive level of accomplishment made him one of the prime points of resistance for writers, such as Raymond Chandler, who wished to develop a grittier, more realistic form of crime fiction. Wimsey's "exquisite and impossible gentility," Chandler famously argued, had no place in the "hard-boiled chronicles of mean streets" that make up so much of post–Golden Age crime fiction. And this is a fair enough observation, although one that fails to do justice to the dark and at times morbid undercurrents of Sayers's fictional world; Chandler's description of the hard-boiled detective as a "hero" and a "man of honor" would certainly apply as well to Wimsey as to Philip Marlowe, although his table manners are no doubt considerably better.[8]

But if Wimsey has no place in the hard-boiled form that seems so suitable to our own fractured era, he nonetheless remains a potent figure. His novels remain in print in multiple editions, no mean achievement for a detective now approaching his centenary, and he has been portrayed on television twice, first by Ian Carmichael in the early 1970s and, more memorably, by Edward Petherbridge in a 1987 series focusing on his romance with Vane (played by Harriet Walter). Nor has Lord Peter's literary life come to an end, as his adventures have been continued by Jill Paton Walsh in four "posthumous" novels. While for the purist these noncanonical novels simply do not count, they are a clear indication that the world still needs Wimsey.

Selected Bibliography

Whose Body? (1923)
Clouds of Witness (1926)
Unnatural Death (1927)
The Unpleasantness at the Bellona Club (1928)
Strong Poison (1930)
Five Red Herrings (1931)
Have His Carcase (1932)
Murder Must Advertise (1933)
The Nine Tailors (1934)
Gaudy Night (1935)
Busman's Honeymoon (1937)

—Eric Sandberg

NERO WOLFE

Rex Stout
(1886–1975)

Nero Wolfe is an eccentric, misogynistic, ponderously overweight middle-aged private detective whose brilliantly nimble mind is much sought after by clients to solve crimes the police cannot. He presides over an all-male household consisting of himself and three assistants in a New York City brownstone famously located on West Thirty-Fifth Street. The household is expensive to maintain, so the clients Wolfe chooses to accept are usually rich and his fees are high. Thanks to his enviably one-sided win/loss record, his pricey services are almost never declined.

This now legendary character, among the most famous detectives in literary history, was the creation of author Rex Stout, who wrote thirty-three novels and thirty-nine short stories featuring the rotund sleuth, beginning with *Fer-de-Lance*

(1934) and ending with *A Family Affair* (1975). Nero Wolfe's adventures have been adapted to film as well as to radio and television. In the millennial year 2000 the extraordinary international success of the Nero Wolfe stories led to their being nominated as the Best Mystery Series of the Century at Bouchercon, the foremost annual convention of mystery writers and readers. The award ultimately went to Agatha Christie's Hercule Poirot books, a clear indication of the august company Stout's detective keeps.

Wolfe shares the spotlight throughout the series with his primary assistant, Archie Goodwin, an independently licensed detective who lives in the brownstone on West Thirty-Fifth while serving as secretary and legman for his corpulent boss. Goodwin is the Boswell to Nero Wolfe's Dr. Johnson, the Watson to his Sherlock Holmes. The narrator of all the Nero Wolfe stories, Goodwin is young, rough around the edges, street smart, and devoted to his employer, who frequently corrects, upbraids, and even insults his young factotum. For his part, Goodwin is not afraid to sound the voice of common sense to the self-styled genius who pays his salary. When funds are getting low, Goodwin is the first to advise Wolfe not to be too fussy about accepting a new client. While the older man might represent an old-world style (Wolfe is Montenegrin by birth), Goodwin is purely American, "a lineal descendant of Huck Finn," according to the noted critic and historian Jacques Barzun.[9]

Next to his astonishing analytical skills, Nero Wolfe is best known for his personal quirks. For one thing, he almost never leaves the brownstone, finding the physical effort far too discouraging. He depends on Goodwin to question witnesses and other key players in the case at hand. When Wolfe finds he must interrogate these players himself, he assigns Goodwin the task of persuading them to come to West Thirty-Fifth Street, where they are ushered into a red leather chair opposite the desk of the great man himself, who frequently excuses himself from rising to greet them.

Another idiosyncrasy: Wolfe is a slave to the schedule that governs his highly ordered life. Four hours every day are spent on his passionately pursued avocation of raising orchids. Following breakfast—prepared by his live-in Swiss chef, Fritz Brenner, who serves as both cook and butler—Wolfe religiously repairs to an upper floor, where his collection of orchids is housed. There, in the company of his full-time orchid maven, the laconic Theodore Horstmann (who also resides in the brownstone, completing the household entourage), he tends his prize-winning collection from nine to eleven. He repeats this ritual from four to six in the afternoon. All other business, including the visits from the obliging witnesses who answer his commanding invitations, must fit around this schedule.

Besides Goodwin, Wolfe employs several other detectives on a freelance basis when Goodwin's plate is already full or when Wolfe wants to keep an investigation secret even from his main assistant. Saul Panzer is unkempt but highly competent, with a sharp memory that is often invaluable to Wolfe; Fred Durkin is less intelligent than Panzer (Goodwin calls him "dumb") but a useful plodder; Orrie Cather is the slickest and handsomest of the freelancers, and perhaps the least likeable.

Remarkably, this set of main characters was already present in *Fer-de-Lance* and remained stable for decades. Nero Wolfe's world is a static one; neither he nor any other character ages, nor does his daily routine change, nor do the house and its furnishings ever seriously alter. Whether the plot involves a group of middle-aged friends terrified that one of their number is out to murder them (*The League of Frightened Men* [1935]), an ingeniously designed murder for which Goodwin is being framed (*Black Orchids* [1942]), the suspected poisoning of an unwed mother (*Champagne for One* [1958]), or any of the dozens of other Nero Wolfe stories, the Depression-era atmosphere in which Nero Wolfe was originally conceived remains. Indeed, the series is pleasingly dated. "Those stories have ignored time for thirty-nine years," Rex Stout said to his biographer. "Any reader who can't or won't do the same should skip them."[10]

Many Nero Wolfe fans find comfort in the books' stability. "Reading a Nero Wolfe," as one commentator put it, "is akin to visiting the home of an old friend or returning to the same inn on Cape Cod each year, nodding in delight at the familiar star-patterned quilt on the same canopied bed in the usual room, finding the idyllic view from the patio unchanged, unspoiled."[11] In the characters of Nero Wolfe and Archie Goodwin, Rex Stout combined the refined detective of the classic British mystery with the hard-boiled American shamus spawned by the Prohibition gangster era. The result was a publishing success story that has rarely been equaled, a mystery series that continues to please, and a posthumous fan base any author would envy.

Selected Bibliography

Too Many Cooks (1938)
In the Best Families (1950)
The Golden Spiders (1953)
The Black Mountain (1954)
The Doorbell Rang (1965)

—Joseph Sgammato

LILY WU

Juanita Sheridan
(1906–1974)

Juanita Sheridan's quartet of Lily Wu novels may fall outside the traditional dates of Golden Age detective fiction, but her amateur sleuth closely follows the model delineated by this genre's most famous female detective, Miss Marple. Both are likened to Nemesis, both are emotionally detached, both use conversation to elicit information, and both employ gender stereotypes for their own purposes. Yet Lily is important in her own right. She is the primary detective in her series, which was a first for fictional Asian women, who were normally cast as subordinates, as in James Norman's *Murder Chop Chop* (1942). Moreover, Sheridan's depiction of Lily circumvents the vilification of Chinese people often found in earlier crime novels influenced by xenophobic "Yellow Peril" theories, such as Sax Rohmer's Fu Manchu novels. Consequently, these mid-twentieth-century novels are crucial texts for exploring race, primarily through the figure of Sheridan's detective.

As racial prejudice was common in 1940s and 1950s America, it is unsurprising that Lily encounters this problem, with characters such as Mrs. Benson in *The Kahuna Killers* being reluctant to treat her as an equal. Lily's cases also regularly involve cultural tensions. The novels' settings contribute to this, with the first, *The Chinese Chop* (1949) being set in New York, whilst the others are set predominantly in a multicultural Hawaii, where Sheridan lived for a time, and where both Lily and her Watson-like friend, Janice Cameron (the narrator of the series) were born. Lily's understanding of Chinese and Hawaiian culture is a key part of her detecting skills. In *The Kahuna Killer* (1951) and *The Mamo Murders* (1952), the crimes originate from, and are exacerbated by, nonnative Hawaiian residents ignoring native Hawaiian traditions and attempting to Westernize the island, in particular by altering the landscape for tourism. Lily's affinity with the relatively poorer native Hawaiians provides her with information the police do not possess, thus helping her succeed in her investigations.

Having another character narrate Lily's investigations further plays into Sheridan's depictions of race, as the reader's perceptions of Lily, especially in the first novel, rely on Janice's presentation of her. Janice's Hawaiian upbringing positively shapes her outlook on race and makes her open to cultural difference, yet even she is culpable for the occasional erroneous assumption when getting to know Lily, which reveals the dangers of relying on external appearances and stereotypes. Postcolonial theoretician Homi Bhabha defines stereotyping as "a form of knowledge and identification that vacillates between what is . . . already known, and something that must be anxiously repeated."[12] A similar process is apparent in Janice's early descriptions of Lily in *The Chinese Chop* (1949), when she is unsure of her new roommate's intentions and frequently relies on the stereotype of Chinese people as deceitful. For example, when the corpse of the rooming-house superintendent is discovered and Lily is waiting to be interviewed by the police, Janice notes how "she looked pathetically tiny and fragile. . . . At the same time I became aware that her fragility was completely deceptive."[13] Yet Lily's "deceptive" appearance is not inherent slyness (as Janice quickly realizes) but a tactic she employs to achieve justice. Similarly, Chinese women are often regarded as quiet and therefore innocuous, and Lily uses this preconception to scout locations, as the other characters overlook her, while her assumed air of stereotypical inscrutable mystery allows her to withhold information during her cases until she wants to disclose it.

The camouflage offered by gender stereotypes is another important part of Lily's detecting arsenal. Male characters frequently focus on Lily's beauty, meaning they underestimate her intelligence. Lily uses this to allay the criminals' suspicions, and her innocent demeanor enables her to discover more information. Janice also emphasizes the delusive nature of Lily's appearance when she tells her, "You look like a beautiful doll, Lily. You sound like Nemesis. Heaven help the woman—or man—who tries to outmanoeuvre you."[14] Moreover, Lily often utilizes the assumption that women are less threatening than men for her own ends. As Janice says in *The Mamo Murders* (1952), "The personality Lily was assuming made her look all of fourteen, about as formidable as a child."[15] As with the juxtaposition of "beautiful doll" and "Nemesis," this reinforces the contrast between Lily's external appearance and her intentions.

However, Lily's ethnicity and gender do make her vulnerable, for unlike her Western counterparts she is unable to quickly gain the police's trust. The first novel epitomizes this, as initially she is under suspicion of murder. Janice highlights Lily's precarious position by noting that she has "the same self-protection as the uncanny stillness of a wild forest creature which knows the stalking enemy is at hand."[16] Usually the detective occupies the role of the hunter, but here Lily is the quarry of both the murderer and the police.

Lily Wu is a fascinating detective. She does not just solve crimes but also helps other characters—and readers—discover their own prejudices and assumptions. She is a detective who feels in many ways familiar yet who broke the mold for the fictional representation of ethnic minorities.

Selected Bibliography

The Chinese Chop (1949)
The Kahuna Killer (1951)
The Mamo Murders (1952)
The Waikiki Widow (1953)

—Kate Jackson

DETECTIVE SERGEANT X

Derek Raymond (Robin Cook)
(1931–1994)

In the United Kingdom, Derek Raymond's Factory novels have long been considered classics of British noir, and they are now beginning to build up a well-deserved international reputation. The five novels in the series are often terrifying, frequently brutal, and always bleak. They feel at times more like open wounds than works of fiction. At the center of each novel, both structurally and morally, is the unnamed narrator, a detective sergeant with the London Metropolitan Police struggling to cope with the urban decay, social disintegration, amorality, and violence of Thatcherite England.

Despite the narrator's refusal to identify himself by name, we learn a great deal about him over the course of the series. His life is as desolate as the world he inhabits, his history one of incessant loss: his parents are dead, and his first serious lover died of an overdose. He was married, and had a child, but his wife went mad and murdered their daughter. Most of his friends on the police force have been either killed or maimed in the line of duty. These losses—particularly the death of his daughter, for which he blames himself—have left his personal life blankly empty: he is a man with a "sparse emotional map."[1] The few friends that remain to him are important, both personally and at times in his investigations, but their sporadic presence only reveals more clearly the hollowness of his life.

When the series begins in *He Died with His Eyes Open* (1984), the sergeant is forty-one years old. He lives alone in an apartment so horrible that a rare day of sunshine only makes it look "newer and nastier."[2] He drinks too much, smokes a disgusting brand of cigarette in the hope that it will make him quit, and lives solely for his job with A14, or Unexplained Deaths, the distinctly unglamorous department responsible for investigating cases that "have been written off upstairs as unimportant, not pressworthy, not well connected and not big crime."[3] He spends most of his time in walking the grimy, rain-swept streets, in a series of cheap and nasty pubs, or between the sickly green-painted walls of room 205 of the "Factory," or the Poland Street police station after which the series is named. He has repeatedly been passed over for promotion and lives in a constant state of conflict with the police hierarchy, who loathe his independence, refusal to respect rank, and unwillingness to treat police work as a career rather than a calling. Beyond these external facts, we come to know the narrator on a more intimate level as well, as we share his nightmares and his sorrow at a world too broken for him to fix.

The main thing that is wrong with the Britain of the Factory novels is that it is *modern* Britain. The narrator is nostalgic for a vanished world (one that may well never have existed), in which the streets were safe to walk, people treated each other with respect, and society functioned, a Britain that had a place for all of its people. Like the narrator's apartment, everything that is new in the new England of the 1980s is either meretricious or degraded. The rich and powerful have abnegated responsibility, leaving governance in the hands of an incompetent and careless bureaucracy (including the police), and the poor and vulnerable have been left utterly exposed to the depredations of a world that simply does not care. These are novels set in the end times: "My work," the sergeant informs us, "tells me that our history is over, we are all over."[4]

The key indicator of the state of this fallen England, this grey and unpleasant land, is the presence of the killers whom the narrator pursues throughout the novels. While he has little patience for criminals, or "villains," of any sort, the sergeant's primary obsession is with these murderers. They are, on the one hand, an embodiment of evil, people who "think nothing of taking life" but whose own "existence fascinates" them; "that's the imbalance that we mean by evil."[5] On the other hand, they are not just amoral aberrations but a symptom of Britain's illness, its failure. As one of the series' many killers claims, "I don't believe that I am the disaster—I think I'm just a reminder that people are living in one."[6]

The unnamed narrator's attempts to catch these killers do not rely on any extraordinarily acute investigative skills, on deduction, or on the accumulation of evidence. In fact, the narrator knows who the killer is early in each novel, and catching them is a matter of intense psychological confrontation that culminates in personal exposure to the concentrated evil of the killer. Despite this danger, the sergeant almost never carries a weapon and rejects the routine brutality that characterizes the police work of many of his colleagues.

Instead, the narrator spends much of each novel developing a powerful empathic connection with the victim of the crime, entering into the grain of their sad and broken lives; experiencing their hopes, their loneliness, and their loss; and coming ultimately to identify—utterly—with them. Hence the title of what is considered by many to be Raymond's masterpiece is *I Was Dora Suarez*, in which the narrator struggles not just to catch and punish Dora's killer but also to "bring her back . . . just as if her death had never happened."[7] This is of course impossible, except insofar as the sergeant's narration is itself the realization of this dream. As we read the novel, Dora comes to life through the scraps and fragments of existence assembled by the sergeant, and for him this is just as important—if not more important—than catching the killer. It is perhaps because of this that the detective remains nameless. His anonymity allows him to move more easily into the lives of the victims, to assume for a time their identities, just as it allows us as readers to move more easily into his life and to take up, however briefly, the burden of his quest for justice.

Selected Bibliography

The Factory series:

He Died with His Eyes Open (1984)
The Devil's Home on Leave (1985)
How the Dead Live (1986)
I Was Dora Suarez (1990)
Dead Man Upright (1993)

Other novels:

The Crust on Its Uppers (1962)
A State of Denmark (1970)
The Hidden Files (1992)
Not Till the Red Fog Rises (1994)

—Eric Sandberg

Notes

INTRODUCTION

1. Kenzo Kitakata, *The Cage*, trans. Paul Warham (New York: Vertical, 2006 [1983]), 51.
2. Marshall McLuhan, "From Da Vinci to Holmes," in *The Mechanical Bride: Folklore of Industrial Man* (London: Routledge and Keegan Paul, 1951), 107–9.
3. Barbara Herrnstein Smith, *Contingencies of Value: Alternative Perspectives for Critical Theory* (Cambridge, MA: Harvard University Press, 1991), 30.
4. Ibid., 84, 96.
5. Ibid., 10.
6. Q. D. Leavis, "The Case of Miss Dorothy Sayers," *Scrutiny*, December 1937, 336, 340.
7. Genesis 4:10, King James Version.
8. Heather Worthington, *Key Concepts in Crime Fiction* (Houndmills, UK: Palgrave, 2011), xii.
9. Ibid., ix.
10. "What Books Are Library Users Borrowing?" Public Lending Right, last modified February 13, 2015, http://www.bl.uk/plr. The exception, Nora Roberts, writes romance, which while undoubtedly popular is more strongly gendered and, arguably, more socially limited than crime fiction.
11. Michael Chabon, "Trickster in a Suit of Lights: Thoughts on the Modern Short Story," in *Maps and Legends: Reading and Writing along the Borderlands* (New York: Harper, 2009). 8.
12. Ursula K. Le Guin, "Preface to the 1989 Edition," in *The Language of the Night: Essays on Fantasy and Science Fiction*, ed. Susan Wood and Ursula K. Le Guin (New York: HarperCollins, 1989), 3.
13. Pierre Lemaitre, *Irène*, trans. Frank Wynne (New York: MacLehose Press, 2014), 349.
14. A seminal text here is L. C. Knights's "How Many Children Had Lady Macbeth?" which marks a division line between an older critical focus on character and more modern textual interests. For more on Knights's essay, see Carol Chillington Rutter, "Remind Me: How Many Children Had Lady Macbeth?" in *Shakespeare Survey*, vol. 57, *Macbeth and Its Afterlife*, ed. Peter Holland (Cambridge: Cambridge University Press, 2004).
15. John V. Knapp, "Introduction: Self-Preservation and Self-Transformation: Interdisciplinary Approaches to Literary Character," *Style* 24, no. 3 (1990): 349.
16. Alain Robbe-Grillet, "On Several Obsolete Notions," in *For a New Novel: Essays of Fiction*, trans. Richard Howard (Evanston, IL: Northwestern University Press, 1989), 28.
17. G. K. Chesterton, introduction, in *Edwin Drood and Master Humphrey's Clock*, by Charles Dickens (London: J. M. Dent and Sons, 1915), viii.
18. Rachel Ablow, "Wilkie Collins," in *The Oxford Encyclopedia of British Literature*, vol. 1, ed. David Scott Kastan (Oxford: Oxford University Press, 2006), 48.
19. Wilkie Collins, "Preface to the 1861 Edition," in *The Woman in White* (Ware, UK: Wordsworth Editions, 2002), xxvii–xxviii.

20. Dorothy L. Sayers, "Aristotle on Detective Fiction," *English* 1, no. 1 (1936): 26, accessed February 11, 2014, doi:10.1093/english/1.1.23.

21. Northrop Frye, "Autobiographical Reflections," in *Collected Works of Northrop Frye*, vol. 25, *Northrop Frye's Fiction and Miscellaneous Writings*, ed. Robert D. Denham and Michael Dolzani (Toronto: University of Toronto Press, 2007), 4–5.

22. Northrop Frye, "Notebook 33," in *Collected Works of Northrop Frye*, vol. 15, *Northrop Frye's Notebooks on Romance*, ed. Michael Dolzani (Toronto: University of Toronto Press, 2004), 75.

23. Salander is not included in this book, an example of the type of necessary yet necessarily inflammatory decision involved in this sort of list making. Few recent crime characters have had a more pronounced public impact than Salander, and few have inspired such fierce identification amongst readers.

24. Andrea Hynynen, "Death and Immortality in Fred Vargas's Crime Fiction," in *Death in Literature*, ed. Outi Hakola and Sari Kivistö (Newcastle-upon-Tyne, UK: Cambridge Scholars, 2014), 254.

25. Vera Caspary, *Laura* (London: J. M. Dent and Sons, [1942] 1987), 79.

A

1. Fred Vargas, *Seeking Whom He May Devour*, trans. David Bellos (London: Vintage, 2005), 66.

2. Ibid., 242.

3. David Platten, "Jean-Baptiste Adamsberg," in *Detective*, ed. Barry Forshaw (Bristol, UK: Intellect, 2016), 120–29.

4. Dominique Meyer-Bolzinger, "Adamsberg, fils de Maigret," *Temps noirs* 15 (2012): 85–100.

5. Rampo Edogawa, *The Early Cases of Akechi Kogorō*, trans. William Varteresian (Fukuoka, Japan: Kurodahan Press, 2014), 25.

6. Ross Macdonald, *The Moving Target* (Glasgow: Fontana, 1974), 10.

7. Ibid., 86.

8. Ross Macdonald, *The Drowning Pool* (London: Penguin, 2012), 131.

9. Ibid., 24.

10. Fredric Jameson, "Philip K. Dick, in Memorium," in *Archaeologies of the Future: The Desire Called Utopia and Other Science Fictions* (London: Verso, 2005), 345.

11. Philip K. Dick, *A Scanner Darkly* (London: Victor Gollancz, 1999), 67.

12. Ibid., 20.

13. Ibid., 48.

14. Ibid., 73.

15. Ibid., 16.

B

1. Sharadindu Bandyopadhyay, "Where There's a Will," in *Picture Imperfect and Other Byomkesh Bakshi Mysteries*, trans. Sreejata Guha (New Delhi: Penguin, 1999), 104.

2. Sharadindu Bandyopadhyay, "The Frontier Diamond," in *Byomkesh Samagra* (Calcutta: Ananda, 2012), 46 (my translation).

3. Sharadindu Bandyopadhyay, "The Gramophone Pin Mystery," in *Picture Imperfect and Other Byomkesh Bakshi Mysteries*, trans. Sreejata Guha (New Delhi: Penguin, 1999), 29.

4. The partnership lasts until the author begins to narrate the adventures himself from "Room Number 2" (1964) onward.

5. Sharadindu Bandyopadhyay, "Primeval Adversary," in *Byomkesh Samagra* (Calcutta: Ananda Publishers, 2012), 433 (my translation).

6. Friedrich Dürrenmatt, *The Inspector Barlach Mysteries*, trans. Joel Agee (Chicago: University of Chicago Press, 2006), 135.

7. Ibid., 50.

8. Ibid., 73, 154.

9. Ibid., 93.

10. Ibid., 176.

11. Umberto Eco, *The Name of the Rose* (New York: Harcourt, 1983), 16.

12. In 1327, Charles Sanders Peirce had not yet described abductive reasoning, precluding Eco and T. A. Sebeok from more accurately describing the reasoning of both William and Sherlock as abduction.

13. Holmes claims he does not guess; it would be more accurate to say that he does not guess incorrectly.

14. Eco, *Name of the Rose*, 26.

15. Ibid., 326.

16. Maj Sjöwall and Per Wahlöö, *The Fire Engine That Disappeared*, trans. Joan Tate (London: Fourth Estate, 2011), 210.

17. Maj Sjöwall and Per Wahlöö, *The Man Who Went Up in Smoke*, trans. Joan Tate (London: Fourth Estate, 2011), 93–94.

18. Sjöwall and Wahlöö, *Fire Engine That Disappeared*, 210.

19. Maj Sjöwall and Per Wahlöö, *The Laughing Policeman*, trans. Alan Blair (London: Fourth Estate, 2016), 119.

20. Arthur W. Upfield, *Cake in the Hat Box* (Sydney: Pan Books, 1983), 131.

21. Arthur W. Upfield, *The Bushman Who Came Back* (New York: Macmillan, 1957), 28.

22. See the BBC Radio 4 Book Club program on *The City and the City* for more on Miéville's self-conscious engagement with the traditions of the genre.

23. China Miéville, *The City and the City* (New York: Del Ray, 2010), 53.

24. Ibid., 242.

25. Ibid., 312.

26. Joseph Skvorecky, *The Mournful Demeanour of Lieutenant Boruvka*, trans. Rosemary Kavan, George Theiner, and Kaca Polackova (London: Victor Gollancz, 1973), 147.

27. Ibid., 24.

28. Joseph Skvorecky, *The Return of Lieutenant Boruvka*, trans. Paul Wilson (London: Norton, 1991), 158.

29. Julian Symons, *Bloody Murder* (London: Faber & Faber, 1972), 153–54.

30. Gladys Mitchell, *St Peter's Finger* (London: Sphere, 1990), 236.

31. Gladys Mitchell, *The Saltmarsh Murders* (London: Hogarth, 1984), 44; Gladys Mitchell, *Laurels Are Poison* (London: Penguin, 1961), 202.

32. Mitchell, *Saltmarsh Murders*, 120.

33. Gladys Mitchell, *The Mystery of a Butcher's Shop* (London: Sphere, 1990), 65; Mary Cadogan and Patricia Craig, "Introduction," in Mitchell, *Saltmarsh Murders*, 5.

34. Mitchell, *Laurels Are Poison*, 8.

35. Mitchell, *Saltmarsh Murders*, 44.

36. Mitchell, *Laurels Are Poison*, 167.

37. Wolf Haas, *The Bone Man*, trans. Annie Janusch (Brooklyn: Melville House, 2012), 130.

38. Wilkie Collins, *The Law and the Lady* (Oxford: Oxford University Press, 1992), 9.

39. Ibid., 116.

40. Ibid., 182.

41. G. K. Chesterton, *The Father Brown Omnibus* (New York: Dodd, Mead, 1935), 16.

42. Ibid., 5.

43. Ibid., 23.
44. Ibid., 54.
45. Ibid., 81.
46. Charles Dickens, *Bleak House* (London: Penguin Popular Classics, 1994), 282.
47. Ibid., 282.
48. Ibid., 680.
49. Ibid., 701.
50. See National Police Officers Role of Honour, "Metropolitan Police: 1829–1899," last updated January 13, 2012, http://www.policerollofhonour.org.uk.

C

1. Ellis Peters, introduction, in *A Rare Benedictine: The Seventh Cadfael Omnibus* (London: Warner Futura, 1997), 456.
2. Andrew Pepper, *Unwilling Executioner: Crime Fiction and the State* (Oxford: Oxford University Press, 2016).
3. Dominique Jeannerod, "Mort du détective et fin de l'Histoire chez Didier Daeninckx," *Australian Journal of French Studies* 44, no. 1 (2012): 34, 36.
4. Didier Daeninckx, *Murder in Memorium*, trans. Liz Heron (London: Serpent's Tail, 2005), 58–59.
5. Ibid., 47.
6. Margery Allingham, *The Crime at Black Dudley* (Harmondsworth, UK: Penguin, 1950), 11.
7. B. A. Pike, *Campion's Career* (Bowling Green, OH: Popular Press, 1987), 8.
8. Margery Allingham, *Mystery Mile* (London: Penguin, 1952), 71; Pike, *Campion's Career*, 8.
9. Melissa Schaub, *Middlebrow Feminism in Classic British Detective Fiction: The Female Gentleman* (New York: Palgrave Macmillan, 2013), 87.
10. Ed McBain, *Cop Hater* (London: Orion, 2003), ix.
11. LeRoy Panek, *The American Police Novel: A History* (Jefferson, NC: McFarland, 2003), 57.
12. Ed McBain, *Cop Hater*, 9.
13. Evan Hunter, quoted in Erin E. MacDonald, *Ed McBain/Evan Hunter: A Literary Companion* (Jefferson, NC: McFarland, 2012).
14. Frederic Dannay and Manfred Lee, "'William Hope Hodgson and the Detective Story' by Ellery Queen," William Hope Hodgson, ed. Sam Gafford, last modified August 10, 2012, http://williamhopehodgson.wordpress.com (Dannay and Lee published under the pseudonym Ellery Queen).
15. William Hope Hodgson, "The Hog," in *The Casebook of Carnacki, the Ghost Finder* (Ware, UK: Wordsworth Editions, 2006), 190.
16. Howard Phillips Lovecraft, *Supernatural Horror in Literature* (New York: Dover, 1973), 85.
17. Clark Ashton Smith, "In Appreciation of William Hope Hodgson," William Hope Hodgson, ed. Sam Gafford, last modified August 3, 2012, https://williamhopehodgson.wordpress.com.
18. In interviews Vázquez Montalbán has described this unusual form of literary criticism as a kind of sarcastic cultural joke, particularly when Carvalho inverts the status of "high" and "low" literature by burning "classics."
19. Manuel Vázquez Montalbán, *Off Side*, trans. Ed Emery (New York: Melville House, 2012), 11.
20. Manuel Vázquez Montalbán, *Murder in the Central Committee*, trans. Patrick Camiller (London: Serpents' Tail, 1984), 19.

21. Manuel Vázquez Montalbán, *The Angst-Ridden Executive*, trans. Ed Emery (New York: Melville House, 2013), 23.

22. Manuel Vázquez Montalbán, *Southern Seas*, trans. Patrick Camiller (New York: Melville House, 2012), 8, 7.

23. Leonardo Padura Fuentes, *Havana Blue*, trans. Peter Bush (London: Bitter Lemon Press, 2007), 69.

24. T. S. Eliot, "Introduction to *The Moonstone*," quoted in Deidre David, ed., *The Cambridge Companion to the Victorian Novel* (Cambridge: Cambridge University Press, 2001), 179.

25. Wilkie Collins, *The Moonstone*, Humanities Text Initiative edition, http://www.hti.umich.edu, 114.

26. Ibid., 155.

D

1. P. D. James, *Original Sin* (New York: Vintage, 2009), 352.

2. P. D. James, *The Black Tower* (New York: Touchstone, 2001), 74.

3. P. D. James, *Death of an Expert Witness* (New York: Touchstone, 1977), 184; P. D. James, *Devices and Desires* (New York: Vintage, 2004), 381.

4. John J. O'Connor, "Odd Pair of British Sleuths," *New York Times*, July 16, 1996, http://www.nytimes.com.

5. Reginald Hill, *Death's Jest-Book* (London: HarperCollins, 2003), 453.

6. Julia Kristeva, *Possessions*, trans. Barbara Bray (New York: Columbia University Press, 1998), 126.

7. Julia Kristeva, *Murder in Byzantium*, trans. C. Jon Delogu (New York: Columbia University Press, 2006), 84.

8. Kristeva, *Possessions*, 75, 97.

9. Ibid., 21.

10. Julia Kristeva, *The Old Man and the Wolves*, trans. Barbara Bray (New York: Columbia University Press, 1994), 68, 177.

11. Kristeva, *Possessions*, 38, 177.

12. Kristeva, *Old Man*, 35, 64.

13. Kristeva, *Murder in Byzantium*, 78.

14. Ewa Plonowska Ziarek, "From the Agency of the Letter to the Agency of the Icon," in *Kristeva's Fiction*, ed. Benigno Trigo (Albany: SUNY Press, 2013), 101.

15. Luiz Alfredo Garcia-Roza, *The Silence of the Rain*, trans. Benjamin Moser (New York: Henry Holt, 2002), 81.

16. Ibid., 32.

17. Luiz Alfredo Garcia-Roza, *A Window in Copacabana*, trans. Benjamin Moser (New York: Henry Holt, 2005), 138.

18. Luiz Alfredo Garcia-Roza, *Blackout*, trans. Benjamin Moser (New York: Henry Holt, 2008), 143.

19. Edgar Allan Poe, *The Great Short Works of Edgar Allan Poe*, ed. G. R. Thompson (New York: Perennial Classic, 1970), 279, 290.

20. Ibid., 293.

21. Ibid., 441.

22. Ibid., 294.

F

1. Elena Baraban, "A Country Resembling Russia: The Use of History in Boris Akunin's Detective Novels," *Slavic and East European Journal* 48, no. 3 (2004): 398.

2. Amanda Cross, *Poetic Justice* (New York: Ballantine, 2001), 89.
3. Amanda Cross, *Honest Doubt* (New York: Ballantine, 2001), 1, 135.
4. Amanda Cross, *The Theban Mysteries* (New York: Fawcett, 2001), 174.
5. Amanda Cross, *In the Last Analysis* (New York: Fawcett, 2001), 197.
6. John D. Carr, *Death Watch* (London: Penguin, 1953), 31.
7. John D. Carr, *He Who Whispers* (London: Hamish Hamilton, 1946), 219.
8. John D. Carr, *The Mad Hatter Mystery* (New York: Collier, 1965), 161.
9. Edmund Crispin, *Holy Disorders* (London: Vintage, 2007), 3.
10. Edmund Crispin, *Buried for Pleasure* (London: Vintage, 2009), 9.
11. Edmund Crispin, *The Moving Toyshop* (London: Vintage, 2007), 87.
12. Crispin, *Holy Disorders*, 174.
13. Crispin, *Moving Toyshop*, 84.

G

1. Andrew Forrester, *The Female Detective* (London: British Library, 2012), 1.
2. Josephine Tey, *The Man in the Queue* (London: Arrow, 2011), 8.
3. Josephine Tey, *To Love and Be Wise* (London: Arrow, 2011), 189.
4. Josephine Tey, *The Singing Sands* (London: Arrow, 2011), 66.
5. Val McDermid, "The Brilliant, Unconventional Crime Novels of Josephine Tey," *Daily Telegraph*, November 15, 2014, accessed July 31, 2016, http://www.telegraph.co.uk.
6. P. D. James, *An Unsuitable Job for a Woman* (London: Faber and Faber, 2005), 12.
7. Ibid., 13.
8. H. R. F. Keating, "Fiction," *Times* (London), March 12, 1977, 11, *Times* Digital Archive, accessed August 8, 2016, http://find.galegroup.com.
9. P. D. James, *The Skull beneath the Skin* (London: Faber and Faber, 2005), 379.
10. Deon Meyer, *Cobra*, trans. K. L. Seegers (London: Hodder, 2015), 174.
11. Deon Meyer, *Devil's Peak*, trans. K. L. Seegers (2005; London: Hodder, 2012), 64.
12. Ibid., 64.
13. Ibid., 117.
14. Anna Katharine Green, *The Leavenworth Case* (New York: Penguin, 2010), 7, 152.
15. Anna Katharine Green, *A Strange Disappearance* (New York: G. P. Putnam's Sons, 1879), 50.
16. Green, *Leavenworth Case*, 7.
17. Ibid., 104.
18. Anna Katharine Green, "The Staircase at Heart's Delight," in *Room Number Three and Other Detective Stories* (n.p.: A. L. Burt, 1913), 182.

H

1. John G. Cawelti, "The Spillane Phenomenon," *Journal of Popular Culture* 3, no. 1 (1969): 9.
2. Kay Weibel, "Mickey Spillane as a Fifties Phenomenon," in *Dimensions of Detective Fiction*, ed. Larry N. Landrum, Pat Browne, and Ray Broadus Browne (Bowling Green, OH: Popular Press, 1976), 115.
3. Mickey Spillane, *The Mike Hammer Collection*, vol. 1, *I, the Jury; My Gun Is Quick; Vengeance Is Mine!* (New York: New American Library, 2001), 7.
4. Geoffrey O'Brien, *Hardboiled America: Lurid Paperbacks and the Masters of Noir* (New York: Da Capo, 1997), 102.
5. See Betty Friedan, *The Feminine Mystique* (Harmondsworth, UK: Penguin, 1965).

6. "Cliff Hardy Series," Peter Corris, accessed July 20, 2016, http://www.petercorris.net.

7. Graeme Blundell, "Peter Corris' hard-boiled detective still solving cases," *Australian*, February 28, 2015, accessed July 29, 2016, http://www.theaustralian.com.au.

8. Sue Turnbull, "Gun Control Review: Peter Corris Uses His Hero Cliff Hardy to Investigate Australian Society," *Sydney Morning Herald*, April 18, 2015, accessed July 17, 2016, http://www.smh.com.au.

9. Petros Markaris, *Deadline in Athens* (New York: Grove, 2004), 2.

10. Ibid., 134.

11. Petros Markaris, *Che Committed Suicide* (London: Arcadia, 2009), 20.

12. Erifyli Maronite, "The Left and Detective Novel," *Eleuterotypia*: *Bibliothêkê*, May 8, 2005, quoted in Apostolos Vasilakis, "Illegal Zone," Greekworks.com, February 1, 2006. http://www.greekworks.com.

13. Voitto Ruohonen, *The Evil with Us: The Image of Society in the Novels of Matti Yrjänä Joensuu* (English summary) (Keuruu, Finland: Otava, 2005), 561.

14. Matti Yrjänä Joensuu, *Harjunpaa and the Stone Murders* (London: Victor Gollancz, 1986), 97.

15. Ruohonen, *Evil with Us*, 561.

16. Val McDermid, *The Retribution* (London: Sphere, 2011), 113.

17. Val McDermid, *Wire in the Blood* (London: HarperCollins, 1997), 20.

18. Val McDermid, *Fever of the Bone* (London: Sphere, 2009), 384.

19. Lee Childs, introduction to *The Mermaids Singing*, by Val McDermid (London: HarperCollins, 2015), n.p.

20. Jimmy Savile was a British celebrity who often appeared in the 1970s and 1980s on TV shows involving young people. After his death he was discovered to have been a serial pedophile, possibly with necrophilic tendencies. Val McDermid says she based the character of Jacko Vance on Savile after she met him and intuited there was something very wrong. (See "I Based Psycho on Jimmy Savile, Says Writer Val McDermid," *Daily Record*, October 29, 2012, on Val McDermid's official website, http://www.valmcdermid.com.)

21. Jo Nesbø, *The Leopard*, trans. Don Bartlett (London: Vintage, 2011), 632.

22. Jo Nesbø, *The Bat*, trans. Don Bartlett (London: Vintage, 2013), 6.

23. Jo Nesbø, *Police*, trans. Don Bartlett (London: Vintage, 2014), 628.

24. Ibid., 627.

25. Arthur Conan Doyle, *A Study in Scarlet* (London: Penguin, 1985), 12.

26. Arthur Conan Doyle, *The Sign of Four* (London: Penguin, 2001), 5.

27. He Jiahong's Hong Jun series includes five novels, with the first two currently available in English.

28. He Jiahong, *Hanging Devils* (Melbourne: Penguin Australia, 2015), 76; Elisa Nesossi, "He Jiahong: Working between Law and Literature," China Story, September 28, 2012, accessed April 15, 2016, https://www.thechinastory.org.

29. He Jiahong, *Black Holes* (Melbourne: Penguin Australia, 2014), 258; He Jiahong, *Hanging Devils*, 91.

30. He Jiahong, *Hanging Devils*, 97–98.

31. Cheng's original Chinese stories are available online: *Cheng xiaoqing zuopingji* (Selected works of Cheng Xiaoqing) at http://www.kanunu8.com/files/writer/9824.html; and *Huosang tan'anji* (Collection of Huo Sang detective stories) at http://www.my285.com/ZT/hs/index.htm. However, the text layout and proofreading leave much to be desired.

I

1. Masaki Kato, "Self-Destruction in Japan," in *Japanese Culture and Behavior*, ed. Takie Sugiyama Lebra and William P. Lebra (Honolulu: University of Hawaii Press, 1974), 274.

J

1. Pauline Hopkins, *Hagar's Daughter: A Story of Southern Caste Prejudice*, in *The Magazine Novels of Pauline Hopkins*, ed. Hazel V. Carby (Oxford: Oxford University Press, 1988), 89.
2. Ibid., 218.
3. Ibid., 240.
4. Stephen F. Soitos, *The Blues Detective: A Study of African American Detective Fiction* (Amherst: University of Massachusetts Press, 1996), 60.

K

1. Seishi Yokomizo, *The Inugami Clan*, trans. Yumiko Yamazaki (Berkeley, CA: Stone Bridge Press, 2007), 17.
2. Deborah Solomon, "The Mother Load: Questions for James Ellroy," *New York Times Magazine*, November 5, 2006, accessed December 21, 2016, http://www.nytimes.com.
3. James Ellroy, *White Jazz* (London: Windmill, 2011), 28.
4. Ibid., 335.
5. Ibid., 24.
6. Ibid., 47, 51, 109.
7. Ibid., 75.
8. Ibid., 266.

L

1. Kalpana Swaminathan, *The Page 3 Murders* (New Delhi: IndiaInk, 2006), 2–3.
2. Ibid., 175.
3. Kalpana Swaminathan, *I Never Knew It Was You* (New Delhi: IndiaInk, 2012), 23.
4. Kalpana Swaminathan, *The Gardener's Song* (New Delhi: IndiaInk, 2007), 39.
5. Partha Chatterjee, "The Monochrome Madonna," *New Indian Express*, June 27, 2010, http://www.newindianexpress.com.
6. Maitreyee B. Chowdhury, "Kalpana Swaminathan's *The Secret Gardener* Has All the Elements of a Good Detective Novel and Yet, It Fails to Grip the Reader," Women's Web, May 16, 2013, http://www.womensweb.in.
7. Carlo Oliva, *Storia sociale del giallo* (Lugano, Switzerland: Todaro, 2003), 180 (author's translation).
8. Giorgio Scerbanenco, *A Private Venus*, trans. Howard Curtis (Oxford, UK: Hersilia, 2012), 145.
9. Giorgio Scerbanenco, *Duca and the Milan Murders*, trans. Eileen Ellenbogen (New York: Walker, 1970), 135.
10. Richard Marsh, "The Man Who Cut Off My Hair," *in The Complete Judith Lee Adventures*, ed. Minna Vuohelainen (Richmond, VA: Valancourt, 2016), 6, 19.
11. Richard Marsh, "Uncle Jack," in *Complete Judith Lee Adventures*, 186; Richard Marsh, "The Miracle," in *Complete Judith Lee Adventures*, 117.
12. Richard Marsh, "Mandragora," in *Complete Judith Lee Adventures*, 269.
13. Richard Marsh, "Conscience," in *Complete Judith Lee Adventures*, 66; Richard Marsh, "The Restaurant Napolitain," in *Complete Judith Lee Adventures*, 224; Richard Marsh, "Curare," in *Complete Judith Lee Adventures*, 334.
14. Hedy Habra, "Lituma's Fragmented Image in Mario Vargas Llosa's Fiction," *Latin American Literary Review* 31, no. 62 (July–December 2003): 15–32, 18; Mestizo refers not just to a person of mixed race but also to the Latin American "regular Joe."

15. Mario Vargas Llosa, *Death in the Andes* (New York: Penguin, 1997), 30.
16. Elizabeth George, *Well-Schooled in Murder* (New York: Bantam, 1990), 234.
17. Ibid., 235.
18. Zak Smith, "Elizabeth George Talks Inspector Lynley, Not Being British and More," *Indy Week*, October 19, 2003, https://www.indyweek.com.

M

1. Georges Simenon, *The Friend of Madame Maigret*, trans. Helen Sebba (London: Penguin, 2006), 99.
2. Georges Simenon, *When I Was Old*, trans. Helen Essler (London: Penguin, 2016), 10.
3. Georges Simenon, *My Friend Maigret*, trans. Shaun Whiteside (London: Penguin, 2016), 151.
4. Georges Simenon, *Maigret's Memoirs*, trans. Jean Stewart (London: Hamish Hamilton, 1963), 25.
5. Simenon, *Friend of Madame Maigret*, 159.
6. Raymond Chandler, *The Little Sister* (New York: Everyman's Library, 2002), 282.
7. Raymond Chandler, *The High Window* (New York: Everyman's Library, 2002), 611.
8. Raymond Chandler, *The Big Sleep* (New York: Everyman's Library, 2002), 17.
9. Agatha Christie, *The Murder at the Vicarage*, in *Miss Marple Omnibus* (London: HarperCollins, 1997), 3:520.
10. Agatha Christie, *The Moving Finger*, in *Miss Marple Omnibus*, 1:225.
11. Agatha Christie, *The Tuesday Night Club and Other Stories* (London: HarperCollins, 2005), 1.
12. Agatha Christie, *A Murder Is Announced*, in *Miss Marple Omnibus*, 1:410.
13. Agatha Christie, *The Mirror Crack'd from Side to Side*, in *Miss Marple Omnibus*, 2:332.
14. Marcia Muller, *Locked In* (New York: Hachette, 2009), 74.
15. Marcia Muller, *The Dangerous Hour* (New York: Warner, 2005), 173.
16. Marcia Muller, *Listen to the Silence* (New York: Mysterious Press, 2000), 139.
17. John D. MacDonald, *The Green Ripper* (New York: Random House, 2013), 20.
18. John D. MacDonald, *Free Fall in Crimson* (New York: Random House, 2013), 160.
19. John D. MacDonald, *The Deep Blue Good-by* (New York: Random House, 2013), 14.
20. Diane Wei Wang, *The Eye of Jade* (New York: Simon & Schuster, 2008), 18, 55, 113.
21. Ibid., 147, 245.
22. Ibid., 234.
23. Sue Grafton, *W Is for Wasted* (New York: Putnam's, 2013), 4.
24. Sue Grafton, *A Is for Alibi* (London: Pan Macmillan, 2005), 245.
25. Sōji Shimada, *The Tokyo Zodiac Murders*, trans. Ross and Shika Mackenzie (London: Pushkin Vertigo, 2015), 152.
26. Marek Krajewski, *The Minotaur's Head*, trans. Danusia Stok (London: MacLehose, 2012), 80.
27. Marek Krajewski, *Death in Breslau*, trans. Danusia Stok (London: MacLehose, 2008), 5.
28. Raymond Chandler, "'The Simple Art of Murder' (1950)," University of Texas, accessed September 6, 2016, http://www.en.utexas.edu.
29. Andrea Camilleri, *The Terracotta Dog*, trans. Stephen Sartarelli (London: Picador, 2002), 160.
30. Colin Dexter, *Last Bus to Woodstock* (London: Pan, 1977), 15.
31. Colin Dexter, *The Way through the Woods*, in *The Fourth Inspector Morse Omnibus* (London: Pan, 1996), 84.
32. Guy Adams, "Morse: The No. 1 Gentleman Detective," *Independent*, Media, April 27, 2007.

N

1. Barbara Pezzotti, *The Importance of Place in Contemporary Italian Crime Fiction: A Bloody Journey* (Madison, NJ: Fairleigh Dickinson University Press, 2012), 184.
2. Carlo Lucarelli, *Lupo mannaro* (Turin, Italy: Einaudi, 1997), 38.
3. Carlo Lucarelli, *Almost Blue*, trans. Oonagh Stransky (San Francisco: City Lights Publishers, 2001), 68.
4. Ibid., 166.
5. Jasper Fforde, *The Eyre Affair* (London: Hodder & Stoughton, 2001), 133–34.
6. Jasper Fforde, *Something Rotten* (London: Hodder & Stoughton, 2004), 160.
7. Jasper Fforde, *Lost in a Good Book* (London: Hodder & Stoughton, 2002), 335.

P

1. Another pseudonym they used was Benito Suárez Lynch.
2. Peronism was the political ideology of General Juan Domingo Perón (1895–1974), three times president of Argentina. It split the population by promoting an underlying class divide. Some viewed Perón as the voice of the poor, while detractors considered him a demagogue, even a dictator.
3. Eva's quick rise to fame and power, and her access to it through her relationship with Perón, were constantly criticized by the upper classes.
4. Sonia Mattalia, *La ley y el crimen: Usos del relato policial en la narrativa argentina, 1880–2000* (Frankfurt am Main, Germany: Iberoamericana/Verbuet, 2008), 116 (my translation).
5. Mary Elizabeth Braddon, *The Trail of the Serpent* (New York: Modern Library Classics, 2003), 359.
6. Ibid., 29.
7. Ibid., 372.
8. Ibid., 411.
9. Earl Bargainnier, *The Gentle Art of Murder* (Bowling Green, OH: Popular Press, 1980), 45; "The Dead Celebrity Rich List," This Is Money, June 28, 2010, http://www.thisismoney.co.uk.
10. Agatha Christie, *Elephants Can Remember* (London: HarperCollins, 2002), 36.
11. Agatha Christie, *Cards on the Table* (London: HarperCollins, 1993), 191.
12. Ibid., 204.

Q

1. Ellery Queen, *Cat of Many Tails* (London: Victor Gollancz, 1974), 9, 10.
2. Ellery Queen, *And on the Eighth Day* (Bath, UK: Chivers, 1998), 237.
3. Anthony Boucher, *Ellery Queen: A Double Profile* (New York: Little, Brown, 1951), 11.
4. Paul Auster, *The New York Trilogy* (London: Faber and Faber, 2004), 3.
5. William Spanos, "The Detective and the Boundary: Some Notes on the Postmodern Literary Imagination," in *Repetitions: The Postmodern Occasion in Literature and Culture* (Baton Rouge: Louisiana State University Press, 1987), 25.
6. Stefano Tani, *The Doomed Detective: The Contribution of the Detective Novel to Postmodern American and Italian Fiction* (Carbondale: Southern Illinois University Press, 1984), 114.
7. Auster, *New York Trilogy*, 62.
8. Ibid., 68.
9. Ibid., 294.

10. John Banville, "John Banville on 1950s-Era Ireland," Benjamin Black, accessed May 23, 2016, http://www.benjaminblackbooks.com/quirke.htm.

R

1. Alexander McCall Smith, *The No. 1 Ladies' Detective Agency* (New York: Random House, 2002), 3.
2. Walter Mosley, *Little Green* (New York: Doubleday, 2013), 8.
3. Ibid., 11, 69.
4. Walter Mosley, *A Red Death* (New York: Washington Square Press, 1991), 197.
5. Ian Rankin, *Let It Bleed* (London: Orion, 2006), 38.
6. Ibid., 122.
7. Ian Rankin, *Blue and Black* (London: Orion, 1998), 190.
8. Arthur Conan Doyle, *Memories and Adventures: An Autobiography* (Ware, UK: Wordsworth Editions, 2007), 225.
9. It should be noted, however, that some crimes simply aren't funny. *The Burglar on the Prowl* unfortunately demonstrates the dangers of mixing comedy with such crimes.
10. Raymond Chandler, "The Simple Art of Murder," in *The Simple Art of Murder*, by Raymond Chandler (New York: Vintage, 1988), 6, 16.
11. Lawrence Block, *The Burglar Who Studied Spinoza* (Harpenden, UK: No Exit Press, 1993), 81; Lawrence Block, *The Burglar Who Liked to Quote Kipling* (New York: Pocket Books, 1982), 23; Lawrence Block, *The Burglar in the Rye* (New York: Signet, 2000), 19.
12. Lawrence Block, *The Burglar Who Traded Ted Williams* (New York: HarperTorch, 2005), 351.
13. Maurizio De Giovanni, *I Will Have Vengeance*, trans. Anne Milano Appel (New York: Europa Editions, 2012), 11.
14. Ibid., 34.
15. Maurizio De Giovanni, *By My Hand*, trans. Antony Shugaar (New York: Europa Editions, 2014), 24–25.
16. De Giovanni, *I Will Have Vengeance*, 21.

S

1. Graeme Thomson, "Guns, Gay Marriage and a Real-Life Murder: The Private Life of Thriller Writer Patricia Cornwell," *Mail on Sunday*, November 8, 2014, accessed July 15, 2016, http://www.dailymail.co.uk.
2. James Kidd, "Profile of Patricia Cornwell," in *Dust*, by Patricia Cornwell (London: Sphere, 2013), n.p.
3. Patricia Cornwell, *Depraved Heart* (London: HarperCollins, 2015), 15.
4. Patricia Cornwell, *Black Notice* (London: Little, Brown, 1999), 80.
5. Paco Ignacio Taibo II, *The Uncomfortable Dead* (New York: Akashic Books, 2010), 78.
6. He also features in three short stories.
7. Dashiell Hammett, *The Maltese Falcon* (Harmondsworth, UK: Penguin, 1966), 112.
8. Ibid., 183.
9. Ibid., 46.
10. Ibid., 199.
11. Ibid., 198.
12. He also appears in the TV-movie series *Spenser for Hire* (1985–1988) and in five "posthumous" novels written by Ace Atkins.
13. Robert B. Parker, quoted in Barry Taylor, "Interview with Robert B. Parker," *City Limits*, April 30, 1987, 93–94.

14. See Robert B. Parker, *Chasing the Bear: A Young Spenser Novel* (New York: Sleuth Speak, 2010).

15. See Robert B. Parker, "The Violent Hero, Wilderness Heritage and Urban Reality: A Study of the Private Eye in the Novels of Dashiell Hammett, Raymond Chandler and Ross Macdonald" (PhD diss., Boston University Graduate School, 1971).

16. Thomas Pynchon, *Inherent Vice* (New York: Penguin, 2009), 1–2, 69, 304.

17. Ibid., 42, 281.

18. Ibid., 96.

19. Ibid., 97.

20. Nicholas Blake, *The Beast Must Die* (London: Vintage, 2012), 281.

21. Ibid., 139–40.

22. Friedrich Glauser, *The Thumbprint*, trans. Mike Mitchell (London: Bitter Lemon Press, 2004), 22.

23. Ibid., 75.

24. Ibid., 179.

25. Friedrich Glauser, *In Matto's Realm*, trans. Mike Mitchell (London: Bitter Lemon Press, 2005), 257.

26. Arnaldur Indridason, *The Draining Lake*, trans. Bernard Scudder (London: Vintage, 2010), 12.

27. Arnaldur Indridason, *Arctic Chill*, trans. Bernard Scudder (New York: Picador, 2009), 48.

28. Arnaldur Indridason, *Hypothermia*, trans. Victoria Cribb (London: Vintage, 2010), 169–70.

29. Arnaldur Indridason, *Jar City*, trans. Bernard Scudder (London: Vintage, 2010), 5.

30. Zygmunt Miłoszewski, *Entanglement*, trans. Antonia Lloyd-Jones (London: Bitter Lemon Press, 2010), 10.

T

1. E. C. Bentley, *Trent's Last Case* (London: Stratus, 2001), 34.
2. Ibid., 19.
3. Ibid., 228.
4. E. C. Bentley, *Trent's Own Case* (London: Stratus, 2001), 314.

V

1. The separate short story *Rosy and John* (2013 [2017]) is the most straightforward of the Camille texts, as it mainly focuses on his investigation.

2. Andrew Pepper, *Unwilling Executioner: Crime Fiction and the State* (Oxford: Oxford University Press, 2016), 228.

W

1. Henning Mankell, *Faceless Killers*, trans. Steven T. Murray (London: Harvill, 2000), 231.

2. Sara Paretsky, *Bitter Medicine* (Chicago: Hodder, 2008), 310.

3. In 1986 Paretsky was also instrumental in founding Sisters in Crime, an organization dedicated to promoting the status of women in the crime fiction world. An early achievement was to challenge the bias against women crime writers (in the United States at least) in the predominantly male reviews of the time.

4. Ruth Rendell, *End in Tears* (Hutchinson: Random House, 2005), 376.
5. Dorothy L. Sayers, *Whose Body?* (New York: Bourbon Street Books, 2014), 2.
6. Dorothy L. Sayers, *Murder Must Advertise* (New York: Bourbon Street Books, 2014), 38.
7. Dorothy L. Sayers, *Gaudy Night* (New York: Bourbon Street Books, 2012), 348.
8. Raymond Chandler, "The Simple Art of Murder," in *The Simple Art of Murder*, by Raymond Chandler (New York: Vintage, 1988), 12, 16, 18.
9. Jacques Barzun, "Rex Stout," in *A Jacques Barzun Reader* (New York: Perennial Classics, 2003), 564–67.
10. John McAleer, *Royal Decree: Conversations with Rex Stout* (Ashton, MD: Pontes Press, 1983).
11. Linda Barnes, "Introduction to *The Golden Spiders*," in *Nero Wolfe Mysteries: Some Buried Caesar; The Golden Spiders* (New York: Bantam Dell, 2008).
12. Homi Bhabha, *The Location of Culture* (London: Routledge, 1994), 95.
13. Juanita Sheridan, *The Chinese Chop* (Boulder: Rue Morgue Press, 2000), 26.
14. Juanita Sheridan, *The Kahuna Killer* (Boulder: Rue Morgue Press, 2002), 68.
15. Juanita Sheridan, *The Mamo Murders* (Boulder: Rue Morgue Press, 2002), 88.
16. Sheridan, *The Chinese Chop*, 62.

X

1. Derek Raymond, *The Devil's Home on Leave* (London: Warner Books, 1993), 72.
2. Derek Raymond, *He Died with His Eyes Open* (London: Serpent's Tail, 2006), 164.
3. Raymond, *The Devil's Home on Leave*, 12.
4. Derek Raymond, *How the Dead Live* (Brooklyn: Melville House, 2011), 11.
5. Raymond, *The Devil's Home on Leave*, 147.
6. Derek Raymond, *Dead Man Upright* (Brooklyn: Melville House, 2012), 20.
7. Derek Raymond, *I Was Dora Suarez* (London: Sphere, 1991), 155.

Index

academics and academia, 52–53, 61–62, 65, 131
adaptation and adaptations, 4, 39, 56, 92, 105–106, 111, 122, 124, 134, 137–138, 140, 152, 154, 168, 176, 180, 182, 198. *See also* films
Adorno, Theodore, 12
aesthetics, 23, 195
age, 20, 109, 123–124, 192
Akechi, Kogorō, 3–4, 105
alcohol and alcoholism, xvii, 63, 73, 89, 107, 126, 133, 135–136, 153; beer, 14, 119, 137; whisky, 48, 51, 153, 188, 191; wine, 49, 53, 82, 166, 196
aliases, xv, 10, 18, 169
alienation, 11–12, 15, 73, 84, 137, 159–160. *See also* detectives, isolation of
Allen, Grant, 113
Allingham, Margery, 38–39, 64
Altman, Robert, 122
anxiety, 12, 73, 84, 140, 147, 200
Archer, Lew, 4–6, 122
architecture, 49, 105, 137–138, 166
Argentina, 76, 143–144, 147
aristocracy and aristocrats, 10, 24, 38–39, 63, 114, 195–196
Aristotle, xiv
art and artists, 42, 46, 49, 54, 69, 135, 166, 182–184, 196
Athens, 83–84
Auden, W. H., 173
Australia, 18–19, 81–82, 89
Austria, 23, 26–27
Ayatsuji, Yukito, 132

Bacon, Roger, 13
Barcelona, 43–44
Beck, Martin, xv, 14–15, 41, 64, 84, 188. *See also* Sjöwall, Maj, and Per Wahlöö
Bengal, 9–10
Bentley, E. C., 181–183, 196
Beresford, Tuppence, 25
Berlin, 46, 76–77, 187
Bern, 11, 175–176
Blake, Nicholas, 144, 172–174
blood-testing, 90
Bonaparte, Marie, 56
book dealers, 46, 161
books (in crime fiction), 3, 14, 25, 43, 45–46, 50, 55, 138, 141–142, 161–162, 177
Borges, Jorge Luis, 56, 143–144
Botswana, 155–156
Boucher, Anthony, 64, 150
the Bow Street Runners, 145
Brazil, 57–58
Brinton, Valeria, xiv, 28–29
Britain. *See* United Kingdom
Brown, Father, xiv, 29–31

Cadogan, Mary, 25
Cagnoni, Fiorella, 139
Calcutta, 9–10
California, 5–7, 121, 129, 157, 192
cameras and photography, 42, 94, 110, 182
Campion, Albert, 38–39, 64, 69
Canada, xv, 1–2, 23, 122, 190
capitalism, 36, 46, 185
Carlotto, Massimo, 111
Carroll, Lewis, 66, 110
Caspary, Vera, xvii
Catalonia, 44–45
Catholicism and the Catholic Church, 22, 26, 29, 153–154, 191
censorship, 4
Chabon, Michael, xiii
chance, 41, 55, 60, 112, 151
Chandler, Raymond, xv, 5, 78–79, 82, 103, 121–122, 127, 132–134, 159, 196

characterization, xv–xvi, 15, 38, 42, 51–51, 79, 115, 120, 127, 166, 169–172, 177, 182, 196
Chesterton, G. K., xiv, 29–31, 63, 144
Chicago, 11, 75, 191–192
children, 2, 14–15, 25, 60–61, 65, 73, 85, 124, 156–158, 164, 167, 169, 177, 185, 192
Childs, Lee, 87
China, 3, 9, 92–94, 189–191
chivalry, 38, 69, 94, 121–123, 127, 132–133, 137, 172
Christie, Agatha, xv, 25, 39, 53, 61–63, 71, 75, 123–125, 137–138, 146–147, 155, 182, 198
Clark, Mary Higgins, 53
clues, xii, xv, 7, 13–14, 19, 40, 71, 75, 83, 105, 110, 121, 125, 146–147, 150–152, 161, 165, 170, 176, 178–179, 182
Collins, Wilkie, xiv, 28–29, 47, 75, 145
the Collins Crime Club, 172
colonialism, 3, 10, 94–95, 156, 200
comedy. *See* humor
communism, 22–23, 44, 53, 79, 84, 179
Conrad, Joseph, 7
consumerism, 36, 111–112, 128
the Continental Op, 79. *See also* Hammett, Dashiell
Cornwell, Patricia, 53, 165–166
corruption, 15, 26, 36–38, 44, 46, 51–54, 75, 77, 81–83, 86, 89, 95, 103–108, 121–122, 136, 157, 168, 171–172, 175, 191
country houses, 25, 47–48, 115, 122, 146
crime scenes, xvi, 34, 48, 73, 91, 143, 146, 161, 163
criminology, xiii, 11, 22–23, 25, 175
criticism: literary xii–xiii, 62; popular, xi; social, 36, 178
cryptography, 13, 63
Cuba, 45–46
Cuff, Sergeant, xiv, 47–48, 63, 75, 88, 137, 145. *See also* Collins, Wilkie

Dalgliesh, Adam, 49–51, 70
de Quincey, Thomas, 75
democracy, 15, 22, 79, 84, 105
Derleth, August, 42
Derrida, Jacques, 56
detectives: academic, 61–63, 65–66; amateur, xi, 3, 38–39, 61, 69, 71, 76, 101, 113, 119, 122, 139, 149, 153, 156–157, 172, 181, 199; anti-detectives, 151–152, 183–185; as antiheros, 83, 89, 97, 107, 115; armchair, 131, 143, 163; assistants, 1, 3–4, 10, 14, 20, 30, 38, 51–52, 54, 60–61, 87, 89, 91, 93, 116–117, 131–132, 135, 140–141, 145, 147, 155, 166, 168, 197–198, 206n4; duos and partnerships, 51–52, 116–118, 122, 137; eccentricity of, 1, 9, 22, 28, 48, 63, 65, 69, 90–91, 95, 131, 133, 138, 182, 197; female, 24–25, 29, 47, 53, 67–68, 71–72, 74, 112–114, 125–126, 129–130, 139–140, 189–193, 199–201; Golden Age, xii, 6, 24–25, 31, 38–39, 43, 52, 63–64, 69–70, 110, 117, 122, 135, 144, 146, 149, 161, 172, 174, 181, 195–196, 199; hard–boiled, xi, xvi–xvii, 4–6, 14, 20–21, 23, 27, 36, 58, 70, 79, 81, 85, 104, 107, 111–113, 121, 125–126, 129, 132–135, 157–159, 167, 169–171, 192, 196–197, 199; isolation of, 5, 21, 55, 71–74, 85, 107, 122, 137, 159–160, 163, 177, 187, 189–190, 192, 202; moral codes of, 6, 60, 80, 95, 112, 121, 168
detection: equipment, 4, 42, 75, 171; as game, 95, 121, 179; methods, 1–5, 11–12, 23, 27, 38, 42, 48, 55–60, 68, 72, 75, 79, 87, 90–91, 93, 110, 112, 117–120, 126, 133, 137, 145, 150–151, 155, 160–161, 177, 179, 181, 186, 191, 198
Dexter, Collin, 49, 117, 138–140
dialects, 45, 52, 55, 128, 191
Dickens, Charles, xiv, 31–33, 47–48, 62, 75, 145. *See also* Victorian literature
dictatorship, 44, 84, 116, 142, 214
disability, 74, 113, 117, 126, 144–146
disguise, 4, 30, 68, 101, 114, 145, 167, 196
divorce, 5, 15, 57, 66, 128, 129, 176, 176–177, 188
domestic violence, 69, 85, 110. *See also* misogyny
Dostoevsky, Fyodor, 57
Doyle, Sir Arthur Conan, xi, 3, 7–8, 33, 75, 90–91, 94–95, 134, 137, 161, 175, 196. *See also* Holmes, Sherlock
drugs: abuse of, 126, 177; cocaine, 9, 107, 131, 171; dealing, 6–8; trafficking, 46, 53, 89, 107; use of, 13, 90–92, 170–172
Dublin, 153
Dupin, Monsieur Auguste, 42, 54–56, 75, 94, 181

Eco, Umberto, 12–14, 59
Eliot, T. S., 47, 157

empathy, 23, 34, 54, 72, 85, 87, 120, 165, 173, 176, 203
England, 28, 30–31, 34, 63, 65, 114, 123–124, 141–142, 202–203. *See also* United Kingdom
Englishness, 39, 124, 137, 174
epistolary form, 47
ethnocentricism, 27
evil, 2, 5, 11–12, 20–21, 28, 33, 40, 43, 77–78, 89, 94–95, 107–108, 112, 126, 128, 133–134, 147, 193, 203–204
exoticism, 19

fairy tales, 2, 144
faith (religious), 13, 31. *See also* religion
feminism, 24–25, 61, 71, 125, 129, 139, 169–170, 192. *See also* misogyny
femme fatales, 81, 122, 129, 157, 171
fiction: fan, 43; genre, 56; historical, 35, 59–60, 69–70, 76–78, 91, 97; horror, 3–4; literary, xiii, 5, 22, 26, 44, 52, 91, 151–152, 172–174, 176; serial, xvi, 3–4, 28, 47, 90, 100, 145; weird, 42
Field, Inspector Charles Frederick, 31
Fielding, Henry, 145
films, 4, 7, 39, 70, 81, 92, 104–106, 111, 119, 122, 124, 137–138, 140, 156, 168, 171, 175, 180, 188, 198. *See also* adaption and adaptations
finger printing, 19, 63, 75, 90, 182
First World War, 22, 42, 52, 147, 175
Florida, 127
food, 15, 43–45, 51, 83, 133, 135, 162, 166, 188
forensics, xii, 34–35, 40, 48, 56, 75, 77, 89–91, 93, 139, 146, 154, 165–166, 172, 176
France, 1, 36, 53, 120
Freud, Sigmund, 5, 24–25, 56–57
Fry, Northrop, xv
Furst, Alan, 78

Gaboriau, Émile, 75
games, 55, 60, 120–121, 144
gangsters, xvi, 77, 112, 120, 157, 160, 199
gender, 28, 62, 68, 70–71, 72, 79–80, 95, 98, 100, 165, 169, 190, 194, 199–200, 205n10.
genre, xii–xvi, 1, 5, 7, 20–21, 27, 36, 64, 86–88, 97, 129, 144, 171, 207n22; Golden Age detective fiction. *See* detectives, Golden Age; hard boiled. *See* detectives, hard boiled; locked room mysteries, 47, 63–64, 77, 105, 131, 149, 179; police procedural, 15, 20, 39–40, 52, 76, 116–117, 130, 140, 171, 185; science fiction, 3, 6, 20, 52, 68; sensation fiction, 28–29; spy thrillers, 4; thrillers, 2, 4, 10, 21, 30, 87, 174, 185
Germany, 76–77, 83, 103, 175
globalization, 12, 53–54, 92, 96, 137, 187, 189–191
gong'an, xiii, 92
Gothicism, 4, 77, 106
Grafton, Sue, 125, 129–130, 192
graphic novels (and illustrated fiction), 4, 106, 115, 122, 134, 152, 176
Greece, 83
Greene, Graham, 78
Grimaldi, Laura, 139
guns and gun violence, 15, 23, 40, 88, 126, 129, 192

Halter, Paul, 64
Hamilton, Laurell K., 114
Hammett, Dashiell, 5, 79, 82, 103, 127, 167–168, 172
Harris, Thomas, xvi, 139
Hastings, Captain, 110, 147
Hawaii, 199–201
Hawks, Howard, 122
herbs, 13, 35, 166
history, xvi, 11, 36, 60, 77, 135; American, 107, 157; Chinese, 190; of detective fiction, xiii, 4–5, 31, 39, 92, 111, 138, 181; English, 91, 203; French, 36–37; Indian, 10; Mexican, 16–17; Polish, 133; Spanish, 44–45
Hitchcock, Alfred, 40, 70
Hole, Harry, 88–90, 194
Hollywood, 107, 132, 149
Holmes, Sherlock, xi, xvi, 7, 9–10, 13–14, 33, 40–41, 56–57, 59, 63, 71, 76, 90–95, 107, 111, 113, 131, 133, 137, 142, 145–146, 149, 160, 167, 171, 175, 181, 190, 196, 198. *See also* Doyle, Sir Arthur Conan
Holocaust, 12, 192
homophobia, 46, 52, 112
homosexuality, 52
Horkheimer, Max, 12
human nature, 11, 30–31, 82, 107, 119, 128, 156
human rights, 53, 93

human trafficking, 23, 53
Hume, Fergus, 114
humor xvii, 1, 24, 26, 30, 44, 52, 81, 95, 110, 120–121, 135, 141, 143–144, 156, 169–170, 181–182, 215n9
hunches. *See* intuition

Iceland, 1, 176–177
immigrants and immigration, 83, 103–104, 112, 116, 165, 177, 194. *See also* refugees
incest, 25, 107
individualism, 15, 45
the interwar period, 24–25, 167, 178
introspection, 89, 182
intuition, 1, 11–12, 35, 49, 54–56, 60, 65, 71, 73, 77, 88, 94, 112, 124, 135, 150, 179
Ireland, 152–154, 173
Italy, 13, 83, 111, 134, 136, 139–140

Jack the Ripper, 127
Jameson, Fredric, 6
Japan, 3–4, 40, 59–60, 97–98, 105–107, 114, 131–132
Jews and Judaism, 12, 36, 40, 46, 77
justice, xii, 8, 11, 19–21, 23, 25, 27, 31, 35, 40, 51, 54, 67–68, 71–72, 77, 79–80, 82, 84, 86, 91, 93–94, 103, 107, 112–113, 122, 126, 133, 135, 148, 158, 164–168, 172–173, 179, 185, 196, 200, 203

Kennedy, John F., 43, 127
Krajewski, Marek, 132–133, 178

Lacan, Jacques, 56–57
Larkin, Philip, 66
Larsson, Stieg, xiii, 114, 180. *See also* Salander, Lisbeth
laws and legal systems, 11–12, 21, 25, 29, 54, 75, 79, 91, 92–93, 107, 112, 127, 179
Leblanc, Maurice, 4, 59
Lector, Hannibal, xvi
legends, 2, 5, 33, 39, 105, 133, 137–138
LeGuin, Ursula K., xiii
Lemaitre, Pierre, xiv, 184–185
LeRoux, Gaston, 3
Lewis, Ted, xvi
Liang, Diane Wei, 92, 189–191
literary allusion, 19, 44, 52, 59, 117, 137, 173
London, xiii, 69, 74–75, 94, 113, 145, 147, 171, 181, 193–194, 202
Los Angeles, 5–6, 55, 107, 121–122, 133, 157–158, 171

Lovecraft, H. P., 42
Lucarelli, Carlo, 111, 139
Lupin, Arsène, 4, 59, 94
Lynch, David, 59

Maigret, Inspector Georges, 2, 84, 97, 119–121, 175. *See also* Simenon, Georges
Mankell, Henning, 20, 179–180, 187–188
Maris, Yannis, 83
Marlowe, Philip, 5, 55, 71, 79, 121–123, 127, 132, 159, 171, 192, 197. *See also* Chandler, Raymond
Marple, Miss Jane, 24–25, 61–62, 123–125, 142, 156, 181, 199. *See also* Christie, Agatha
martial arts, 58, 112
masculinity, 66, 68–69, 78, 83, 93, 99, 120, 129, 147, 166, 171–172, 199
Matsumoto, Seicho, 97–98, 130
McDermid, Val, 70, 86–87
McGee, Travis, 122, 127–128
McLuhan, Marshall, xi
the mean streets, 6, 40, 55, 76–77, 82, 112, 196. *See also* urban spaces
medicine, 12, 35, 84, 94, 163, 165, 179, 191
the medieval period, 13, 34, 38, 91, 137
metafiction, 62, 151, 196
Metropolitan Police, xiii, 31–32, 67–68, 145, 202
Mexico, 16–17
migrants and migration. *See* immigrants and immigration
misogyny, 15, 24, 40, 80, 83, 121, 128, 131, 197
missing persons, 69, 82, 104, 156
modernity, 38, 44, 94–95, 121, 138, 156, 167
monks, 13, 34–35
Moore, Allan, 57
morals and morality, 11, 19, 22, 28–30, 32, 35, 40, 44, 55, 65, 71, 75, 77, 79, 90, 92–93, 95, 101, 102, 107–109, 120, 122, 124, 128, 133, 161, 168, 175, 179, 187, 202–203
Moriarty, Professor James, 91, 94. *See also* Doyle, Sir Arthur Conan
Morse, Inspector, 49, 117, 136–138, 160
Moscow, 59
motive, xv, xvii, 11–12, 27, 31, 93, 95, 98, 101, 104, 141, 152
"The Murders in the Rue Morgue," 3, 31, 54, 57–58. *See also* Poe, Edgar Allan

music, 2, 26, 49, 53, 65, 88, 92, 131, 138, 159, 160, 188; opera, 13, 65, 113, 133, 137, 163, 188
myths. *See* legends

Naples, 162–164
narrative: first–person, 20, 110, 121, 127, 166, 169; form, xii, xiv–xvi, 13, 26, 52, 75, 95, 121–123, 127, 133, 136, 150, 161–162, 166, 171–172, 185; and time, 129, 192, 199; voice, 101, 147. *See also* narrators
narrators, 4, 9, 13, 27, 43, 47, 100, 113, 131–132, 150–152, 178, 198–200, 202–203. *See also* narrative
national identity, 5, 10, 60, 123, 138, 156. *See also* nationalism
nationalism, 10, 158. *See also* national identity
nature, 6
Nazism, 22–23, 59, 76–77, 89, 175
neoliberalism, 116, 185
neopolicial, 16
the Newgate Novel, xiii, 145
New York, 11, 40, 61, 74–75, 145–146, 149, 151–152, 161, 197, 200
Newman, Paul, 6
noir, xvi, 14, 55, 76, 83, 111, 133, 152, 162, 170–171, 185, 202; Scandinavian, 36, 178
Norway, 88
nostalgia, 60, 106, 115, 126, 137, 174, 203

Oedipus, 5, 25
One Thousand and One Nights, xiii
Oxford, 24, 65–66, 116, 137–138

Paretsky, Sara, xvi, 125, 191–193
Paris, 1–2, 30, 36, 53, 57, 74, 84, 119
perpetrators, xiii, xiv, 3, 19, 27, 30, 35, 54, 61, 77, 85, 88, 103, 106, 113, 132, 143, 167, 173, 185
Peru, 114–116
philosophy, 55, 57, 95, 135, 172; Confucianism, 60, 95; existentialism, 5, 11–12, 23, 55, 169; nihilism, 12
Pirkis, Catherine Louisa, 113
plot. *See* narrative form
Poe, Edgar Allan, xii, 3, 31, 47, 52, 54, 55, 75, 94, 137, 151
poetry, 43, 49, 50, 65, 69–71, 97, 110, 137, 172–174
Poirot, Hercule, 24, 54, 56, 110, 137, 142, 146–148, 190, 198. *See also* Christie, Agatha
poison, 23, 113, 146
Poland, 133, 178–180
policial revolcionario, 45
politics, 13, 34, 43–45, 66, 73, 80, 82, 104, 107, 127, 135, 158, 172
popular culture, 4, 10, 49, 95, 135
popular fiction, 3, 79, 127, 165, 174
pornography, xvi, 111
postcolonialism, 10, 94, 200
postmodernism, 59, 111, 127, 151–152, 171
Prague, 22–23, 76–77
priests, 29–30, 86, 119, 153
profiling, 87, 140
Pronzini, Bill, 64
prose style, 19, 66, 107, 120
prostitution, 37, 58, 104, 109, 111, 133, 163
psychoanalysis, 5, 24, 53, 55–56
psychology and psychologists, 3, 11, 30, 53, 56, 58, 69, 86–87, 147, 150, 170, 173
"The Purloined Letter," xii, 56–57

Qui, Xiao Long, 92

race and racism, 18–19, 40, 104, 112, 116, 152, 157–158, 199–200. *See also* xenophobia
radical crime fiction, 36–37, 185
Rawson, Clayton, 64
realism, 2, 23, 27, 40, 43, 64, 121
reason, 1, 4, 9, 13–14, 19, 27–28, 30, 53, 55–56, 60, 63, 85, 95, 105, 150, 182
Rebus, Detective Inspector John, 122, 159–160, 194
refugees, 24, 95, 189. *See also* immigrants and immigration
regional identities, 1, 43–44, 135
relationships, personal, 26, 37, 50, 55, 69–70, 73, 81, 85, 87, 88, 107, 115, 120, 126, 130, 135, 159–160, 166, 176–177, 184–185, 188, 196
religion, 13–14, 30, 35, 150. *See also* faith (religious)
revenge, 21, 60, 79, 115, 124, 138, 173, 179
revolutions, 17, 72, 93, 189–191
Reykjavik, 177–178
Rinehart, Mary Roberts, 75
Rio di Janeiro, 57–58
Road Hill Murders, 48
Robbe-Grillet, Alain, xiv

Robicheaux, Dave, 122
Rohmer, Sax, 200
rural settings, 1, 93, 105–106, 123, 138, 187
Russia, 27, 59–60, 73, 77

sadism, 12, 80, 86
Salander, Lisbeth, xv, 114, 206n23. *See also* Larsson, Stieg
San Francisco, 125–126, 131, 167
Sayers, Dorothy L., xiv, 24, 39, 49, 63–64, 75, 146, 195–196. *See also* Wimsey, Lord Peter
Sciascia, Leonardo, 140
science, 13, 95
Scotland Yard, 49, 66, 116, 141, 145, 172, 173
Second World War, 5, 10–11, 36, 69, 76–78, 105, 107, 111
serial killers, 87–89, 131, 139, 159, 185
sexism, 98, 169. *See also* misogyny
sexuality, 3, 13, 25, 28, 40, 52, 80, 107, 113, 127
Shanghai, 94–96
sign language, 114, 145
Simenon, Georges, 2, 84, 97, 119–120, 175. *See also* Maigret, Inspector Georges
Sjöwall, Maj and Per Wahlöö, xv, 14–15, 41, 64, 188. *See also* Beck, Martin
Smith, Clark Ashton, 42
Smith, Derek, 64
social change, xvi, 39, 84, 92, 117, 124–127, 170, 194
social class, 32, 34, 38, 48, 67, 101, 116–118, 124, 144, 173–174; class prejudice, 75, 95; lower and working, 81, 115, 117, 121, 145; middle, 9, 28, 39, 95; upper, 39–40, 123, 173
social norms, 2, 27, 29
South Africa, 72–74, 187
Spade, Sam, 5, 79, 121, 127, 167–168, 171, 192
Spain, 44–45, 83
sport and exercise, 26, 45, 51, 82, 107, 127, 169
Stevenson, Robert Louis, 159
Strand Magazine, 90, 113–114
suburbia, 5, 81–82
suicide, 19, 46, 55, 61, 63–64, 71, 84, 89, 98, 111, 113, 146, 163, 173, 185
the supernatural, 2, 30, 41–42, 63, 141, 162–164
Sweden, 14–15, 84, 187
Switzerland, 91, 174–176, 198
Sydney, 81–82, 89

Tarantino, Quentin, 111
technology, 41, 51, 113, 135, 139–140, 142
television series, 4, 6, 10, 20, 40–42, 59, 70, 92, 105, 111, 119, 122, 124, 134–138, 156, 165, 175, 188, 194, 197–198. *See also* adaptation and adaptations
terrorism, 104, 135
Tokyo, 97–98, 105–106, 131–132
transgender, 69, 163
translation, 26, 36, 46, 77, 95–96, 111, 134, 143, 175, 190
Turkey, 103

undercover agents, 7, 55, 67, 101
United Kingdom, 67, 70, 116, 202–203. *See also* England
Upson, Nicola, 70
urban spaces, 6, 82, 85, 93–94, 96, 111–112, 115, 137, 140, 152, 157, 202. *See also* the mean streets
utopianism, 17, 46

Vallorani, Nicoletta, 139
Van Dine, S. S., 63, 149
Vane, Harriet, 196–197. *See also* Wimsey, Lord Peter
Verasani, Grazia, 139
victims, xiv–xv, 15, 23, 34, 37, 45, 50, 54–55, 65, 70, 73, 84–86, 89, 93, 95, 97–98, 110–111, 115, 129, 131, 135, 137, 139, 160, 163, 168, 173–174, 185, 203
Victor, Metta Fuller, 100
Victorian era, 28–29, 62–63, 67–69
Victorian literature, 32, 47, 110, 145. *See also* Dickens, Charles
video games, 122
Vidocq, Eugène, 145
vigilantism, 79, 179
violence, xvi, 5–6, 51–52, 69, 76, 79–80, 108, 111, 121, 133, 136–137, 159, 169, 185, 202

Walsh, Jill Paton, 197
Warsaw, 23, 178
Warshawski. V. I., xvi, 191–192
Waters, Sarah, 146
Welles, Orson, 182
Whicher, Inspector Jonathan, 48

William of Ockham, 13
Wimsey, Lord Peter, xiv, 24, 49, 59, 63–64, 69, 181, 195–197. *See also* Sayers, Dorothy L.
Wodehouse, P. G., 162, 196

xenophobia, 83, 199. *See also* race and racism

Yorkshire, 51–52, 145
Ystad, 187–188

About the Editor and Contributors

Eric Sandberg is an assistant professor in literature at City University of Hong Kong. He loves crime fiction but also writes about modernism, adaptation, and the contemporary novel.

* * *

Juha-Pekka Alarauhio is a university teacher at the University of Oulu, Finland. His interests lie, broadly, within literary hermeneutics and, more specifically, in the writings of Matthew Arnold.

Nathan Ashman is associate tutor at the University of Surrey (UK). His research interests include James Ellroy, crime fiction, and contemporary cultural studies.

Kerstin Bergman is a Swedish crime fiction scholar and literary critic, and the author of *Swedish Crime Fiction: The Making of Nordic Noir* (2014).

J. C. Bernthal is associate lecturer at Middlesex University (UK) and author of *Queering Agatha Christie: Revisiting the Golden Age of Detective Fiction* (2016).

Katherine E. Bishop teaches literature at Miyazaki International College in Japan. Her research interests include aesthetics, empire, and ecology.

Kenneth K. Brandt is professor of English at the Savannah College of Art and Design. His *Jack London: Writers and Their Work* is forthcoming.

Patricia Catoira is associate professor of Latin American Studies at Montana State University. Her current research focuses on violence and detective fiction from Latin America.

Paul Cobley is professor in language and media at Middlesex University (UK) and is the author of a number of books, including *The American Thriller* (2000).

Inger H. Dalsgaard is associate professor in American studies at Aarhus University, Denmark, and the editor of two volumes on Thomas Pynchon for Cambridge University Press.

Anindita Dey teaches literature at Debraj Roy College, Assam, India. Her PhD is on detective fiction, and she is currently working on a book on Indian detectives.

Chad A. Evans studied detective fiction under Josef Skvorecky at the University of Toronto. His *Vincent Calvino's World: A Noir Guide to Southeast Asia* (2015) looks at crime as reality fiction.

Milla Fedorova is associate professor at Georgetown University, Washington, D.C., and author of *Yankees in Petrograd, Bolsheviks in New York* (2013).

Laura Foster completed her PhD at Cardiff University, Wales, in 2014. Her research interests include representations of the workhouse, Victorian periodicals, and crime narratives.

Katarina Gregersdotter is associate professor at Umeå University, Sweden. She has published articles and books on Anglo-American and Scandinavian crime fiction and popular culture.

Ludmiła Gruszewska-Blaim is associate professor at the University of Gdańsk, Poland. She has published books on English and American literature, utopian cinema, and college mystery fiction.

Felicity Hand teaches postcolonial literature at the Universitat Autònoma de Barcelona. She is also editor of the electronic journal *Indi@logs: Spanish Journal of India Studies.*

Janine Hatter is lecturer at Sheffield Hallam University (UK). Her research interests include nineteenth- to twenty-first-century Gothic and crime and sensation fiction.

Ruth Heholt is senior lecturer in English at Falmouth University (UK). Her research interests include crime fiction, the supernatural, and the Gothic.

Heike Henderson is professor of German at Boise State University, Idaho. Her research interests include crime fiction, intercultural relations, and literary representations of food and cannibalism.

Johan Höglund is reader in English Literature at Linnaeus University, Sweden, and director of the Linnaeus University Centre for Concurrences in Colonial and Postcolonial Studies.

Alexander N. Howe is professor of English at the University of the District of Columbia. His research interests include American literature, detective fiction, psychoanalysis, and film.

Winona Howe, retired professor of English at La Sierra University, Riverside, California, has published articles on film studies, folk tales, Wilkie Collins, Charles Dickens, and Arthur Upfield.

Andrea Hynynen is a research fellow at the University of Turku (Finland). Her research interests include French crime fiction, gender, sexuality, and identity.

Maysaa Husam Jaber is lecturer of English literature at the University of Baghdad. Her research interests focus on hard-boiled crime fiction and gender and crime.

Kate Jackson is an independent scholar whose work on Golden Age crime fiction has appeared on her blog http://www.crossexaminingcrime.com, in *Crime and Detective Stories Magazine*, and in *Mystery Scene Magazine*.

Agnieszka Jasnowska is an independent scholar and reviews editor of *parallax*. Her research interests include Victorian literature and culture, detective fiction, and identity politics.

Alison Joseph is creator of detective nun Sister Agnes and author of three novels featuring a fictional Agatha Christie. She has adapted Maigret stories for BBC Radio.

Julia Karolle-Berg is associate professor of German at John Carroll University near Cleveland, Ohio. Her current research focuses on early German-language detective novels.

Zofia Kolbuszewska teaches at Wrocław University, Poland, has published on forensic imagination and the Gothic, and edited the volume *Thomas Pynchon and the (De)vices of Global (Post)modernity*.

Linda Ledford-Miller teaches literature of the Americas (English, Spanish, and Portuguese) at the University of Scranton, Pennsylvania. Her interests in crime fiction include food, space, and place.

Jakub Lipski teaches English literature at Kazimierz Wielki University in Bydgoszcz, Poland. He does research on the long eighteenth century, crime fiction, and the Gothic.

Sheng-mei Ma is professor of English at Michigan State University, specializing in Asian Diaspora and East-West comparative studies. The most recent of his seven single-authored books in English is *The Last Isle* (2015).

Merja Makinen was associate professor at Middlesex University (UK). She works on Agatha Christie and feminist crime fiction. She is the author of *Agatha Christie: Investigating Femininity* (2006) and *Feminist Popular Fiction* (2001).

David Malcolm is a professor of English literature at the University of Gdańsk in Poland. His espionage novel *The German Messenger* was published in 2016.

Rebecca Martin is professor of English at Pace University in New York with research interests in crime writing, film studies, and the literary Gothic.

Neil McCaw is professor of Victorian literature and culture at the University of Winchester (UK) and author of books including *Adapting Detective Fiction* (2010).

Corinna McLeod teaches world literatures at Grand Valley State University in Michigan. Her areas of scholarship include national narratives, postcolonial literatures, and fictions of empire.

Claire Meldrum teaches film and literature at Sheridan College in Oakville, Canada. A PhD candidate at Wilfrid Laurier University, her research focuses on nineteenth-century American detective fiction.

Carolina Miranda is senior lecturer at Victoria University, Wellington, New Zealand, with interests in translation and twentieth-century Latin American literature. She has published on crime fiction from Argentina, New Zealand, and Spain.

Michelle D. Miranda is associate professor at Farmingdale State College in New York and author of *Forensic Analysis of Tattoos and Tattoo Inks* (2015).

Nina Muždeka is associate professor of Anglophone literatures at the University of Novi Sad, Serbia. Her interests include genre theory and the contemporary novel.

Wendy Jones Nakanishi teaches at Shikoku Gakuin University in Japan and has published two crime novels: *Imperfect Strangers* (2015) and *Progeny* (2016) under the name of Lea O'Harra.

Meghan P. Nolan is assistant professor of English at SUNY Rockland, author of *Stratification* (2008), and writer of identity-driven poetry, creative nonfiction, and mystery.

Joanne Ella Parsons teaches literature at Bath Spa University and Falmouth University (UK). She is the coeditor of *The Victorian Male Body* (2018).

Fiona Peters is reader in crime fiction at Bath Spa University (UK) and author of *Anxiety and Evil in the Writings of Patricia Highsmith* (2011).

Barbara Pezzotti is assistant lecturer in Italian studies at Monash University, Melbourne. Her most recent book is *Investigating Italy's Past through Historical Crime Fiction, Films and TV Series* (2016).

Leigh Redhead is a PhD student in creative writing at the University of Wollongong, Australia, and author of the Simone Kirsch private-eye series.

Lucia Rinaldi is senior teaching fellow at University College London. She is author of *Andrea Camilleri: A Companion to the Mystery Fiction* (2012).

Satomi Saito teaches Japanese literature and culture at Colgate University, New York. He is now completing a book manuscript on genre and narrative in Japanese popular media.

Niklas Salmose is associate professor of English literature at Linnaeus University, Sweden, currently researching the Anthropocene. He is also a filmmaker and a publisher.

Johanna Sandberg teaches academic English and English for specific purposes at the Hong Kong Polytechnic University. She recently translated Hjalmar Bergman's classic novel *The Markurells of Wadköping* (2016).

Stefano Serafini is a PhD student in comparative literature at Royal Holloway, University of London. He is currently researching late nineteenth-century Italian crime fiction.

Joseph Sgammato teaches English and film at SUNY/Westchester Community College in Valhalla, New York.

Agnieszka Sienkiewicz-Charlish completed her PhD on Ian Rankin at the University of Gdańsk, Poland, in 2015. She coedited *Crime Scenes: Modern Crime Fiction in an International Context* (2014).

Catherine Simmerer is a graduate student at Marquette University, Milwaukee. She has contributed to the American Chesterton Society as both writer and transcriber.

Paolo Simonetti is research fellow at "Sapienza" University in Rome. He coedited *Dream Tonight of Peacock Tails: Essays on the Fiftieth Anniversary of Thomas Pynchon's* V.

Selim Şimşek is lecturer in Rize, Turkey. His research interests include German studies, broadly speaking.

Rebecca Gordon Stewart is associate lecturer in English literature at Bath Spa University (UK) and coeditor of *Crime Uncovered: Anti Hero* (2016).

Zachary Tavlin is the Kollar Fellow in American Literature and Art History and the Richard M. Willner Memorial Scholar at the University of Washington.

George Twigg is an independent scholar who was recently awarded his PhD for a thesis on biopolitics and race in the novels of Salman Rushdie.

Carlos Uxó is senior lecturer at Monash University, Australia. He edited *The Detective Fiction of Leonardo Padura Fuentes* and is currently preparing a monograph on Cuban crime fiction.

Minna Vuohelainen is lecturer in English at City, University of London. Her current research focuses on Gothic and crime fiction, spatiality, and fin-de-siècle popular culture.

Beth Walker is a writing specialist at the University of Tennessee at Martin, specializing in revision and girls' detective fiction.

Samantha Walton is senior lecturer in English literature at Bath Spa University (UK) and the author of *Guilty but Insane: Mind and Law in Golden Age Detective Fiction* (2015).

Carol Westron is author of contemporary crime fiction. She is an expert on the Golden Age and reviews for Mystery People and the British Library.

Renata Zsamba is assistant lecturer at Eszterházy Károly University in Eger, Hungary. She studies British Golden Age detective fiction and the socialist crime fiction of Hungary.